READING
KARL
BARTH

READING KARL BARTH

New Directions for North American Theology

KURT ANDERS RICHARDSON

Baker Academic
Grand Rapids, Michigan

Published by Baker Academic
a division of Baker Publishing Group
P.O. Box 6287, Grand Rapids, MI 49516-6287
www.bakeracademic.com

Printed in the United States of America

Library of Congress Cataloging-in-Publication Data
Richardson, Kurt A. (Kurt Anders)
    Reading Karl Barth : new directions for North American theology / Kurt Anders Richardson.
        p.   cm.
    Includes bibliographical references and index.
    ISBN 0-8010-2729-2 (pbk.)
    1. Barth, Karl, 1886–1968. I. Title
BX4827.B3R49 2004
230'.044'092—dc22   2004008707

Contents

PREFACE

Books in theology have authors with legacies that are yet to be made and are often made in the making of a book. This text is the product of a lengthy sojourn with Barth. Barth's work is an immense testimony to the truth of the gospel of Jesus Christ during one of the richest lifetimes enjoyed by any theologian in the history of the Christian church. I come to Barth's work, *Church Dogmatics, Romans, Anselm,* and others, with particular interest in bringing to light some of their leading passages.

This book is written as much to let Barth shed light on the contemporary work of theology as to shed light on Barth. Those who regard Barth as ultimate should realize that Barth would not have allowed such a categorization. Those who dismiss Barth should recognize that such actions are entirely misplaced. The great interpretations of Barth and the global reach of his writings testify to his position in the canon of Christian theologians. We will consult him appreciatively and critically just as we do Athanasius, Augustine, Luther, and Calvin. But Barth also belongs to the moderns, theologians who have contributed to the formation of historical consciousness and know quite fully what the Reformed adage *finitum non capax infiniti* means: "The finite cannot comprehend the infinite." As Barth matured as a theologian, he realized that this work requires dialectical thinking, always with God's revealed prerogatives as primary, but most important, within the incarnational structure of all Christian knowing, which dares to speak where philosophy has attempted and failed at supplying a resolution. In the incarnation of the Word of God, God's revelation in person, in the person of Jesus Christ, the infinite has comprehended the finite and vice versa through the reconciling work of this one and only Son of God. More than the model of revelation and its rich trinitarian implications, the incarnation that makes possible the reconciliation of God and humankind stands for the entire covenantal working of God in the world for our sake and above all for his own sake. We are included and invited to participate in his gracious self-giving in order to fill the world with the knowledge of the God who loved the world so much that he gave his one and only Son, through the creating and resurrecting power of his Spirit.

For my first sense of the great Swiss theologian, I credit my beloved and esteemed teacher Harold O. J. Brown, who enjoyed Barth, learned from him, and quite naturally revealed to his students how useful he was in a context not altogether favorable toward him. I also must mention my esteemed Doktor Vater, Jan Milíč Lochman, the great Czech theologian of the postwar years whose departure from our midst cannot remove the memory of his passion for truth and tolerance. To these my teachers in theology I dedicate this book.

As I have written this book, numerous colleagues and students have had a profound impact on my reading of and thinking on Barth. The following must be mentioned here: Stan Grenz, Craig Blaising, John Franke, Clark Pinnock, Frank Clooney, Travis Kroeker, George Hunsinger, Bill Placher, Millard Erickson, Sarah Coakley, Bruce McCormack, Donald Bloesch, Mark Heim, Elmer Colyer, Donald Dayton, Glenn T. Miller, Hans-Martin Barth, Fred Sanders, Timothy George, Daniel Hardy, Peter Ochs, David Novak, David Ford, Mabiala Justin-Robert Kenzo, KK Yeo, Philip Chia, Gary Deddo, Mark Boda, Janet Clark, Dennis Magary, Garth Rosell, Wes Wildman, Erik Panikian, Faye Bodley-D'Angelo, Todd Pokrifka, Christian Winn, Alexandra Meek, Peter Heltzel, Naomi Gray, Patrick Gray, Curtis Evans, Ken Hardin, Steven Squires, Alan Wong, Jamie Skillen, Jason Robinson, Michael Ford, Andrew Gabriel, Stuart Harsevoort, Dallas Friesen, and Jason van Vleet. Along with these are my editors at Baker Academic, Robert N. Hosack and Melinda Timmer, whose encouragement and patient attention to all the details of theological book publishing are exemplary. Above all, I must thank my partner in life and labor, Dolores, whose love and constancy is the delight of my Christian sojourn, and our children, Erik, Kristin, Matthew, and Kelsey, who have accompanied us on this sojourn and are learning the mercy and grace by which we live.

INTRODUCTION

This book commends a reading of Karl Barth as part of the great spiral of *fides quaerens intellectum* (faith seeking understanding) that is the church's practice of scriptural reasoning and doctrinal understanding. Barth wrote *Church Dogmatics* as an ongoing project of occasional theology.[1] Each volume was an occasion to begin again with a fresh recovery of the Word of God in consideration of a different doctrinal locus. Ever since the sixteenth-century divide between Protestant and Catholic, evangelical theologians have written their "regular" and "irregular" theological projects *coram Deo* (before the face of God), offering their texts to the judgment of God, since no tribunal of human judgment is sufficient to pronounce finally upon any human being's work. Instead of *imprimatur* and *nihil obstat,* the evangelical theologian and the churches have had to rest content with provisional judgments on provisional published formulations and declarations. All of the church's documents, save Scripture, are revisable testimonies, however stable they may be as faithful witnesses to the truth once for all delivered in Jesus Christ. Barth did not believe in the finality of the *Dogmatics,* but he did believe in it as his testimony to the faithfulness and obedience required of any theologian in the church of Jesus Christ.

The kind of reading of the *Dogmatics* offered here is peculiar to the nature of their writing and as such is a constrained reading. In attempting to grasp what Barth finally intended in these four volumes, one must pay attention to the fact that the point at which they stop becomes a lens through which properly to understand the whole. Barth was interested only in how revelation can be heard to speak on its own terms into all of life by re-creating that life in the confession of faith and the obedience of the church. He could not

---

1. *CD* is divided as follows: I—2 pts.: doctrine of Word of God; II—2 pts.: doctrine of God; III—4 pts.: doctrine of creation; IV—5 pts. (1, 2, 3.1, 3.2, 4): doctrine of reconciliation; V—index.

help but be captured by an ever-new, ever-refining understanding of it. The divisions of these volumes into multiple subvolumes of sixteen "chapters" and seventy-three "paragraphs" require the customary front-to-back reader of the *Dogmatics* also to read them back to front. Because Barth allowed himself to be constrained by increased understanding, we too are constrained by his constraints—at least in the matter of reading him.

The fourth volume then becomes this lens, this route to understanding Barth from back to front, an extroverted reading that is a turning *(Kehre)* back to the beginning, not by means of a return to an a priori of the first volume, but one that allows later determinations to read former ones according to the focus of the later ones. A prioritizing or privileging of the fourth volume of the *Dogmatics* is not indicative of some break with what proceeds, although it is the full development, unfolding through its four parts, with matters already clarified in Barth's massive treatment of God's election in the second half of volume 2. In Jesus Christ, who is both the electing God and the elect man for us, we have the clearest delineation of what is ours and what is his, the bonds of our existence in him, and his determined action toward us. The election of grace is God's unilateral determination of himself to be for us and ultimately to begin his new work in us.

But the basic structure of the divine and human relationship only comes to full, although radically simple, formulation in the fourth volume: "*Extra nos—pro nobis—in nobis*" (outside us—for us—in us). As Barth's discussion of God's election gives way to dealing with the command of God, the responsibility that God has taken upon himself for the sake of human beings, there is a gradual letting go of an earlier emphasis on *participation* in God in favor of gracious *correspondence* to God in human obedience. In the second half of *Dogmatics* II/2, there is, surprisingly, not only the first discussion of Barth's ethics based on the exemplarity of Christ in his atoning work for us but also a massive development of his theological method. This is brought out in the fifth chapter of the present book. Far from a kind of gnostic dualism, gracious correspondence to God through the obedience of faith is a deepening of what Barth was after in his emphasis on *analogia fidei* (analogy of faith) in the first volume. Through the christological concentration of the *Dogmatics*, Barth moves away from notions of divine-human interpenetration according to a trinitarian model with respect to faith and obedience, just as he will move away from divine-human hypostatic union according to incarnational models with respect to the church. Particularly with respect to the latter, a correspondence model of divine-human relations in Christ cannot be suggestive of a christological heresy since the church is not the body of Christ with its own head and members but with Christ alone as its head, and therefore the church is not a new incarnational form of Christ.

The entirety of Barth's theological existence was characterized by a trajectory and goal of his conceptuality from and loyalty to Reformation doctrine in its Protestant and Catholic dimensions. In particular, his constancy with reference to Luther and Calvin and to the traditions that emerged out of them never left him. Barth knew that on its own principles Christian theology must itself be *semper reformandum* (ever reforming) these traditions, particularly his own Reformed tradition. Barth is not interested in anything but the continuous reform of his church and in turn of all the churches. None of the churches' formulations are irreformable since the church never stands incorrigibly under its Lord in obedience to his Word. Thus, from the first notes of the *Church Dogmatics,* after the abortive *Christliche Dogmatik,* to the end of IV/4, Barth is acutely sensitive to the demands of the Holy Spirit, who is Lord of the Word, to bring the church into ever-greater vital conformity to the truth of that Word. Reform, whatever the cost, must ever be undertaken since the cost of contradicting that Word can only be a loss. Since the fundamental exchange between God and the human is constituted by the truth of the Word, contradiction of the truth can only amount to an incapacitation of the church and the believer to live according to that Word. Barth found himself to be tested by that Word—the Word of revelation, of God's self-objectification, of gracious election, of creation, of justification and sanctification, and finally of faithful obedience—in all the living, freeing, loving Word of the Triune God in and through Jesus Christ. Likewise, we are tested in reading Barth backward and forward through the *Church Dogmatics.*

At first this is a dizzying prospect. Encounter with the density of Barth's words and the manifold richness of his witness to the Word is nothing short of a plunge into an ocean of discourse. Yet it is not the ocean that is God's life with us and our life with him but an oceanographer's and geographer's record for plying one's way through the ocean and the land masses bounded by it that is interpretation of the reality of Jesus Christ. Barth is the greatest theological geographer of the twentieth century and perhaps also of the two preceding centuries.

It takes courage to read Barth. This is because the principle of *semper reformandum* is so real for him. At once affected by his embrace of the great Christian traditions in theology, one may imagine that—given his opposition to liberal theology and to neo-Protestantism and also his early rejection of overly subjective trajectories of Pietism—Barth should be read as central to Christianity's mainstream. Indeed, as the English translation was being completed on the final volume of the *Church Dogmatics* (hereafter, *CD*), his editors, Thomas F. Torrance and Geoffrey W. Bromiley, wrote their final tribute to Barth in their preface: "The great Church Father of Evangelical Christendom, the one genuine Doctor of the universal Church [whom] the modern era has known. . . . Only Athanasius, Augustine, Aquinas and Calvin have performed comparable service in the past, in the search for a unified and comprehensive basis for all theology in the grace of God."[2] But then one comes across his reforming commitments,

---

2. *CD* IV/4:vi. *CD* = Karl Barth, *Church Dogmatics,* ed. G. W. Bromiley and T. F. Torrance, trans. G. W. Bromiley, 2d ed., 4 vols. plus index in 14 vols. (Edinburgh: T & T Clark, 1975–81).

and one realizes there is no doubt that Barth, as fully as he has embraced the tradition, is himself not a traditionalist. Much in the tradition is at stake when we embrace the reforming principle inherent in Barth's theology.

The operative word in the title of this book is *reading*, and it carries with it a theological program that seeks to be fully Christian while acknowledging the multiple ways in which Barth will be read.

Scripture Readers Reading Barth

Readerly reports of Scripture readers live with even more than Nicholas Wolterstorff explores in the liturgical address and response "The Word of the Lord . . . Thanks be to God." A constant battle is produced by confusion over tradition, theology, spiritual books, theological histories, and so on read in light of Scripture. There is no sense in which Barth has anything more than authority derived from Scripture, the Reformed traditions, and the wider Christian community. To read the *CD* is more than a literary act or even a philosophical one; it is a religious act because Barth's work is so fundamentally shaped by his testimony to the Word of God.

What is at issue in reading theology is twofold: (1) We need to determine whether a text in contemporary theology is an endeavor to enhance the basic claims of Christian orthodoxy. (2) Then we need to determine the degree to which this goal has been achieved. There is no question that Barth has intended the first; hence, there is a wide spectrum of response to his work in the *CD*. Readers raise many good questions about the development of his thought in the *CD* and regarding works other than the *CD*, particularly his Romans commentary in two editions, work on Anselm, works on ethics, historical theology of the nineteenth century, and work on Schleiermacher. But what we are most concerned with here is the deposit of his dogmatic reasoning and the ways in which this deposit is and will be received.

As a Reformed Protestant theologian, Barth holds to the particular relation between Scripture and all other statements of doctrine and interpretation in the history and life of the church. Compared to Scripture, all these other statements are always only of relative authority and applicability. Barth's formulations about Scripture and the permanent form of its truth develop throughout the *CD*. But he takes a different view of the other statements, from creed, tradition, and the most exemplary of theologians. Even the great creeds are not a product of revelation and therefore reflect at best the temporary authority of the churches at the time of their writing. Only as they are reaffirmed and added to across the centuries does their relative authority have binding force. Yet they remain relative vis-à-vis Scripture, the prime vehicle of divine revelation.

It is difficult to find a matter from the history of church tradition on which Barth does not offer lengthy discussion and considered dogmatic judgment. Barth certainly can be read for various dimensions of his work: exegetical, biblical, Reformed, ecumenical, sacramental, political, and even metaphysical and postmetaphysical theologies. But through the entire project of the *CD,* he is most interested in aiding the church with its dogmatic understanding and pedagogy. Dogmatics is, after all, instruction in the Christian faith under, from a Reformed perspective, the five guiding principles of *sola gratia, sola scriptura, solo Christo, sola fide,* and *soli Deo gloria*—all inseparable from one another and, from the perspective of the church's articulation, coequal. These principles do not stand alone. They are markers of a linguistic and critically realistic approach to the church's and the theologian's knowledge of God through his Word.

Reading Barth, one is not pressed to see multiple sources of theology constantly at work, as with those who direct constant attention to some quadrilateral (revelation, tradition, reason, and experience—or variations on this theme). The *CD* attends to these, but the source of theology is always singular: the Word of God. Barth regards this as the form and content of everything the church has to know and say. Instead of sources of theology, the other components in a real sense are considered and brought under judgment by the theology of the Word of God. Often this judgment is highly critical, since the grace of God corresponds with the desperate human need for grace. The human aspects will always reflect the divine judgment standing behind the divine promise of grace. But since grace is promised and realized in Jesus Christ, nothing of the human or of nature in general is the same.

Other purported "sources" of theology could not possibly accomplish this or function in this way. Tradition, reason, and experience are always vitally and profoundly present, but they do not function as sources. This is nowhere more in evidence than in Barth's treatment of natural theology, beginning with Romans, extending through the controversy with Brunner, and crystallized in his discussion of the knowledge of God in *CD* I/1. For Barth, the universally critical function of the Word of God as the sole source of theology means that at the same moment in which natural theology is rejected, a theology of nature is established. By the same token, while rejecting experiential and traditionalist theologies, Barth's *CD* answers and fulfills the demands for profound theologies of experience and tradition.

The reader of Barth must attend to the fact that Barth is both unsystematic and an exemplar of his own pedagogical principles as a knower of God through faithful reading of Scripture, faithful hearing of the Word of God. Barth did not conceive of the *CD,* outline the publishing project, and systematically insert settled "scientific" content into the beautifully complex architecture of an outline over the space of nearly four decades. Barth, the reader of the Word of God, keeps returning to an ever-new handling of the content of the Word of God.

The burden of this book is to point out some primary points of such expansive learning. As a result of his continued reading, Barth put some of his formulations behind him. On account of Christian living itself, Barth's theology works as a living witness to knowledge of God in relation both to the

Word of God and to the presence of God. This task is constantly beginning again. The importance of this is to understand not only Barth but also how he views all future theology: Each theologian of the Christian church is called to begin again, somehow to witness to the ever-new truth of God's Word in Jesus Christ.

Dogmatics as the pedagogy of faith is never adequately expressed by exegesis alone, whether of the Scriptures or of tradition or of the *CD*. Correct grammatical, syntactical, and historical understanding is certainly necessary. But in and through what is understood, we are led to what will be understood, new judgments engendered by knowing God and his Word for the sake of his being known and our obedience here and now. No one from history does this for us, and we cannot do it for future historical figures with whom we have no part to play beyond our lifetimes.

The church has had to regard what it calls "historical faith" as heresy, mere belief that authorities—supremely Christ and the apostles and what they taught was saving truth—do not save in themselves. Salvation comes only by believing in and living by the Word of God, which speaks to our generation while we live and move and have our being. Not to be confused with "historic faith," the once-for-all-delivered Word of God with the testimony of the Holy Spirit always produces faith and its own proclamation in each generation. Hence, historical faith and, *mutatis mutandis,* historical theology, even of the great twentieth-century theologian (Barth), are not adequate either for faith or for theology.

A book that reflects a reading of Karl Barth, paying attention to many other readers of him, can hardly be more than a report on readerly understanding. Since Barth's dogmatics is a lengthy discursive theology of witness to the Word of God and to the knowledge of God in Jesus Christ, one must beware of atomized accounts of the *CD*. Essential to appreciating the *CD* is Barth's discourse. Readers may try to reduce Barth to a comprehensive outline of essential words and their meanings according to Barth or to impose a grid of hermeneutical categories on the *CD*. But those doing so will miss and even distort the purpose of the *CD,* which is to be read in all of its energetic discursiveness and linguistic vibrancy—out of both the German original and the adequacy of the complete translation. In view of this, the present book has sought to quote passages that exemplify Barth's meaning and language, eschewing fragmentation and summarization, behind which the theologian and his text disappear.

One way of seeking a readerly approach to the *CD* is a work by George Hunsinger, *How to Read Karl Barth.*[3] Hunsinger acknowledges that his book makes most sense after one has read the entire *CD*. Nevertheless, he hopes that his *Wegweisung*, "showing the way," will assist readers in discerning the

---

3. George Hunsinger, *How to Read Karl Barth: The Shape of His Theology* (New York: Oxford University Press, 1991).

logics of Barth's work. Hunsinger performs an admirable service in proposing six motifs that guide the entire ten volumes of the *CD*. For a practical
hermeneutic of application, he also focuses on four dimensions of truth that
he detects in Barth.

The problem with such an approach (and Hunsinger surely knows this) is
that his reliable lens is primarily synchronic and serves to resist the irreducibly
diachronic character of the successive volumes of the *CD*. Certainly, the topical divisions, the loci of the *CD*, call for synchronic categorizations, but only
as one angle of approach. Hunsinger's motifs have another problem, however,
and that is their hermeneutical rather than particular theological quality. He
has oriented them to revelational categories: Trinity, Christology, soteriology,
eschatology. While he is sensitive to the particularity of the *CD* in each of these
cases, the hermeneutical categories dominate (e.g., actualism, particularism,
objectivism, personalism, realism, and rationalism).

In recent years, Hunsinger seems to have gravitated to a simpler and more
grounded christological model for reading the *CD*—which rings far truer to the
character of the *CD*. Not long after the appearance of Hunsinger's book, however, Bruce McCormack's celebrated genetic history of Barth and his theology
appeared, also guided by a complex hermeneutical category of "critically realistic dialectic."[4] As the first volume (based on an outstanding dissertation)
of a planned two-volume work, McCormack's historical theology of the great
twentieth-century theologian takes us through Barth's career before he wrote
the *CD*. Biographical in shape, McCormack's work is intimately acquainted
with Barth's exegetical and expositional moves as his publications appeared
and were read by his contemporaries. By the end, McCormack displaces his
hermeneutical analysis with the christological and theological categories of
Chalcedon and election.

Of readers in the English language, John Webster has excelled in providing
orientation to Barth and the *CD*. The reliability of his knowledge of Barth and
also of Barth's great German student, Eberhard Jüngel, is widely acknowledged.
Webster is alert to the progression of ideas in the *CD* and therefore its unsystematic nature. This becomes particularly notable when Webster, like Jüngel,
points out how the doctrine of election becomes definitive for understanding
the relation of God to creation in ways quite untypical of Reformed theology.
Webster follows Jüngel in making the same comparison of groundbreaking,
tradition-altering work between II/2 and IV/4.[5] Barth's singular emphasis on
divine election known and mediated through Jesus Christ is unique in the way

---

4. Bruce L. McCormack, *Karl Barth's Critically Realistic Dialectical Theology: Its Genesis and
Development, 1909–1936* (Oxford: Clarendon, 1995).

5. John Webster, *Barth* (New York: Continuum, 2000), 88; cf. also Webster's most helpful
"Reading the Bible: The Example of Barth and Bonhoeffer," in *Word and Church: Essays in Christian Dogmatics* (New York: T & T Clark, 2001), 87–110, where he points out the commonality
of the two theologians in seeing sanctification as an essential component of all scriptural exegesis.
Reading "is not personalizing or immanentizing Scripture, drawing it into the reader's psychic

it articulates both God's election of Christ and his election of humanity in this one person (Christ) and in the history of this one person.[6] In divine election, the full dimensions of revelation come into focus, what Thomas Torrance has so acutely highlighted concerning the knowledge of God according to the *CD:* God's being in action and God's act in his being.[7]

Instead of concentrating (as the tradition has) on abstract notions of God's unconditioned omnipotence, Barth enunciates the exclusive trinitarian and christological grounding of election. This results in the double *homoousion:* Jesus Christ, being one with the Father and being one with humanity. As we have occasion to consider later in this book, the relationship between Barth's view of election and his view of baptism is based on the being and act of God in Jesus Christ. On account of Christ, divine work and human work are fundamentally distinguished.

The dialectic of Barth's theological exposition could not be more apparent. Some of the modes of thought in I/1 and I/2 imply convergence or even interpenetration of the divine and the human in the church and its service. Yet in *CD* IV Barth emphatically leaves each (the divine, the human) to its own nature and integrity—except in the one case of Jesus Christ. Divine action is thus fully divine; although it is entirely turned toward the human, it remains fully divine. By the same token, human action remains fully human. The two modes of action are asymmetrically reconciled on account of divine action, but human action is liberated and given its own integrity in Christ and through the Holy Spirit. This is fully worked out in *CD* IV.

What is already worked out (in I/1 and I/2) in the ethical implications of election is the distinctively human action in obedience afforded to believing humanity through the Word of God. On account of the knowledge of God and of divine action through this Word, human beings are set free to act in ways that correspond to divine action. What we say in agreement with the Word of God also has an active coefficient in deeds of obedience that imitate the divine deeds of grace and reconciliation. Jüngel will assist us, along with Webster, to appreciate the role of ethical action in Barth. Particularly, Jüngel will show how this action is so fundamental to the model of correspondence (*Ensprechung*) of divine and human action.

The present book makes no pretensions of exhaustively citing Barth's readers or elements from the whole *CD*. It does try to lay out several crucial lines of

---

sphere, or perhaps the social sphere of the meditating community. . . . The affections are involved, but they are shaped; and what prevents ignorance and lack of discipline is not methodological rigour, but something infinitely more taxing: what Barth called the *epochē* [fixed point] of the interpreter in favour of the word of the living Christ" (106–7). Indeed, the present work will raise into focus Barth's continuing development of theological method in light of the reality of the living Christ to the faithful theologian.

6. Cf., *CD* II/2:45–172.

7. Thomas F. Torrance, *Karl Barth: Biblical and Evangelical Theologian* (Edinburgh: T & T Clark, 1990), 190–97; cf. *CD* II/1:257–321.

argument and development for understanding Barth's project. There is little here in the way of discussing *CD* III, the immense treatment of the doctrine of creation. In many respects, because the Protestant tradition is so focused on revelation, salvation, and theological method, the doctrine of creation is underdeveloped. Barth's contribution goes a long way to rectify this. Yet *CD* III is only beginning to receive the treatment it deserves; that awaits another volume. What is attempted here is further clarification of the revelational logic in the *CD* as a whole.

The upshot of what is contended here is the necessity of a back-to-front reading of the *CD,* following the normal pattern of coverage. Moves that Barth makes right up through IV/4 are essential to comprehending his entire enterprise. If readers miss even the last volume (IV/4) or render it somehow a mere appendage, they violate Barth's witness and his intent to conform his thought to the content of revelation, even if that means assuming the role of a solitary reformer. He knew he was in historic good company. The reading of the *CD,* back to front, is of course an impossibility; one can only do so imaginatively. Nevertheless, contemplative imagination must make a readerly journey of reversing one's steps, making a "turning" (*Kehre*). This will afford one an indispensable vantage point for seeing how Barth modifies and corrects his own project as he proceeds on the *theologia viatorum* that is the *Church Dogmatics.*

Reading is also about the cultural "location" of the practice. This book includes a tentative discussion of what it means to be reading Barth in North American theological contexts. The author of the present book can only report on a cluster of factors that affect him as an evangelical, a Protestant, an ecumenist, an American writing as a colleague and believer together with other theologians. The book also concludes with reflections on doing pilgrim theology. The *CD* is brought ever new into contexts that make it new. At the same time, it is irreducibly an artifact of twentieth-century historical theology. Barth has left us with such an immense testimony and sound theological judgment as a Christian theologian that we will henceforth ever bear with his limitations and errors.

We write pilgrim theology, now partially in imitation of Barth. Yet we write pilgrim theology because, like every other theologian of the Christian traditions, Barth cannot bear witness for us and we cannot bear witness for him. Corrected misreadings of Barth—as helpful and as necessary as they are to proper understanding and future labor—are not at all what theological witness means. Witness is the fulfillment of one's own calling to offer to Christian proclamation sound theological judgment, both critical and constructive. Such judgment concerns fundamental challenges to understanding and action confronting Christian churches worldwide and particularly in one's own world. What the *CD* does is provide resources and an example for how theologians are to work in their own time.

The exemplarity of the *CD* makes it the continuing reliable resource that it is—evidenced by the increasing number and breadth of those of Christian background turning to it for help. But, of course, the *CD* only immediately turns to its own source of help and instructs us to be bold in our own petitions to the living and almighty God: *Hilf uns in unsre Not!* Help us in our need!

1

Theologian
of the
Twentieth Century

Twentieth-Century Theology as Historical Theology

Christian theology is the continuous practice of interpreting and proclaiming the gospel of Jesus Christ in its fullest sense as it encompasses Old and New Testaments and its own historic legacy. And although theologians properly begin and ever return to the gospel as uniquely and solely embodied in the Scriptures of the New Testament, they are also drawing upon the traditions of theology within the many churches of the church of Jesus Christ. Each generation of churchly theologians, lay and ordained, working inside and outside theological institutions, communicates in some way with the past and with the future in the matter of Christ and his significance. As theologians compose their specialized testimonies to faith in their Lord and as their lives expend themselves in communicating this testimony, their works pass into the great library of historical theology. Although it is difficult to know when contemporary theology becomes historical theology, it is safe to say that contemporary theologians must prepare themselves, for at best their own contributions become "historical" in their own lifetimes. Because of the conversational nature of theology—a conversation of agreements and disagreements—it is a product of and contribution to identifying problems and proposing solutions to the process of Christianity's attempts to understand and to communicate its knowledge of God and his relations with creatures. In light of this, twentieth-century theology, like that of previous centuries, has become installed in this great library. For theology to succeed in its duty to the gospel, each generation of its published testimonies must defer to the next: This is its destiny but also its necessity.[1]

How then is the library of historical theology useful to the contemporary theological conversation?[2] Orienting theologically to the gospel, particularly along Protestant and evangelical lines, but also ecumenically, theology requires at least two approaches: one diachronic and the other synchronic. The synchronic approach to theology acknowledges how theologians often interpret Christian doctrine with minimal reference to historical development. Other than some general considerations to patristic, medieval, reformational, and modern epochs, many theologians work with a nearly atemporal approach to theology. In a single paragraph, references from the sweep of two millennia of Christian theology are made because certain texts and formulations of Christian theology have become "canonical."[3] Beyond denoting the official list of scriptural books, "canonical" is a rich term and can also mean that a particular Christian church and its official teachers have either by council or practice adopted a particular phrase, such as *homoousion* or *sola fide,* or a particular book, such as Athanasius's *De incarnatione* or Calvin's *Institutes.* At work here in theology is the rule of Vincent of Lérins: *ubique, semper, ab omnibus.* Next to Scripture, these are the tools of theology that reflect what is believed: "everywhere, always, and by everyone." Such canonical materials for theology are of historical interest and gain intergenerational if not timeless authority; they are constantly appealed to as being not merely free from heresy but ever instructive of the faith.

One of the leading contributions on how theology works synchronically is by the Yale theologian George Lindbeck.[4] In his influential paradigm of theological approaches, he offers three types: (1) cognitive-propositionalist, emphasizing truth-claims; (2) experiential-expressive, emphasizing religious experience; and (3) cultural-linguistic, emphasizing rules of religious life. That theology should treat doctrines as embodying propositional truth is, essentially,

---

1. Certainly, this would not substantially alter the way in which historical theology is done, in the likes of Jaroslav Pelikan, *Christian Tradition: A History of the Development of Doctrine,* vol. 5: *Christian Doctrine and Modern Culture (since 1700)* (Chicago: University of Chicago Press, 1991).

2. Cf. Richard A. Muller, *After Calvin: Studies in the Development of a Theological Tradition* (New York: Oxford University Press, 2003); Dermot A. Lane, ed., *Catholic Theology Facing the Future: Historical Perspectives* (New York: Paulist Press, 2003); Bernard L. Ramm, *The Evangelical Heritage: A Study in Historical Theology* (Grand Rapids: Baker, 2000); Alister E. McGrath, *Historical Theology: An Introduction to the History of Christian Thought* (Malden, Mass.: Blackwell, 1998); and Aidan Nichols, *The Shape of Catholic Theology: An Introduction to Its Sources, Principles, and History* (Collegeville, Minn.: Liturgical Press, 1991).

3. For extensive discussion of "canon" as a theological term with multiple significance, see William J. Abraham, *Canon and Criterion in Christian Theology: From the Fathers to Feminism* (Oxford: Clarendon, 1998).

4. Cf. George Lindbeck, *The Nature of Doctrine: Religion and Theology in a Post-Liberal Age* (Philadelphia: Fortress, 1984).

an ancient approach. Although Lindbeck regards this first approach as suffering from exaggerated claims, he acknowledges that taking Scripture as revelation is a powerful motivation to formulate theological truth claims propositionally. Scripture is read and interpreted with primary attention to its uniquely authoritative canonicity, not to its historical qualities. This sets in motion the entire synchronic approach with respect to all well-received theological works. Theological texts from every era can be employed for their propositional claims to truth. The second type of theological approach, experiential-expressive, while also coming under negative scrutiny by Lindbeck, is nevertheless a determinative aspect of theological reflection. Rather than classifying Christian religious experience according to a set of general religious experiences, the Christian theologian would rather give attention to unique and yet common experiences of Christian believing.[5] Friedrich Schleiermacher, whom Lindbeck identifies as an exemplar of approaching Christian faith through generalized experience, is an ambiguous reference: In his *Speeches*,[6] Schleiermacher refers to a common core of "prereflective" experience, but in his later *Glaubenslehre*,[7] his focus is to interpret uniquely Christian doctrines in terms of their basis in Christian experience. The third approach, most approved by Lindbeck and dependent on Ludwig Wittgenstein and Clifford Geertz, sets out religion in linguistic terms as a "language" learned and performed by those shaped by it within particular communities of discourse and behavior. Like a language with its own embedded rules of meaning and effective communication, Christian rules of knowing and acting are interpreted by theology to help guide succeeding generations in the practice of these rules. Although many theologians would resist reducing theology in this way, none would mistake the effectiveness when its practitioners use theological statements to provide guidance in worship and preaching and to establish boundaries of community.

The diachronic in the conversation that is theology follows and contributes directly to conversation partners and readers who will interact with a newly published theological text within a year and then within a decade of its influence, if it provokes wide comment and change.[8] In the diachronic method, theologians accept a special limitation and a special opportunity. The limitation

---

5. Although the "inclusivist" approach to salvation in Christ is contested, an implication of this theological approach is the realization that the different religions reflect incommensurable truths about diverse religious ends. Thus, Buddhist nirvana is a reality, but not the reality of the new creation promised by Christ and his apostles. Cf. S. Mark Heim, *The Depth of the Riches: A Trinitarian Theology of Religious Ends* (Grand Rapids: Eerdmans, 2001).

6. Friedrich Schleiermacher, *On Religion: Speeches to Its Cultured Despisers,* trans. Richard Crouter (New York: Cambridge University Press, 1996).

7. Cf. Friedrich Schleiermacher, *The Christian Faith,* ed. H. R. Mackintosh and J. S. Stewart (Philadelphia: Fortress, 1976).

8. Alisdair MacIntyre is particularly alert to the increased influence of historical consciousness and contemporaneity in philosophy and ethics. Although the encyclopedic methods of modern scholarship are not desirable for their minimalist approach to commitment, he decries the "incommensurability" of the multiple voices of contemporary scholarship. While I would

is that every theological contribution, no matter how influential over time, is addressed primarily to its own time of publication. Its author is overwhelmingly moved to write for the conversation partners and recent publications of the time. And when that theologian passes from the scene, the theological currency of his or her works also passes from the scene. This is not to say that their work is irrelevant to later times; otherwise no one would do synchronic theological work. But every reader of the now-deceased author's works is limited to what has become the archival remains of that author, not only in works continuing to be published or still procurable but also—if some segment of the Christian community is so moved—through an established archive of every available source of the esteemed theologian's work and life. For a generation following the death, a new generation of theological students relies on testimonies of those who were shaped by the presence of the theologian who taught them or was the conversation partner of their own teachers. But then the survivors also pass from contemporary life, and the next generation must resort to the archive for every exposure to the witness, whether for the primary source or even the secondary sources of those who lived and worked with the theologian in question. The archiving of Barth is a limitation that every contemporary theologian must accept.

There is also a special opportunity that I just mentioned with respect to the diachronic approach: to develop new theological expositions, to engage in new theological debates that pursue the uncovering of truth, and to cultivate the motivation to action that can only be and must be achieved in one's own lifetime. Theology is both an exercise of memory and an exercise of construction. Of course, one can no longer master a single field of theology; there are too many traditions and too many interdisciplinary approaches both in classical divinity terms as well as more recent developments, such as the theology of nature or comparative theology of religions. In one's own lifetime, matters of personal faith in Jesus Christ, adherence to Christian community in practices of worship and mission, identification of spiritual gifts that tend toward theology, and the realization of the contemporary expressions of the various strands of theological tradition all spur one on to one's own theological goals of writing, teaching, and, if so gifted, preaching. Although each generation of theologians has much to learn from Barth—indeed, one could spend most of one's time just learning more from him—one may also follow his example to do the old and the new thing, which he did in his own theological project. Like Barth, one must gain sufficient independence, for

---

regard this as a correct description of our situation, Western cultures are developing democratic rules of social engagements that cope quite well with the competing voices of contemporary discourse. See Alisdair MacIntyre, *Three Rival Versions of Moral Enquiry: Encyclopaedia, Genealogy, and Tradition,* Gifford Lectures delivered in the University of Edinburgh in 1988 (Notre Dame, Ind.: University of Notre Dame Press, 1990).

the sake of the church and its theology, to engage debates arising at the front edge of faithful thought and action.

I would urge that we pay closer attention to Barth's own sense of what it meant for him to be a theologian and to make his contribution in the *Dogmatics* and other writings. He asks his readers to read him and then to move on. One reads him and moves on, always returning to him as to other great contributors, but one moves on. This is what it means to be a pilgrim theologian, finding the path marked out for one in one's own lifetime. But let us consider our access to Barth through his archive.

An archive[9] is not a person and cannot convey a personal presence. But an outstanding one for Karl Barth does exist, supervised for several decades by Hinrich Stoevesandt and now by Hans-Anton Drewes, at Brudholzallee 26 in Basel, Switzerland. That there is a Barth archive provides for the retrieval system of this man's late-nineteenth- to mid-twentieth-century theological and personal artifacts. His scholarly and many personal remains have become the stuff of the archaeology of ideas: for some, modern, late modern, or postmodern; for others, types of Reformed and ecumenical theology, indeed, Catholic and Orthodox.[10]

The retreat and resort to a theologian's archive can become like a pilgrimage—a passionate attendance to a privileged class of documents and memora-

9. I am thinking here particularly of the reflections in Jacques Derrida, *Archive Fever: A Freudian Impression,* trans. Eric Prenowitz (Chicago: University of Chicago Press, 1998), in which he explores memory, temporality, technology, and religious experience through access to archival institutions. This is a fascinating discussion of public places instituted for the exploration of a private individual who is only virtually present and continuously archived in the hopes of new discoveries for those who wish to make their own discoveries of the life under study. Interestingly, archives already have a biblical frame of reference (Ezra 5:17; 6:1) as well as annals of Israel (e.g., 1 Kings 14:19; 2 Kings 1:18; 1 Chron. 27:24; 2 Chron. 20:34; Ezra 4:15; Neh. 12:23; Esther 2:23) and indicate some concern for historicity in the very accounts of Scripture. As practiced in "archivization," the archive exists for the sake of the belief in facts, claims Carolyn Steedman, *Dust: The Archive and Cultural History* (New Brunswick, N.J.: Rutgers University Press, 2002).

10. Bruce McCormack, the foremost historical theologian of Barth's life and work writing in the English language, contributes to the Barth archive's website a discussion of why he finds Barth of such interest to Americans, citing five points: (1) Barth's earnest biblical and classic doctrinal interests offer the prospect of a "rebirth of genuine Protestant theology in America." (2) The nondogmatic characteristic of Barth's *Dogmatics* claims that every medium of revelation is never identical with God himself, and every theology, therefore, is fundamentally fallible and must be open to self-correction. (3) Barth's theology is not a cultural or religious discipline and instead is bound exclusively to God and his self-revelation in Jesus Christ, and as such it must obediently attend to its divine, Christocentric service. (4) Barth's dogmatics and his ethics are inseparably bound together for an integrated life of faith shaped by obedience to God and not reducible to political programs that at best are provisional and limited. (5) Barth's commitment to the local church enables the subject of theology to strengthen both laity and clergy in a reordering of priorities. Speaking of his *Doktor Vater,* the late professor Edward Dowey of Princeton Seminary, McCormack looks forward to a Barth renaissance in the United States but acknowledges that this has not yet been fulfilled. Cf. www.unibas.ch/karlbarth/.

bilia. But an archive is not the next best thing to the living theologian. It is not a mausoleum. The full significance of an archive as an extraordinary institution of sources begins to emerge when the life of the memorialized has come to an end. Thus, a theologian's archive is a singularly modern phenomenon, at once a library and a museum of a private and public life. In Barth's case, the archival development coincided with history coming to a head after the Cold War and the democratization of Western culture. Barth was a great man whose sense of destiny drove him to explore the knowledge of God. The archive presents vastly more than the publication of the collected works of a theologian. It has become an intellectual node in the consciousness of the world. Like the archives of other greats, Barth's is a place to which one may retire for intensive research or even for pilgrimage. It is a place that gathers its information not only by the author but also in terms of the other. Its collections show not only much of the documentary context of the records and publications of the great person; they also present ways in which it is obvious or not so obvious that the world influenced this man or, more importantly, was influenced by him.

As precious as the archive of the deceased is for the purposes of "reconstruction" of that life, for enacting memory, and for the accurate interpretation of all the dimensions of his thought, it is much more the case that the archive signals the full "academization" of the one no longer with us. We are certain that nothing more will be said by the author, and we can now sift through what we are allowed to sift through, to weigh and to categorize the artifacts on the way to authoritative representations.

What really counts in our reading of Barth, as one of the key figures of historical theology, is that he also exists as a key figure in church history. The significance of this affords us the opportunity to explore a theology of history. This raises a couple of crucial problems that divinity studies have pushed aside and that can no longer be pushed aside: How does the theological dimension of narrative appropriate the historical? How does the narrative dimension of history appropriate the theological? Something of a massive healing is necessary here, which connects us in an important way to the third section of this chapter on the postmodern reading of Karl Barth.

Since the mid- to late-nineteenth century, Christian historiography, the writing of Christian history, underwent both specialization and a theological chastening. In terms of specialization, it became a faculty or topic unto itself. More significantly, theological studies have recognized the impossibility of writing what was deemed to be a necessary singular narrative of the progress of the Christian religion and a telling of events from a "biblical perspective," where the acts of God are presented as clearly in evidence from particular events. Hence, fewer and fewer Christian historians were willing to offer readings of providence in their historical narrations and arguments.

In its own way, the detachment of history from theology was also conspicuous. Historical narrative, of course, has always been a stress point in theology. In the history of doctrine, theologians rarely appropriate anything more than the barest historical outline of the life of Jesus. They claim historical events as essential to the truth claim of Christianity but let Scripture, commentary, and sermon narrate those claims. Narrating the history of Jesus in light of Christology is just one of the ways in which history was problematic for theology.

When theology and church history performed a unified function, a number of theological determinations were in force. Not only was divine providence in history being affirmed but also a sense that Scripture had already begun to narrate history, beginning with prehistory in the protology of the world and prophetically completing the narrative of history through eschatology. In addition, not only was Christianity a hearing of divine revelation at all times present to it by the work of God's Spirit and the reception of it by human acts of faith, but also, since the human being is created in the image of God, the mind could exist simultaneously in the presence of creatures and in the presence of the Creator. Immanence and transcendence were characteristic of human consciousness, and therefore, the influence of the transcendent could be read off the immanent through the aid of the biblical narrative, the illuminating Holy Spirit, and the vital faith of the believing theologian-historian. Although there have been attempts at a theology of history (e.g., Paul Tillich), the inadequacy becomes apparent in that the kingdom of God merely becomes the "meaning" of history, but we still find no narrative.[11] Indeed, since Paul had declared that the Israelite history of the Scriptures was written so that Christians might learn from their example (1 Cor. 10), how could there not be a sacred history essential to doctrine?

Two factors, one modern and one postmodern, enter into the question of Christian history and theology in the past century. First, our sense of the secular means that a certain realism about this characterization is necessary. Indeed, Barth and Bonhoeffer along with many of their contemporaries readily affirmed the secular not only as godlessness but also as naturalness—whether anthropologically or cosmologically defined. Second, it is also more than appropriate to reject false "metanarrative" and maintain criticism of the uses of grand histories that tell stories of origins and historical destinies as employed by fascism and communism in the twentieth century. Through this second phenomenon, many have found a way to a kind of postsecularism, but not yet with an adequate theology of history.

A theology of history is necessary because it is a way of taking responsibility for the acts of Christians as well as interpreting them according to revelation and faith, for the purpose of memory and Paul's goal of learning from their example. There are no Christian exemplars without a theology of history. But if there are Christian exemplars because of a theology of history, then this theology will also include churches and their institutions. In criticizing metanarrative, it

---

11. Cf. Hartmut Rosenau, "Das Reich Gottes als Sinn der Geschichte—Grundzüge der Geschichtstheologie Paul Tillichs," in *Reich Gottes,* ed. Wilfried Härle and Reiner Preul, Marburger Jahrbuch Theologie 9 (Marburg: Elwert, 1999), 63–83.

is not so much the Scriptures that come under the deconstructive edge but the imperial and nationalistic Christian histories that do. In this sense, one must be extremely cautious about critiques of secular social theories that offer only a reconstructionism of premodern, Constantinian abominations.

If Barth is going to serve as an exemplar, then we must come to grips with the theological duty of history. A number of questions come before us: What does it mean that Barth is proving to be one of the key theologians in the history of the Christian church? What does it mean that at a particular moment of crisis the Barmen Declaration had to be written? Like other theological and moral crises in the history of Christianity, the painfulness of confessing sin and failure, while not appearing to be part of a preferable narrative, is nevertheless vitally biblical and essential for worship; paraphrasing Luther, repentance can be regarded as our greatest act of worship because in doing so we agree with God that he is right and we are wrong.

Charting the Life of This Swiss Theologian

The contours of Barth's life are straightforward and well known. The son of Anna Sartorius and Fritz Barth, Karl was born in the city canton of Basel, Switzerland, in 1886. His father, a devout man and dedicated seminary professor in Bern in New Testament and early church history, exercised a profound influence on him. For university training in theology, Karl Barth, in good fashion, made his rounds to Bern, Berlin, Tübingen, and Marburg. After his vicarage at a Reformed church in Geneva from 1909 to 1911, he entered the full pastorate of the working-class parish of Safenwil. Shortly thereafter he married the able violinist Nelli Hoffman. Together they had one daughter and four sons.

While doing the work of a pastor in proclaiming the gospel and building community, Barth underwent two crises, one positive and the other negative. The positive crisis was letting the Bible speak, letting it shape him and his message entirely. This he explored with his lifelong friend and fellow preacher Eduard Thurneysen. The negative crisis was his realization of his professors' great error in supporting Germany's ambitions in World War I. Barth was struck by the transformation of academic religion "into intellectual 42-cm. cannons."[12] Not only had the theologians endorsed the war, but they had also given religious praise for the experience of war itself as a source of moral rejuvenation and necessary heroism. Here he realized that liberal theology was not oriented to the purposes of God in Jesus Christ, and he traced the problem back to Friedrich Schleiermacher. Liberal theology was not truly progressive in terms of the revolutionary power of the gospel. Barth realized that God

---

12. Eberhard Busch, *Karl Barth: His Life from Letters and Autobiographical Texts,* trans. John Bowden (Minneapolis: Augsburg, 1976), 81.

held the sole prerogatives in the world, and yet he gives to human beings their freedom, willing that they might respond to the most radical reality of all, himself revealed in Jesus Christ. Taking leave of liberalism, Barth began to explore Scripture and tradition intensively. Out of this exploration would grow the manuscript of his great Romans commentary, which appeared and caused explosions of theological reaction throughout the German Christian world in 1919. In 1921, Barth was appointed professor of Reformed theology at the University of Göttingen and later to chairs at Münster (1925) and Bonn (1930). He published works critiquing nineteenth-century Protestant theology and produced a celebrated study of Anselm.

The *Church Dogmatics* are so extensive that they constitute a kind of archive in themselves—albeit an intentionally and unavoidably incomplete dogmatics of the Christian faith. They are his faithful deposit of theological artifacts from five decades of his career as a theologian. To read them is to become a kind of archaeologist, digging into the record of Barth, the archivist of his own career as a teaching and preaching theologian. One must constantly pay attention to multiple generations of an idea, to architecture of the work, and to an array of puzzling minor objects that have no connection with our present—the many contemporaries with whom Barth was debating at the time of his writing.

This book does not contain Barth's biography—indeed, in some ways no book on his theology should do so as long as no critical biography exists. Only fragments of such a biography are available. Eberhard Busch's *Life of Barth* is something of an archive in itself. A topical history, that of Barth's relation to the Jews, has been critically produced.[13] Barth, the Swiss theologian of the twentieth century and a rigorous independent like his forebear Zwingli, prepared to joust and to fight on the cantonal theological battlefield. Barth is a Winkelried,[14] ready to take the spears of the enemy into his middle in order that the little army of the Lord might see the triumph of the kingdom of God. Barth the preacher and man of action, who initiated the assault against Protestant liberalism in the second decade of the twentieth century and virtually authored all of the Barmen Declaration, reentered Switzerland in 1934 after dismissal from his post at Bonn for disloyalty to Hitler and continued writing the *CD*. But to add insult to injury, in 1939, the University of Münster withdrew the doctoral title it had previously awarded to Barth.

Barth's politics as well as his dogmatics marked the following three decades of extraordinary activity. He would admit the lateness of his reaction to anti-Semitism in Germany such as to be ineffective in taking on that battle. From the beginning Barth advocated total military and social resistance to Nazi

---

13. Not yet translated but singularly significant: Eberhard Busch, *Unter dem Bogen des einen Bundes: Karl Barth und die Juden, 1933–1945* (Neukirchen-Vluyn: Neukirchner Verlag, 1996). The fifteenth chapter deals with the guilt of Christians in the mass murder of the Jews.

14. This Swiss hero, Arnold von Winkelried of Unterwalden, is celebrated for his famous cry, "I will open a passage!" in the 1397 battle of Sempach against the Hapsburgs.

totalitarianism on the battlefield and in cultural encounters. He did this to the consternation of many of his fellow Swiss citizens, since the threat of a Nazi invasion during World War II was great. Once Hitler had been defeated, Barth was the first to call his Swiss nation to reconciliation with the Germans and to offer a merciful hand of aid. As a social democrat and possessing a certain antipathy toward American economic power and ideology and religion, Barth often equated the United States and the Soviet Union in regard to a threat to the security of the world. He refused to make anticommunism a mark of postwar Christian ethics. Had he been a decade younger and lived a decade longer, seeing the events of the Prague Spring (1968) and the retrograde nature of social and political conditions in the Soviet bloc in contrast to the relatively great benefits of the Western democracies, one would expect he would have changed his mind. Indeed, he would suffer the indignity of social opprobrium on the occasion of his retirement lecture at the University of Basel from introductory remarks by the city's mayor. Barth rightly eschewed offering any alignment of Christianity with a particular political party or system. What counts is Christ's lordship over the church and the believers' witness to that authority.

After retirement, Barth continued to lead seminars and to write. Unfortunately, as Charlotte von Kirschbaum's strength diminished so did Barth's output. But the contribution of his thought had been immensely well developed. Indeed, with Kirschbaum's assistance, so much that would not have been possible became reality. As much as through any, his legacy would be advanced by two great students: Thomas Torrance for the English-speaking world and Eberhard Jüngel for the German-speaking. They would have their influence because they are brilliant theologians in their own right, so conspicuously influenced by Barth, and yet so penetratingly perceptive of what Barth was after in the *CD*. To these three figures we now turn.

The Fruit of Kirschbaum

The immensity of Barth's project cannot be considered without reference to the aid and companionship of Charlotte von Kirschbaum. Although the presence of Kirschbaum throughout Barth's middle and later career is difficult personally, she was adopted into the circle of the family life and remained there until both their deaths. Indeed, she is buried with Karl and Nellie at their family site in the Bruderholz cemetery in Basel.

Various assessments of Kirschbaum's relation to Barth have been offered, ranging from Kirschbaum being a kind of administrative assistant to authoring large parts of the *CD*. Likely she was influential somewhere between these two poles, but certainly, out of devotion to him, she gave her energies selflessly to the fulfillment of his theological vocation. She accompanied him on virtually all occasions pertaining to his great career, aiding him in his preparations, and most of all accompanying him into the solitude that writing such a vast amount of text required. We can be assured that there is nothing of the *CD* and the other writings that lack her hand in their substance and shape. This is not to say that she generated theological ideas in the way that Barth did, as her own work shows,[15] but that Barth found in her and she in him an extraordinary partnership that produced its own creative nexus. In Barth's own words toward prefacing *CD* III/3:

> I should not like to conclude this Preface without expressly drawing attention of readers of these seven volumes to what they and I owe to twenty years of work quietly accomplished at my side by Charlotte von Kirschbaum. She has devoted no less of her life and powers to the growth of this work than I have myself. Without her co-operation it could not have been advanced from day to day, and I should hardly dare contemplate the future which may yet remain to me. I know what it really means to have a helper.[16]

Stemming from her training as a Red Cross nurse, Kirschbaum had directed her energies to her self-teaching in theology, including its primary languages. She must not be overlooked, although some criticism existed for quite a long time that Eberhard Busch had given her too much attention in his *Life of Barth*.

So far as we can tell, Kirschbaum's path as Barth's "helper" rather than as a noted theologian in her own right was not at all regrettable for her. Indeed, it was a self-affirmation that had cost her good relations with her own family in Germany.[17] Left destitute by her father's death in World War I in 1916, she suffered such deprivation that her health was permanently damaged during the time immediately following. Her pastor had been Georg Merz since before her confirmation, and after the war he invited her into the circle of his friends and colleagues, which included the celebrated author Thomas Mann.

Merz had struck up a friendship with Barth after being impressed by the Romans commentary, eventually published by Christian Kaiser Press in Munich (1919) as a result of Merz's advocacy as adviser to the press. Their friendship was such that Merz became godfather of the Barths' fourth child. Thus, through the close ties of the two, Kirschbaum was introduced to Barth, and the new relationship found its potentiality by the summer of 1924 in connection with Barth's Swiss friends, the Pestalozzis, whose chalet outside Zurich was a favorite retreat for a large circle of acquaintances. Barth's closest theological colleague, Eduard Thurneysen, recognized the circumstantial limitations in which Kirschbaum found herself and rec-

---

15. Cf. Charlotte von Kirschbaum, *The Question of Woman: The Collected Writings of Charlotte von Kirschbaum,* trans. John Shepher (Grand Rapids: Eerdmans, 1996); cf. also Renate Köbler, *In the Shadow of Karl Barth: Charlotte von Kirschbaum,* trans. K. Crim (Louisville: Westminster John Knox, 1989).

16. Quoted from *CD* III/3:xii–xiii, in Kirschbaum, *Question of Woman,* 1.

17. Kirschbaum, *Question of Woman,* 5.

ommended that she gain formal administrative training, for which the Pestalozzis paid.

By the time Barth was invited to his professorship in Münster in 1925, Kirschbaum was ready to assist him, which she did in February 1926.[18] She immediately went to work on all the texts he was developing at the time: a new edition of *Romans,* his to-be-published Göttingen lectures, a commentary on Philippians, and his *Die christliche Dogmatik im Entwurf.*[19] The last she would help him entirely rework and retitle, becoming the first volume of the *CD* by 1932. The way in which she undertook her task at Barth's side could hardly be better expressed than by the recollection of another friend of the two, Gertrud Staewen, recalling that Kirschbaum was

> possessed by a scintillating, concentrated energy that was never loud but was always present. This energy, this zest for life, she had decided, entirely and completely, to exist only for one single human being, for his life, for his work, for his well-being and his peace of mind, for his friends and students.[20]

Kirschbaum was intensely conscious of her lack of formal academic training, which drove her to finish her university preparatory high school diploma. With this work finally complete, she resumed her labors for Barth at the beginning of his sabbatical in April 1929 and would contribute unending assistance to him until ill health finally prevented her in 1964.

From the time of her absorption into the Barth family in October 1929, Kirschbaum became the perfect partner to Karl Barth in all his labors as a theologian. She made abstracts of books she read for him, prepared manuscripts of lectures on a daily basis, produced a massive note-card index for the *CD,* attended and summarized lectures of Barth's opponents, and most significantly did background research for him. These contributions made virtually all of his work possible. As the books were produced, their adjoining desks provided the physical structure for their conversations, which were transformed into the very words of the texts.[21] In view of this, it must be said that the work of Karl Barth is the product of not one but two theologians. Having stated this, however, there is no question of ferreting out particular passages of the *CD* wholly attributable to Kirschbaum. This she made impossible. The completed work was always what she wanted in her calling, Barth's *CD.* Only her failing health prevented the great work, which would have finished with a dogmatics of the Spirit in the consummating work of God. But a life cannot produce finished work, and so she could not, and neither could Barth.

---

18. Ibid., 8.

19. Karl Barth, *Die christliche Dogmatik im Entwurf,* ed. Hinrich Stoevesandt (Zürich: Theologische Verlag, 1982).

20. From Köbler, *In the Shadow of Barth,* 32; Kirschbaum, *Question of Woman,* 9.

21. Köbler, *In the Shadow of Barth,* 11.

Theological Genetics in Torrance and Jüngel

Before we move to a fundamental cultural question with respect to receiving the work of Barth—whether we are postmodern in our outlook—we should deal with a few influential perspectives on him. These are the "genetic" works on Barth, those of Torrance, of von Balthasar, and supremely of McCormack. Each of these is a particularly engaging exercise in the formation of thought and character of the theologian. Although we do not have a critical biography of Barth, these works certainly contribute toward that end. Each is the product of a special kind of almost devotional labor to display just how estimable the life's work may be.

The contribution of Thomas Torrance begins with his work on the early Barth and extends throughout his own work during the great productivity of his emeritus years through the centenary (1986) of Barth's birth. His work has inspired significant followers.[22]

There is yet one kind of reflection on Barth that continues to stand in an extraordinary relation to him and his work, the writings of Eberhard Jüngel. He is a great one in his own right who nevertheless characterized Barth as one among those who "condemn us to understand him." While Jüngel has produced highly significant theological work on the knowledge of God and recently on justification, his work on Barth's view of the Trinity and other Barthian themes are easily as significant. For a long time, seeking a compatibility between Barth and Bultmann, reflection on Barth won out.[23] Regarding Jüngel, the English-language world of theology is especially indebted to the work of Oxford theologian John Webster—now recently moved to Aberdeen—who has retranslated in a much more felicitous way Jüngel's book *God's Being Is in Becoming*.[24] As Webster describes Jüngel's contribution, "Like nearly everything which he has written on Barth, it is interpretation of the highest order."[25] Expounding that God's absolute freedom makes the creation capable of receiving his self-revelation, Jüngel also asserts that God in his freedom establishes actual personal relations with human creatures based on the internal relations within the Trinity, both *ad intra* (to the inside) and *ad extra* (to the outside). This is significant in view of the many works exploring Barth's view of God and that of process theology. Indeed, as is typical of Jüngel, he finds in the life and person of Jesus Christ, just as Barth did, the entire framework for a proper ontology of God. With respect to Jüngel, we want to note his estimation that, from *Romans* on,

---

22. E.g., Alister E. McGrath, *Scientific Theology: Reality*, vol. 2 (Grand Rapids: Eerdmans, 2002).

23. Whose fruits are perhaps most evident in Jüngel's notable student Ingolf Dalferth, whose contributions on Barth include the critical realism so crucial to McCormack's study.

24. Eberhard Jüngel, *God's Being Is in Becoming: The Trinitarian Being of God in the Theology of Karl Barth: A Paraphrase*, trans. John Webster, 2d ed. (Grand Rapids: Eerdmans, 2001), based on the 4th ed. of *Gottes Sein ist im Werden* (Tübingen: Mohr, 1986).

25. John Webster, "Translator's Introduction," in Jüngel, *Being Is in Becoming*, xviii.

Barth's influence is demonstrably singular in importance. He declares not only that theology changed because of Barth but also that his work constitutes one of the most important intellectual works of the twentieth century.[26]

Theology in Postmodernity

The connection between deconstruction and the apophatic in theology has been highly suggestive for Barth interpreters. This comes at the point of the reflection of the theologian and the philosopher, in this case often Jacques Derrida. What is the nature of theological writing at the hands of a particular theologian? If in the end there are only particular theologians, there is no re-ified "theology" at all but the clustering of various communities of theologians, to the extent that any one of them has an audience.

But one must be careful of reading Barth out of context as it were, or more to the point, out of himself, ecstatically. That Martin Heidegger read *Romans* and was profoundly affected by the depth of its actuality is not a crediting of Barth with Heidegger's philosophical program of interpreting Being. The affinity certainly is at the point of the intensity of reflective practice, but the connection dissipates beyond that. The theologian's and the philosopher's grappling with their subjects, indeed, with their own souls, bear the traces of genius and help form our awareness of their particular biographies as we read what they have written.

To the extent that Derrida[27] is pursuing the deconstruction of certain grammatical and syntactical conventions that aid in production and installation of social authorities, he extends the genetic project of Friedrich Nietzsche. And deconstruction is legitimate as critique of authorities and the way people may appeal to these authorities to aid in grander projects of history and narrative that compel adherence and faith. The other side of the postmodern reading clusters around the tendencies of Heidegger's movement of penetration and intensification with respect to letting Being be. At these levels, practices of reflection, of reading and of writing, and of proclaiming all bear the marks of a family of intellectual practice and even of stylistic expression. The anthropology of the theologian in the twentieth century is conceived and self-conceived in ways that resemble one another.

What is significant about a connection between Barth and deconstruction is the work that is done to free texts not from single meanings as much as from certain monolithic claims—sometimes even against the will of their authors

26. Eberhard Jüngel, *Barth-Studien* (Zürich: Benziger, 1982), 60.

27. Isolde Andrews, *Deconstructing Barth: A Study of Complementary Methods in Karl Barth and Jacques Derrida* (Frankfurt am Main: Peter Lang, 1996), 103–7, successfully deflects the criticism of Barth's dialectic as Hegelian because Barth never pushes to a synthesis that collapses difference into a universal oneness. *Analogia fidei* does what attention to *Différance* does.

or great interpreters. Scripture is both God and man speaking together; other texts are negotiated conjunctions of subjective and objective determinants. To the extent that modern systematic thought, either in theology or in philosophy, tended toward radical resolutions—such as "God is Being," or "revelation is experience, the duality that is better reconciled while remaining duality rather than resolved into a single substance"—made systematic thinking scandalous.

Rather than a critical, philosophical resolution of difference where the text of Scripture as revelation is lost to the texts of religion, Barth establishes the dichotomous book of man and book of God, which are reconciled in Jesus Christ and faith in him. Deconstruction could correspond to that moment when one hears Scripture as nothing other than word of humanity or even when one hears Scripture as nothing other than Word of God.

One of the guiding characteristics of postmodernity is the cultural collapse of secular universalism. A leading commentator writes of the result:

> For radicals to discard the idea of totality in a rush of holophobia is, among other more positive things, to furnish themselves with some much-needed consolation. For a period when no very far-reaching political action seems really feasible, when so-called micropolitics seem the order of the day, it is relieving to convert this necessity into a virtue—to persuade oneself that one's political limits have . . . a solid ontological grounding, in the fact that social totality is in any case a chimera. It doesn't matter if there is no political agent on hand to transform the whole, since there is in fact no whole to be transformed. It is as though, having mislaid the breadknife, one declares the loaf to be already sliced. Totalities, after all, have to exist for someone; and there would now seem [to be] nobody for whom the totality was a totality.[28]

One could say that philosophy of the God's-eye view or that of supremely competent scientific theory of one form of Cartesianism or another is not furnished for human beings and that there has been a final realization of this. That Barth was committed to a chastened sense of human competency is rooted in the Reformed tradition rather deeply. That this makes his theological project postmodernist is another matter. There have been many angles of approach either to explaining or to elaborating postmodernity. Suffice it to declare here that something political and something religious is fundamentally at issue.

Politically, the transitions are rather over. What began in liberal and radical revolution and even earlier in the impotency of social hierarchy concludes in the late-twentieth century with the failure of all rival systems. Some kind of identification between civilization and democracy becomes a settled matter. But this settled matter results in minimal social values for the sake of social

---

28. Terry Eagleton, "Where Does Postmodernism Come From?" *Cànon literari: Ordre i subversió*, ed. J. Pont, Actes del colloqui internacionel (Lleida: Institut d'estudis Ilerdencs, 1998), 29–45, 36–37.

flexibility and in the convergence of multiple beliefs as a result of the most fundamental liberal value: freedom of conscience.

Religiously, although modern secularity and postmodern pluralism or relativism have been deemed excruciatingly low points, they are not the whole story. These religious realities are rooted in the earlier movements of Reformation and post-Reformation, where religious dissent and the search for authenticity of Christian faith prompted first toleration and then liberalization in religious and legal theory. In the first instance, secularity is the conscientious objection to irreconcilable interecclesial conflict, and pluralism is the conscientious reception of multiple ecclesial bodies within a single civil order.

The conflicts that led to these states of affairs were not merely the failure of politics; they were the striving to interpret the Christian faith with greater authenticity. Failure to understand this often leads to recalcitrant nostalgia for an ecclesiastical golden age—a medieval one, which of course is no more real than a pre-Raphaelite painting. The trajectory of Christian culture has simply been in the direction of liberty of conscience on theological grounds and the unavoidability of religious plurality, first, for the sake of one's own conscience, and then also for the sake of everybody else's. The power of a critical and/or secular perspective is always rooted in some religious original, in this case the power of repentance or of conversion. Critical judgment and secularity have always been disingenuous when claiming to have no religious or theological nature.[29] That the modernist belief in and quest for certainty of knowledge is rooted in late medieval and Reformation beliefs in certainty of religious knowledge is a highly important connection. For the Reformers, of course, the belief in certainty rested on the fundamental critique of the Roman ecclesia and the way it cast its own authority. The certitudes of magisterial authority were relocated in Scripture and certain self-referential hermeneutical practices of interpretation. That this move was made is not so surprising, given the hermeneutics of Christian belief. What is surprising is the secular detachment of certainty in philosophical rationality. Such certainty was divine from the outset and therefore mythical or at least something that divine providence alone could have in omniscience. But the idea that omniscience had inscribed itself in nature meant that some native clarity of vision could attain certainty of knowledge. One can lament the history of secular certainty, but one must also remember the theology from which it sprang.

The demise of social hierarchies, the backbone of the premodern order, was occasioned by the political influence of nonnoble persons who began assuming responsibility for the social order. This would become the old liberalism in the face of the new in nineteenth-century experiments with socialism and in the face of a false conservativism in the fascist experiments. The cooptation of the term *liberal,* so ironically by ideologues of a socialist persuasion, continues to beg the

---

29. The most effective exposé of this is accomplished by John Milbank, *Theology and Social Theory: Beyond Secular Reason* (Cambridge, Mass.: Blackwell, 1991).

question as to a future recovery by a contemporary variety of old liberalism. In the meantime, in many respects they are neoconservatives.

But the most important feature of liberal culture is the constitutionalizing of liberal ideals, the installation of these principles in the reasoning practices at the fundamental levels of religion and politics. The fact that the political and religious order of culture could become so effectively led by a new order of things has put this reality into a constant state of contentiousness, but for its own benefit, I would argue.

Postmodernism makes much of the demise of the so-called grand narrative. This I take not as Scripture, the ancient text of the people of God, but of the way in which Christianity came to inhabit particular cultural traditions, such as the Roman one, with its own grand narrative inaugurated by the likes of Virgil. The belief and inscribing of a providential narrative including special divine guidance and great men, whose piety always tips the scales of fate in favor of the great nation, come under severe critique in the face of reforming theologies and liberal ideologies.

Christian faith has always been a matter of answering questions regarding belief or unbelief. By the eighteenth and nineteenth centuries, Christianity's own critics were questioning the legacy of the religion in the most fundamental way. Was Christianity evidence of "religious individualism" and "historical relativism"? From the standpoint of disbelief in reviewing the claims of Christianity either personally or historically, one option simply had to be voluntarism. To the extent that belief is a voluntary act and not by definition coerced, unbelief could be justified conscientiously by anybody not persuaded by the Christian message. Strategies of stigmatizing unbelief in the Christian message by generalizing that message to the point of a theism/atheism dichotomy and creating a negative politics of unbelief have simply failed. Something voluntarist is inherent to the Christian message, and it dares not fault conscientious unbelief. To this extent, the fact that the teachings of the New Testament canon threatened no apostate with death by human instrumentality is sufficient grounds for claiming this.

From Barth's own beginnings as a student and critic of "modern theology," religious individualism, and historical relativism,[30] he is postmodern in the sense of believing that one must go beyond this position to something truer, something that grasps the reality of God more fully. Religious individualism is not so much a wrong path as an incomplete one. Historical relativism is not so much an untruth as merely a partial truth. The big question is whether Barth employs premodern methodology to advance his theological aims. Let us remember, however, that Barth employs what he learned as a modern student of theology

---

30. Claus-Dieter Osthöver, *Die Lehre von Gottes Eigenschaften bei Friedrich Schleiermacher und Karl Bart* (New York: W. de Gruyter, 1996), 103, citing Barth's early essay "Moderne Theologie und Reichsgottesarbeit" (1909) from *Gesamtausgabe*, vol. 3: *Vorträge und kleinere Arbeiten, 1905–1909,* ed. H.-A. Drewes and H. Stoevesandt (Zürich: Theologischer Verlag, 1992), 344.

against the very modernism of his training. His then is a modern solution to the problems of modern theology. Does this make him postmodern?

Some of what Christoph Schwöbel describes might lead one to a different conclusion. Barth, he declares, consciously inverts the methodological inversions of modern epistemology. In discussing Barth's study of Anselm, Schwöbel centers on the famous *fides quaerens intellectum* as the signal of this inversion: "The being of God must be understood as the ground for knowledge of God." "The actuality of the Word of God determines the possibility of theology."[31] Barth's theology is neither premodern (Roman Catholic) nor modern (neo-Protestant) since theology cannot emerge from either a prior condition in human nature or a prior condition in the nature of the church. Only in the ever-new work of the Spirit through the Word can the church and the human know God on God's terms.

John Webster's quotation of John Milbank—who regarded Barth as at once indifferent to philosophy but still locked into a modernist "duality of reason and revelation," running the risk of "allowing worldly knowledge an unquestioned validity within its own sphere"—is not adequately answered.[32] Webster rightly counters postmodernist readings that would reduce Barth to linguistic style by reminding readers that Barth was first and foremost a theologian who was wholly given over to "the world of God."[33] He reminds us that Barth conducted himself as a theologian according to the maxim of "doing theology as if nothing had happened."[34] This means that the vagaries of pressing contemporary conversations must be made relative to the greater interest of understanding the gospel on its own terms. Instead, Webster points to three words of Barth that sum up the relation to postmodernism: "It is given."[35] God graciously gives Jesus Christ to be known to humanity in the church. This positive givenness goes far beyond the perpetual indefiniteness of postmodernism. Probably the richest quote Webster offers from Barth comes from his theological history of the nineteenth century. He reminds us of the newness of each generation of the church:

> Every *period* of the Church does in fact want to be understood as a period of the *Church,* that is, as a time of revelation, knowledge and confession of the

31. Christoph Schwöbel, "Theology," in *The Cambridge Companion to Karl Barth,* ed. John Webster (Cambridge: Cambridge University Press, 2000), 17–36, quoting 30.

32. John Milbank, "Suspending the Material: The Turn of Radical Orthodoxy," in *Radical Orthodoxy: A New Theology,* ed. John Milbank, Catherine Pickstock, and Graham Ward (London: Routledge, 1999), 2, quoted in John Webster, "Barth, Modernity, Postmodernity," in *Karl Barth: A Future for Postmodern Theology?* ed. Geoff Thomason and Christiaan Mostert (Hindmarch: Australian Theological Forum, 2000), 8.

33. Webster, "Barth, Modernity, Postmodernity," 11.

34. Karl Barth, *Theological Existence Today! A Plea for Theological Freedom* (London: Hodder & Stoughton, 1933), 9, quoted in ibid., 13.

35. *CD* I/1:12, quoted in Webster, "Barth, Modernity, Postmodernity," 19.

one Christian faith, indeed, as a special time, as this time of such revelation, knowledge and confession.[36]

Thus, rather than over and over sounding an alert of epochal change, Christian theology and its theologians of each generation find ever-new, ever-fresh expressions of the Holy Spirit in their time. And this they will not fail to do because the mercies of God and indeed the people of God are "new every morning" (John Keble, 1822).

Let us take up Graham Ward's profoundly engaging work on Karl Barth,[37] which is perhaps the most thoroughgoing engagement by a postmodern theologian. The close reading of Barth together with Emmanuel Lévinas and Derrida represents a kind of exegesis of segments of Barth's work that are more helpful than the more thematic treatments. Barth should be read not in terms of systematic uniformity but always as a developing theologian. Rather than subjecting him to lengthy summarization, one should work on segments of his text, truly "hear" him, and look for connections with one's own theological situation. This Ward has done, and masterfully.

Ward's resources have been the *CD* I/1, I/2, II/1, III/2, especially II/1, and also *Romans*. In conversation with Barth, Ward brings in a host of representative texts from Lévinas and Derrida, along with a collection of philosophical contemporaries and immediate predecessors from Barth's time. As the backdrop for the book, Ward hearkens to his student days with their discussion of religious language. He shows the trace of Reformation theology, which is compelled to reflect on the medium of revelation, the human word, and to theologize not only on the medium but also on God's will to mediate himself and his Word through human words and human flesh. Ward is interested in discerning Barth according to his time, and a biographical sense therefore pervades his approach. He is aware that Barth did not engage in debates about the function of language in philosophy, but he finds it intriguing that Barth did his work on the Word of God during such a cultural foment. His interest in Barth can be summed up as the "reaction against idealisms" in the espousal of an absolute meaning able to stabilize and guarantee all reference. Ward continues, "Derrida terms this an immediate access through language to the defined and meaningful 'logocentrism.'"[38] By this is meant a belief that words effectively depict reality. In many respects, logocentrism is a way of regarding the Cartesian belief in the achievement of absolute clarity of thought as the

---

36. Karl Barth, *Protestant Theology in the Nineteenth Century: Its Background and History* (London: SCM, 1972), 15, quoted in Webster, "Barth, Modernity, Postmodernity," 21.

37. Graham Ward, *Barth, Derrida and the Language of Theology* (Cambridge: Cambridge University Press, 1995); cf. William Stacey Johnson, *The Mystery of God: Karl Barth and the Postmodern Foundations of Theology* (Louisville: Westminster John Knox, 1997). In many respects, North American postmodern theology owes its origin to Mark C. Taylor, especially in *Erring: A Postmodern, A-Theology* (Chicago: University of Chicago Press, 1987).

38. Ward, *Barth, Derrida and the Language of Theology*, 4–5.

moment of arriving at certain knowledge and therefore at truth itself. Barth's approach to language, whether of Scripture or theology, is that it both says and does not say what can be said about God. This is the case because of the "new particularism" that Barth introduced in Christology, where the divine Word and the human word are united in the person of Jesus Christ. Precisely where universalistic philosophy parted ways with Christian theology, theology is at the point where it must part ways with the error of failing to recognize the erring of all linguistic acts: No one achieves a universal perspective. The myth of stable, uncontestable facts as a result of experimental methods employed in the physical sciences should never have been regarded as a proper standpoint by theologians.

The Reformation theology of the Word in Barth's theology flows out of the combining of Luther's Word from "outside us," internalized by the work of the Holy Spirit, and Calvin's Word illuminated by the same Spirit. Ward perceives a "grid" in Barth "composed of two antithetical axes. The first is the form, nature and epistemology of language as they are revealed directly by God. The second is the relationship between word [*Wort*], talk [*Rede*] and utterance [*Sprache*] which mediate, for the Church, this immediacy."[39] This grid, according to Ward, stands behind the entire unfolding of the *CD* and its exposition of the knowledge of God in creation, reconciliation, and redemption. What binds the two axes together is the *analogia fidei* (analogy of faith)—which I am not sure Ward gets exactly right—whereby the form of faithful knowing is made to correspond to God's self-knowing as revealed in Scripture. The agent of this faithful knowing, this fashioning of a correspondence, is the Holy Spirit. This correspondence is not discernable between our souls and God but entirely in the revelation of the Word of God and the knowledge that comes by faith alone made possible by that revelation alone.

Ward's interest in *CD* II/1, particularly its fifth chapter, is crucial: In this volume (to which this book will turn later), Ward reads Barth's intent to present the knowledge of God as an apophatic process that results in positive content. He perceives what Torrance perceived a generation earlier in the act of God reclaiming human language for himself when revelation is received by faith and experienced as "a reflection [Abbild] of the Godhead."[40] Nevertheless, Barth presupposes a Kantian epistemology, a dichotomy between the noumenal and phenomenal; the knowledge of God is the overcoming of this divide through the action of God. God reclaims language for himself in the act of imparting certain knowledge of his work in creation, reconciliation, and redemption. "True correspondence or analogy is restored."[41] Through a "nomenclatural or passive-copy theory of language" possible only through revelation and no other way, Barth effects a positivist correspondence view

39. Ibid., 14.
40. Ibid., 24.
41. Ibid., 27.

of language. What begins entirely in the coherencies of a "perfect correspondence" between Scripture and reader ends with a correspondence theory of
knowledge.[42] Ward understands this movement according to Barth as nothing
short of redemption from the fall.

Wanting to know how this correspondence is achieved requires a resort to
the incarnation of the Word of God in Jesus Christ. The incarnation "is the
meaning and the hermeneutic for understanding all language."[43] This is the
"Christological particularism" that becomes a universal through the transform-
ing presence of this Word in the world. Such transformation is no less than
a recovery of the primordial Word in words so that language itself is caught
up in an eschatological process of being redeemed. This primordial nature
of language is reflected in the correspondence between God's word speaking
creation and Adam's word calling identity into being:

Genesis 1:
6 And God said, "Let there be . . ."
7 . . . And it was so [וַיְהִי־כֵן].

Genesis 2:
19 . . . and whatever the man called every living creature, that was its name
[הוּא שְׁמוֹ].

But at this point Ward is tempted to reverse Barth's order of relations between Christology and language and to make the latter somehow primary. In
other words, some kind of theological realism is first of all necessary to make
the christological claims. This is unfortunate since Barth understood that any
explication of a theological hermeneutic would be an outgrowth of revelational
actuality in the process of reading Scripture. Ward then turns to the theoretical
context in which Barth worked, the German *Geist* of the late nineteenth to
mid-twentieth centuries with its ponderings of the nature of language—whether
or not Barth had paid attention to this context. More significantly, Ward is
interested in a context for his discussion of Lévinas and Derrida. The trick
then will be showing a connection between these two and Barth.

The connection Ward thinks he finds is located in Marburg, Germany. It
was in this academic city[44] that the turn of the twentieth century collected
some of the most powerful minds in philosophy and theology and to which
the student Karl Barth aspired as the pinnacle of his training. In the Marburg
School, certain leading ideas of *Sprachphilosophie* are transformed by the best

---

42. Ibid., 28.
43. Ibid., 31. It is clear that Kevin Vanhoozer, *Is There a Meaning in This Text? The Bible,
the Reader, and the Morality of Literary Knowledge* (Grand Rapids: Zondervan, 1998), is after
something like Barth's recovery of language in recovering the author through divine authorship
of Scripture, but this is largely unacknowledged.
44. In Germany, Marburg especially is known as "the university with a city."

of the Jewish philosophers (e.g., Rosenstock, Rosenzweig, and Buber), constituting a "methodological change which involved not simply a move from neo-
Kantianism to phenomenology, but a shift from transcendental subjectivity to
dialogicalism."[45] Reflection on the earliest biblical sources that convey speech
as both word and act,[46] as the relational space between the "I-Thou" of com-
municants, "identified with languages as address, discourse or *Rede*." In this
discourse, "two forms of Logos encounter each other—God's and creation's."[47]
This development produced a movement beyond the *Sprachphilosophie* determined by "an I-It epistemological model which develops an abstract and static
picture of language," and the new *Redephilosophie* "based upon an I-Thou
ontological model" and developing a linguistically oriented phenomenology.[48]
Ward's discomfort with this movement dialogue "is conceived as a sacramental
act" and seems to him not to allow for analogy—an unfortunate slippage away
from relational to objective concepts. What Ward is concerned about is the
Jewish claim to a dialogical relation with God that precedes the historical Jesus,
whereby "no grounds are provided for the uniqueness of Jesus Christ."[49] This
becomes, as in the case of Rosenzweig, an *analogia entis* (analogy of being)
orientation. The presence of God in all language signifies at the most fundamental level that a process of self-redemption, an eschatological principle, is
built into creation. This is the true becoming of Being, but with reference to
the spoken word, even when it is inscripturated. Through this focus, the word
becomes simultaneous to us, and we overcome our error of always transform-
ing references to the dialogically personal into the monologically objective.
According to Ward, here is where Barth and the Marburg school, particularly
through Buber, have their point of contact. Ironically, the contact includes
influence from Barth's side to even Heidegger with the publication in 1919 of
Römerbrief.[50] But Ward claims that the difference between the first and second
editions of *Römerbrief* was his encounter with Marburg's *Redephilosophie.*

The curious thing about Ward's thesis is his attempt to show that Barth
distances himself from belief in the immediate experience of revelation in favor
of "the true nature of interpretation."[51] But where Ward errs is in conflating the
immediate human encounter of the *Deus dixit* (God said) of Scripture with the

---

45. Ward, *Barth, Derrida and the Language of Theology*, 64.

46. דָּבָר, as both verb and substantive, especially the latter with the sense of "annunciation"
and "Word of God," and in human terms where the translation "word" can just as well be "event"
or "thing" that took place, as in, e.g., Gen. 15:1; 18:14; 22:16; 24:30; 44:7; Pss. 22:1; 56:4;
59:12; 105:8. But I would also add the other word for speech act, אָמַר, by which God creates,
promises, commands obedience, blesses, and curses (e.g., Gen. 1–3).

47. Ward, *Barth, Derrida and the Language of Theology*, 64.

48. Ibid., 66.

49. Ibid., 74.

50. Ibid., 80; drawing on Steiner's work, Ward points out Heidegger's adoption of Barth's
exegetical style.

51. Ibid., 88.

interpretation (exposition of Scripture), which is the impossible yet necessary description of God speaking. Ward is fixated on Barth's negativity regarding the loss of direct knowledge of God once possessed by the human *imago Dei* (image of God) but now lost on account of the fall. Yet Ward strangely goes beyond the second edition of *Römerbrief* to find references in Barth to what he regarded as the already immediately present knowledge of God in the revelation of Jesus Christ, by the Holy Spirit working with the Word. This is a significant deficit in Ward's analysis. Thus, when Ward comes to speak of the *analogia entis*—appearing already in Barth's work superseded by the *CD, Die christliche Dogmatik im Entwurf* and the earlier *Göttingen Dogmatics*—he claims that Barth is fixated on a faith that "bears upon a relationship with God that does have both noetic and ontological implications."[52] Where Ward seems to run afoul is at two major points: (1) his wish to "place Barth in the context of German philosophy of language (and discourse),"[53] and (2) his entire project of using Barth's reflections on theological language in chapter 5 as a primary lens through which to view the knowledge of God. Ward confuses Barth's declaration of two words, the Word of God and the word of humanity, with "two antithetical languages"[54]—where they are located and how they function theologically is actually quite foreign to Barth. The juncture in Ward's presentation where he wishes to engraft Barth with postmodern philosophy, particularly in Lévinas and Derrida, is the "problematic" of discourse that is a "crossing through and the resurrection of discourse itself."[55] Indeed, the rest of the book is an attempt to show this connection. Tragically, where this connection must be exposited entirely in a christological way, Ward never proceeds to this on its own terms but within the relation to the problematic, which he wishes to identify in Barth along postmodernist lines.

It is not that I object to bringing the theologian and the theological task into conversation with philosophy, postmodern or modern, but it again and again is in reducing theology to a philosophical problem. Ward's project is more subtly conceived: The philosophical problem is actually supposed to be a theological one with theological answers, however imperfect. Ward has paid close attention to certain genetic streams in the development of postmodern philosophy, including Heidegger. While Ward well identifies Buber's critique of Heidegger, he reads Buber as extending the ontological tradition from Plato to Hegel, where man stands ultimately in "relation to the neuter" (Being).[56] Lévinas will draw heavily on this point and perceives in Heidegger a modernist

---

52. Ward, *Barth, Derrida and the Language of Theology*, 100; most curiously, Ward claims that in Barth's book on Anselm, he "works out the distinction between *analogia entis* and *analogia fidei*—although neither of the terms appear."

53. Ibid., 102.

54. Ibid.

55. Ibid., 103.

56. Ibid., 121.

whose Romanticist totalism paved the way for Nazism. Ward also delineates how Lévinas misreads Heidegger,[57] whose later work contributes to the rise of postmodernist philosophy by becoming a "champion of difference" in his ontology of relations. Curiously, but crucially, "most of Lévinas's key terms can be traced back to Heidegger." Indeed, "his work can be viewed as a Jewish midrash on Heidegger's."[58] But where Heidegger will not venture into theology, Lévinas does, particularly in his works *Totality and Infinity* and *Otherwise than Being*. The difference this makes is literally the movement beyond Heidegger's terminality in thought and to Lévinas's drive to an ethical eschaton.

The great question is the kind of move beyond an agnostic space between belief and unbelief, where Heidegger found himself. It is a theological one for Lévinas and Derrida, but only because the status of knowing is different for all three. Since belief in the self or in God or in Being is not dependent on scientific knowing, the questions are, In theology, how does such knowing that is the knowing of God arise? What is to be done if it does not arise at all? What is to be done if the knowing is a knowing that God is not? This would strike Barth as an exploration in natural theology and would appear to be utterly irrelevant to his theological purposes. For Lévinas, out of the experience of otherness, the infinite keeps insisting on itself. The theology of this is rooted in the *imago Dei*, which indicates the bond between the divine and the human. Ward also wants an inclusion of Christian believing in the Jewish triad of "I and you and the Third who is in our midst," but this may not comport well with Barth.[59]

At this point in Barth, the Christology of the Word can be quite misunderstood for its implications regarding human language. Ward discusses Barth's primary emphasis on revelation as "event" (*Ereignis*—indicating some affinity with Heidegger's sense of the term) of divine penetration into creation, the rupture that is a unique activity next to all others, including other things that happen *(geschehen)* in a narrative.[60] Ward is surely right: "The miracle of [Christ's] advent institutes the *analogia fidei*, whereby the Word is communicated to human being in words." The question arises, however, as to whether this event takes place for God's sake or for the sake of language. If it is for the latter, then language must have a Christology in order for otherness to erupt in our awareness, indicating the Word within the words. If, on the other hand, the rupture of the word through Christ is the moment of God's prerogatives in absolute freedom, then we do not have a strong case of philosophical comparability. Lévinas's analogy of apperception of transcendence disrupting the

---

57. But Emmanuel Lévinas, *Of the God Who Comes to Mind,* trans. Bettina Bergo (Stanford: Stanford University Press, 1998), 92, states, "You know, when I pay homage to Heidegger, it is always costly to me, not because of his incontestable brilliance, as you also know."

58. Ward, *Barth, Derrida and the Language of Theology,* 123.

59. Ibid., 146.

60. Ibid., 152–54, finding support in George Hunsinger, *How to Read Karl Barth: The Shape of His Theology* (Oxford: Oxford University Press, 1991), 11.

totality of what otherwise is, is not in the first instance what is going on in Barth's christologically defined *analogia fidei* with respect to "creaturely reality." Ward acknowledges that "Lévinas does not espouse the particularism of Barth's Christology"[61]—but this is the very point, that for Barth, the rupture itself is particularistic, not a rupture already taking place in all language but one that indicates the rupture of all judgments.

The unique objectivity of God in Christ does not render Lévinas's apophatic theology of language untrue. Indeed, Barth might have an affinity for it, but there is simply no overlap. Although Ward is not making a missiological statement like Emil Brunner, there is a latency of natural theology in this entire exercise. This is perhaps why, in the end, Derrida is skeptical of the Lévinas project, which he regards as an effort to detect traces of deity in things, not much different from Augustinian searches for a *vestigia trinitatis* (vestiges of the Trinity). If it were the case that some kind of postmodern sensibility was causing Barth's approach, then he would evidence the attempt at a connection between the general and the particular, but this he resolutely does not do. This is not to overlook the particularism of Israel's faith, her God, and her election; yet expositions of such faith have also included the foreign material of natural theology. Lévinas simply would be no exception, although his route to natural theology is radically different from modern or premodern approaches. Thus, Lévinas and Barth can both view revelation as a rupture that "fissures the Kantian unity of apperception." Both also can have a similar view of self, but where they diverge is the way they encounter revelation. Lévinas has no corresponding particularism in Scripture or the figure of God in Scripture. What Ward wants to relegate to a "Christological difference"[62] is actually not christological but rather a particularistic difference over the uniqueness of revelation.

In Lévinas, all the virtues of Israel's God are in evidence, but the experience and truth of God through revelation are grounded elsewhere, in the communicative anthropology and sociality. Yet Ward wants to find a kenotic dimension common to both Lévinas and Barth—and if Lévinas were speaking out of a linguistic of YAHWEH as אֵל עִמָּנוּ (Immanuel, God with us, e.g., Isa. 8:8), he would find kenosis. The "ethics of kenosis" is certainly common to both, but not kenotic theology: God's self-emptying servitude in the covenantal revelation of gracious presence as YAHWEH and Christ (cf. Isa. 53 and Phil. 2:6–11). Ward impressively exposits Barth's christological particularism as though similar to Lévinas's ethical and anthropological particularism, but the structural-theological point of contact is lacking. I venture several explanations: This is to avoid the modernist misuse of the Name, the classic Judaic reticence in using the Name, and also classic philosophical habits of discussing the being of God. But for Lévinas, the Other is the stranger, to become a neighbor; for Barth, the Other is Jesus Christ, to be the Savior. A particularism that situates

---

61. Ward, *Barth, Derrida and the Language of Theology,* 156.
62. Ibid., 157–58.

between transcendence and immanence and even a messianism are common to both, abandoning modernist conceptions of totality and anthropologies of self-sufficient, logocentric reasoning. But is not their difference subversive of this project? For Barth, the messianism is always this Stranger-become-Savior; for Lévinas, the messianism is always every stranger-become-neighbor. It is this very point that Derrida criticizes in Lévinas.[63]

In discussing Lévinas, one cannot ignore his profound indebtedness to Scripture. He is fixed on themes that open up to great potential for theological dialogue beyond the boundaries of Judaism. God *found* is always also God sought, as seen in the text of Isaiah 65:1, where God declares:

נִדְרַשְׁתִּי לְלוֹא שָׁאָלוּ נִמְצֵאתִי לְלֹא בִקְשֻׁנִי
אָמַרְתִּי הִנֵּנִי הִנֵּנִי אֶל־גּוֹי לֹא־קֹרָא בִשְׁמִי׃

> I was ready to be sought out by those who did not ask,
>   to be found by those who did not seek me.
> I said, "Here I am, here I am," to a nation that did not call on my name.

Lévinas thought it necessary to work at the level of theoretical questions rather than those arising from Scripture and faith because the latter stand behind the former anyway. Theoretical questioning forgets this priority, although Lévinas would just as soon not refer to a priority.[64]

In discussing a new set of parallels between Derrida and Barth, the acute awareness of time and the resulting absence of presence potentially bring the two together. But now the framework of exchange and negotiation has displaced the framework of communication. Derrida, accusing Lévinas of being an empiricist, believed he detected a latent Platonism in his thought. Lévinas makes such moves, Derrida claims, because he takes his own metaphors too seriously where the face of the other becomes the presence of otherness, even if only as a trace of presence, and therefore a new claim for knowing "Being" *(ousia)*.[65] Ward makes the observation that Lévinas has actually imported a kind of *analogia entis* that, Barth protested, reduces God to anthropology.[66] This is unfortunate since the failure of metaphysics to secure the certainty of the knowledge of Being should have cancelled the attempt to import any claim of this kind into the discourse. The problem is that a metaphysics of presence cannot be philosophically demonstrated or privileged, thus leaving

---

63. Ward continues his comparison with Lévinas and Barth in trinitarian terms but is forced, even forced in the extreme. This is in no way a dismissal of Lévinas's brilliant expositions but a coming to terms with the greater incomparability between Lévinas and Barth, in spite of Ward's curious listing of Scripture-based terms that he calls "the same for each—sin as atheism and egology, 'revelation,' 'God,' 'prophet,' 'Messiah,' 'eternal,' 'creation,' 'born again'" (ibid., 169).

64. Lévinas, *Of the God Who Comes to Mind*, 85.

65. Ward, *Barth, Derrida and the Language of Theology*, 181.

66. Ibid., 188.

merely a form of acting on faith. This is the case with presence since there "is neither pure encounter, nor pure constitution, only the world 'in which the absence-presence of God *plays.*'"[67] Anything more than this ambiguity in the rupturing of silence that is all discourse is impossible. If anything more is offered in the way of God, it is no longer philosophy but theology in the form of a realized eschatology.[68] Derrida's critique effectively silences Lévinas, who no longer exercised self-critique here but also allows him, as it were, to move forward by faith. As such, Derrida is a necessary supplement to the reception of Lévinas.

Ward finally acknowledges the basic difference between Lévinas and Barth at the point of general and special revelation: The former recovers *analogia entis* in acts of saying, the latter *analogia fidei* in the radical particularity of God in Jesus Christ.[69] Lévinas ultimately comes to the immediacy of God's being, following the trace of language in his own type of negative theology. More than the dynamics of language itself, Ward must acknowledge that the entire reception of biblical revelation by Barth on such things as sin and free will, divine grace and election, drive him far beyond what general communicative events deliver about God—and even beyond events that the Scripture text engenders. Ward perceptively highlights Barth's refusal to regard revelation on general terms, and this means rejecting even negative theology and the attempt to derive some positive benefit from it. Breaking with any Hegelian understanding of a synthesis of positive and negative reasoning toward the knowledge of God, Barth insists on the knowledge of God solely in the "power of his movement" *(die Kraft seiner Bewegung).*[70] This is where, for Ward, the "supplement" of Derrida's "economy of *différance*" enters in.[71]

For Derrida, truth and meaning are ever-open questions closed only by a divine event or death. Everything in human knowing therefore is "partial and provisional." Because of this, even knowing a trace of God's immediate presence or the metaphysical Word are not possible in the temporal acts of human communication, whether spoken or textual. The focus, however, should be on "immediate presence" for human knowing. God and the Word are accessible only through mediation, whether because of radical temporality along Derrida's reasoning or because of God's sovereign purpose according to Barth's. Ward again perceives that Derrida "necessarily constructs a transcendental argument and requires the possibility of immediacy in order for mediacy to have any meaning at all."[72] Derrida is focused on the restrictions of the time for revelation, rejecting any final content to either positive or negative theology

67. Jacques Derrida, *Writing and Difference,* trans. Alan Bass (Chicago: University of Chicago Press, 1978), 107, quoted in ibid., 188.

68. Ward, *Barth, Derrida and the Language of Theology,* 189.

69. Ibid., 204–5.

70. *CD* II/1:201, 226.

71. Ward, *Barth, Derrida and the Language of Theology,* 208.

72. Ibid., 214.

in the form of eschatology (in contrast to Lévinas's focus on the spatiality of face-to-face encounter in communication). As such, removing the present from any actual contact with the final future defers truth before the end to an excruciating remove. This is at the heart of his criticism of Lévinas's realized eschatology: The end is not present until the end. One can hardly resist a pause for reflecting on two great passages of eschatological knowing:

ἐκ μέρους γὰρ γινώσκομεν καὶ ἐκ μέρους προφητεύομεν· ὅταν δὲ ἔλθῃ τὸ τέλειον, τὸ ἐκ μέρους καταργηθήσεται. . . . βλέπομεν γὰρ ἄρτι δι᾽ ἐσόπτρου ἐν αἰνίγματι, τότε δὲ πρόσωπον πρὸς πρόσωπον· ἄρτι γινώσκω ἐκ μέρους, τότε δὲ ἐπιγνώσομαι καθὼς καὶ ἐπεγνώσθην.

For we know only in part, and we prophesy only in part; but when the complete comes, the partial will come to an end. . . . For now we see in a mirror, dimly, but then we will see face to face. Now I know only in part; then I will know fully, even as I have been fully known.

1 Corinthians 13:9–10, 12

Ἀγαπητοί, νῦν τέκνα θεοῦ ἐσμεν, καὶ οὔπω ἐφανερώθη τί ἐσόμεθα. οἴδαμεν ὅτι ἐὰν φανερωθῇ ὅμοιοι αὐτῷ ἐσόμεθα, ὅτι ὀψόμεθα αὐτὸν καθώς ἐστιν.

Beloved, we are God's children now; what we will be has not yet been revealed. What we do know is this: when he is revealed, we will be like him, for we will see him as he is.

1 John 3:2[73]

As it turns out, since part of what Derrida is working against are eschatologies of metaphysics, he moves to a highly generalized eschatology. Like Lévinas, he avoids Scripture's particularity of the Word of God. The antimetaphysics strategy of Derrida (deconstruction through constant referral to *différance*), whereby metaphysics is subverted as surrogate theology, is relatively success-ful.[74] Hegel's dialectical progressions, both semiotic and historical, are the particular focus of Derrida's strategy. *Différance* for Derrida is that which stands radically outside all dialectical relations, where opposites define one another through their relations. *Différance* is that which cannot be enclosed

73. Our knowing in Christ "in whom are hidden all the treasures of wisdom and knowl-edge" (ἐν ᾧ εἰσιν πάντες οἱ θησαυροὶ τῆς σοφίας καὶ γνώσεως ἀπόκρυφοι [Col. 2:3]) cannot be confused with his fullness or his knowing. Indeed, these *treasures,* while open and benefiting us fully, are not fully accessible in view of hope that does not yet know, has not yet seen, has not yet heard. Far from being a kind of gnostic knowing, the greater dis-analogy of our present knowing is the truly eschatological "not yet" of all presences and all events. The rejection of metaphysics by coming to grips with eschatology is not a pursuit of truth but a reaction against its unjustifiable claims to possess truth in its finality.

74. Cf. esp. Jacques Derrida, *Speech and Phenomena,* trans. and ed. David B. Allison (Evan-ston, Ill.: Northwestern University Press, 1973).

within dialectical process, and as such it relativizes or destabilizes every conception of process at the level of metaphysics—this is the "economy of *différance.*" Derrida effectively uses metaphysical insights to subvert projects of metaphysical systematization.

The question here, as Ward elaborates, is whether Derrida is performing a kind of apophatic move in theology (negative theology, in the tradition of Dionysius and Meister Eckehart and, indeed, even Heidegger). He points out Derrida's own sensitivity to this in Derrida's denial that this is the case while allowing the possibility that he is doing so. Ward recognizes Derrida's use of the metaphysical against metaphysics in what amounts to a recognition of human fallibility and injury, of undecidability. The temptation at the heart of all metaphysics, taking metaphors too seriously, as more than linguistic relations, and elevating them to transcendent truth, is nothing short of recognizing that *analogia entis* does the same thing.[75] Instead, metaphorical function is at the heart of linguistic mediation; forgetting this is simply to fall into the temptation of exalting metaphor. At this point death enters into Derrida's negotiations with Lévinas. The eschatology of death displaces that of hope. The perishing—the present along with the activity of desire—disrupts all attempts at stable knowledge and corresponds to the very nature of language at its limits. Ward reflects, however, that what language cannot do, God does in the particularity of Jesus Christ, especially in the name that stands for the Word in the words.[76] In fact, Derrida is a negative theologian who in the course of time moves from the *apophasis* (negation) to the *kataphasis* (affirmation) of what it claims to know about God—even if only a trace of God.

By way of conclusion, Ward draws Barth and Derrida together through a challenge to the critics of Barth's account of revelation.[77] Barth's dialectical reasoning can be expressed through any of three terms: presentation, representation, and performance. In divine presentation, actually divine self-presentation, Ward is a bit confused when he says, "It is unclear how His presence is presented to us."[78] But surely what Barth has in mind is the original, continual, but radically sin-obscured self-revelation of God in creation. Like all free initiatives on God's part, humanity is held accountable and is under judgment because of this dimension of revelation:

διότι τὸ γνωστὸν τοῦ θεοῦ φανερόν ἐστιν ἐν αὐτοῖς· ὁ θεὸς γὰρ αὐτοῖς ἐφανέρωσεν. τὰ γὰρ ἀόρατα αὐτοῦ ἀπὸ κτίσεως κόσμου τοῖς ποιήμασιν νοούμενα καθορᾶται, ἥ τε ἀΐδιος αὐτοῦ δύναμις καὶ θειότης, εἰς τὸ εἶναι αὐτοὺς ἀναπολογήτους.

75. Ward, *Barth, Derrida and the Language of Theology,* 224.
76. Ibid., 233.
77. Ibid., 235, quoting Richard Roberts's criticism of the dialectical *analogia fidei* in "The Doctrine of Time in Karl Barth," *A Theology on Its Way?* (Edinburgh: T & T Clark, 1991), 144.
78. Ward, *Barth, Derrida and the Language of Theology,* 237.

For what can be known about God is plain to them, because God has shown it to them. Ever since the creation of the world his eternal power and divine nature, invisible though they are, have been understood and seen through the things he has made. So they are without excuse.

Romans 1:19–20

What Ward misses here is crucial. The incapacitation of human knowing what can be plainly (φανερόν) known about God is indicative of a radically noetic flaw because God actively makes himself known (ἐφανέρωσεν) through creation. Paul virtually belabors the point by specifying which "invisible" (ἀό- ρατὰ) (cf. Col. 1:15f.) attributes should be known: "eternal power and divine nature" (ἀΐδιος . . . δύναμις καὶ θειότης) through "the things [God] has made" (τοῖς ποιήμασιν). Very poignantly, the agency of revelation is the work of God: God presents himself by entering the world as its Maker. The effectiveness of this revelation is indicated by the moral indictment of inexcusability (ἀναπο- λόγητος).[79] The creation is so evidently knowable as the creation of this God, everywhere and always mediating the traces of this God, and yet this God is so evidently and culpably not known. Indeed, because of this incapacitation, a different form of mediation, a representation rather than a presentation, is needed to make the knowledge of God effectively known. God wills to be known through Jesus Christ and as Redeemer, not merely as Creator.

God comes to us in Jesus Christ, not just to present himself again as Cre- ator, although the Son is the Mediator of the divine work of creation itself (John 1:1–4; Col. 1:15–20), but as representative of God to man and of man to God. Just at this point Ward might have brought out the importance of the Chalcedonian formulation to explicate more fully the incarnational and redemptive significance of this representation. The incarnation (John 1:14; Rom. 1:3) is the ontological basis for the chief attribution of Christ as the Mediator between God and humanity (μεσίτης: 1 Tim. 2:5; Heb. 8:6; 9:15; 12:24). Although the activity of the mediation is asymmetrical,[80] God initiates the mediation entirely for his sake and ours; ontologically, the relations are entirely mutual and are expressed by means of the double *homoousion* (of the same substance).[81] By virtue of the incarnation, the Son is *homoousios* with the

---

79. In the New Testament, this term appears only here and in Romans 2:1; it stands in relation to the legal term under negation, ἀπολογέομαι, which is one's speech of defense in the face of accusation or judgment.

80. Ward, *Barth, Derrida and the Language of Theology,* 239, seems to discern this when he notes the distinct terms Barth uses, where Christ "represents" *(vertreten)* us to God and where Christ "enters" *(eintreten)* into our sphere to represent God.

81. As the formula reads: "consubstantial with the Father as touching his Godhead, and consubstantial with us as touching his manhood." Recent christological study has explored and expanded on Chalcedonian formulations: Aloys (Alois) Grillmeier, with Theresia Hainthaler, *Christ in Christian Tradition,* vol. 2: *From the Council of Chalcedon (451) to Gregory the Great (590–604),* part 4: *The Church of Alexandria with Nubia and Ethiopia after 451,* trans. O. C. Dean

Father and also *homoousios* with humanity.[82] The Son is both "one nature" with God and "one nature" with all human beings. Elect to this destiny, this God is this man, this man is this God, so that a dual representation is effectuated in a human life, this man's life, who ever lives to perform this representation. At the level of revelation where we access it, it in the first instance is memory installed in the texts of Scripture. Here, too, Ward gets it only half right, since Barth is also emphatic about the Holy Spirit's role in making present what the textual memory of Scripture does not do in the form of mere print. Ward is correct about a "forgetting of the language in order to describe again a form of representation that cannot be represented" but can only be "continually negotiated."[83] But "in fact" God makes this possible in the communicative relationality and mediatorial activity of the Holy Spirit.

This leads to the third dimension of revelation: performance. By this I think Barth intends the performance of self-revelation that corresponds to an act of faithful knowing. Ward points out the epistemological tension in Barth between the empirical reception of transcendent reference in theological language and "an alternative, immediate form of knowing" that, however, remains unexplained.[84] Ward knows that Barth's answer to this tension is to be found in his explication of *analogia fidei,* where the knowledge of the believer not only corresponds with God's self-knowledge but also participates in it. Without specifically referring to Barth's dialectic, this is the heart of the theological matter. And yet in the midst of Barth's dialectic, where divine speech constantly calls into question and relativizes human speech and language reflecting divine prerogative, Barth displays an "undialectical certainty" that appears to undermine part of his theological claim. One could ask Ward then what *dialectical certainty* would be. Equally odd, Ward blames Barth for not distinguishing "metaphorical from non-metaphorical language use." Theology is made to absorb epistemological terms without redefining those terms. What seems to be going on is that Ward simply resists what Barth is trying to do. Ward nicely sums up Barth: "By faith, we read this epistemological vocabulary as properly and originally belonging to a divine and not a human epistemology."[85] What Ward objects to as the performance of theology, Barth intends to resolve with reference to God's performance of self-demonstration, which

---

(Louisville: Westminster John Knox, 1996); J. Van Oort and Ulrich Wickert, eds., *Christliche Exegese zwischen Nicaea und Chalcedon* (Amsterdam: KOK Pharos, 1992); and Uchenna A. Ezeh, *Jesus Christ the Ancestor: An African Contextual Christology in the Light of the Major Dogmatic Christological Definitions of the Church from the Council of Nicea (325) to Chalcedon (451)* (Bern: P. Lang, 2003).

82. It is in just this formulation that Barth's uniting of the two interpretations of the incarnation as "hypostatic union" is best highlighted. The Son is *enhypostasis* as the specific man Jesus, and simultaneously, the Son is *anhypostasis* as the personed union of divine and human natures.

83. Ward, *Barth, Derrida and the Language of Theology,* 238–39.

84. Ibid., 241.

85. Ibid.

constrains us to gratitude and indebtedness and therefore to the knowledge of God the Father as our Lord, because in eternity God is the Father of His own eternal Son and with Him the source of the Holy Spirit. Further, the fact that according to that self-demonstration God Himself is and does everything for the man who still owes Him everything . . . , that self-demonstration constrains us to adoration of His faithfulness and grace and therefore to the knowledge of God the Son as our Lord . . . , that God is Himself eternally the Holy Spirit, proceeding from the Father and the Son, and of one essence with them both . . . to hope, and therefore to the knowledge of the Holy Spirit. . . . In this way the self-demonstration, and in this way the proclamation and action of God through His Word in the covenant concluded with man, is grounded in God Himself. In this way and on this ground it has its compelling force. Because God is in Himself the triune God, both in His Word and in the work of creation, reconciliation and redemption, we have to do with Himself. It is therefore impossible for us to postpone the decision—which means the encounter with Him—on the grounds that He is perhaps quite different from the One who proclaims Himself and acts in this way. And because God is in Himself the triune God, in this His Word we have to do with the final revelation of God which can never be rivaled or surpassed. It is, therefore, quite impossible to ask about other lords alongside and above this Lord. In the life of God as the life of the triune God things are so ordered and necessary that the work of God in His Word is the one supreme and true lordship in which He gives Himself to be known and is known.

. . . In the heart of the truth in which we know God, God knows Himself; the Father knows the Son and the Son the Father in the unity of the Holy Spirit. This occurrence in God Himself is the essence and strength of our knowledge of God. . . . It is certainly a hidden occurrence . . . in which man as such is not a participant, but in which he becomes a participant through God's revelation and thus in a way inconceivable to himself . . . our knowledge of God acquires truth as the internal expression of that inner truth. . . . We laud and magnify Him in the hiddenness of His self-knowledge, on the strength of which alone the knowledge of God can ever become real. Our knowledge of God is derived and secondary. It is effected by grace in the creaturely sphere in consequence of the fact that first of all, in itself and without us, it is actual in the divine sphere—in the sphere of God as the sphere of His own truth, or the inner truth ever of our knowledge of God, who is always inaccessible to us as such. We stand here before the root of the necessity to fear God because we may love Him, to revere Him in His mystery because He has made Himself so clear and certain to us. . . . We stand here before the root of the problem of the objectivity of God. We have already seen that without the objectivity of God there is no knowledge of God . . . , that without God's objectivity to Himself there is no knowledge of God; without the truth of a primary objectivity of Him who reveals Himself to us there is no truth of His secondary objectivity in His revelation. . . . It does not mean any renunciation or surrender, but only the confirmation and exemplification of His divine nature. . . . To say this, however, is to say that His unveiling in His works and signs always means for us His veiling too, that His revelation always means His hiddenness, that love towards Him cannot be without fear before Him, that the clarity and certainty of His existence bestowed upon us cannot be without His remaining a mystery to us . . . , that even in His revelation we know Him only in consequence of the fact that knowledge of God is real as God's own hidden work in His being as the triune God from eternity to eternity.[86]

Ward is correct in observing that Barth does not develop a theology of theology—that would be to counteract Barth's counteraction against most modern theology (thus dismantling its self-sufficiency). Barth instead is intoxicated with divine self-sufficiency that is at once free, providentially gracious, and covenantal. To awaken to faith in the Triune God means to be included derivationally in God's self-knowledge. But Ward has therefore either not perceived or not comprehended Barth's determination to write a revelational theology of divine initiative from first to last. Instead, the continuity between God's self-revelation and faith by the gracious work of God is no different from knowing God by the gracious work of God. Indeed, God's gracious work makes this knowing possible. Finally, Ward prefers that we agree with Barth based on the unavoidability of "flawed logic" of explanation and follow "a logic of the movement of Barth's theological discourse itself."[87] This he likens to the "unknowledge" of Derrida's *différance* when compared with knowledge claims in philosophy and science. Ward suggests this based on the words of Jesus, "I am with you always," and their double sense, anticipating Derrida's "double position" of the now and not yet of eschatological faith.

Instead of Lévinas's theological traces of divine presence in all human events of linguistic exchange, Derrida proposes the eschatological in all such events, and to this Ward ascribes "the interminable process of *analogia fidei*."[88] What Ward means by this is the way in which Barth's theology is a continuous uniting of past, present, and future in theological statements, knowing that human statements about God's revelation are always partial and stand under divine judgment. But there is only a certain minimum to which this refers. Ward claims that Derrida helps Barth philosophically by showing us the philosophical teleology to which Barth resorted. But is this the case? In a lengthy excursus on orthodox dogmatics of the seventeenth century, Barth exposes its lack of theological consistency in its understanding of analogy. It took its cues from *analogia entis* in medieval Scholasticism and not, as it should have, from the revelation of God's gracious initiative in Christ—*analogia gratiae*. This is the only proper understanding of analogy, Barth argues:

> We have therefore attempted to understand and form the doctrine of analogy otherwise than the older orthodoxy did, and as . . . it must be understood and formed, if we are already aware that Christology really is and must remain the life-centre of theology, of all theology, and if we are also aware that the correct interpretation of Christology, as presented even by the older orthodoxy, is to be

86. *CD,* II/1:48–50.
87. Ward, *Barth, Derrida and the Language of Theology,* 243.
88. Ibid., 246.

found in the doctrine of the justification of the sinner by faith alone. For the point at issue is that it is not a good thing to operate in theology with a twofold truth. The point at issue is that in the doctrine of God, in the doctrine of the knowledge of God by Jesus Christ, we must think and speak and argue from the Word of God and not from elsewhere.[89]

But the context of Barth's discussion is the question of the veracity of our knowledge of God: How do we know that our knowledge of God is true? This is something that linguistic phenomena and their philosophical interpretation in no case can answer. Why Ward seeks an answer here in Derrida or in Lévinas is laudable at the point of apologetics but not at the point of coordinating with Barth's intentions as a theologian. Barth is acutely aware that in resting entirely on revelation and grace he is propounding a circularity of truth in the knowledge of God—*circulus vertatis Dei*. But this is so that in every case theology as the human testimony to the true knowledge of God may always emanate from faith and indeed be a demonstration that our faith has stood up to trial and received the corresponding comfort of God.

No other sphere of knowing can possibly contribute to this knowing of God.

> In respect of the *circulus vertatis Dei* we have no last word to speak. We can only repeat ourselves. We can, therefore, only describe Him again, and often, and in the last resort infinitely often. If we try to speak conclusively of the limits of our knowledge of God and of the knowledge of God generally, we can come to no conclusion. . . . And the question always remains whether we stand in faith so that this can be said of us, and therefore whether we are actually partakers of true knowledge of God. In this matter we have definitely no last word to speak. If we think we have, we have already pronounced our own judgment, because we have denied faith. For this very reason, the reference to Jesus Christ cannot and must not on any account try to have on our side the character of a conclusive word. Jesus Christ is really too good to let Himself be introduced and used as the last word of our self-substantiation. . . . We are again caught up in the attempt (the attempt of unbelief) to anchor in a safe harbour, whereas in faith it is a question of putting out to sea at Christ's command. We are not referring to Christology. We are referring, christologically speaking, to Jesus Christ Himself. . . .
>
> But this sphere is the sphere of Jesus Christ. Grace is not a general possibility, to which as such we can systematically recur and from which we can withdraw. . . . Grace is the "grace of our Lord Jesus Christ" (2 Cor. 13:14 [13]). If we appeal to it, we not only acknowledge that we are in need of restraint or of assurance in regard to our own action, but we have confessed that our action (in our case, a line of thought) reveals a vacuum within us which is decisive for the whole, shewing it to be either correct or utterly futile. We have confessed that we cannot fill up this vacuum, not even with a central concept, either by restraint or

89. *CD* II/1:242.

by assurance. We have confessed that there, in this vacuum of our action and line of thought, stands Jesus Christ: not a christological article which we can now utilize as a key to turn this last lock, and therefore not as a last word in our mouth; but Jesus Christ Himself as the pre-eminent Judge and Saviour of our action.[90]

Here we realize that absent from Ward's entire discussion is a dimension absolutely critical to Barth's thinking: personal faith in Jesus Christ. Barth's way of thinking on this matter was not in any way philosophically conceived; indeed, he was emphatic that this had nothing to do with defining christological concepts. Instead, the dynamic of faith is a guiding principle throughout the entire *CD*. With Barth, theology is also and always and supremely personal testimony, the dialectically dynamic second feature of the knowledge of God. The first and primary is God's revelatory and gracious action to communicate his own self-knowledge to the believer through Jesus Christ. Faith is the knowledge and personal communication of the knowledge that God has revealed graciously to all believers—the *analogia fidei*. Barth's theology is a reflection of "the divine reality by which the *circulus vertatis Dei* in which we move is encompassed."[91] Barth knows that knowledge claims based in revelation and faith are a tremendous risk, but to describe them otherwise or to resort to philosophical self-substantiation, simply cannot be done. The knowledge of God in Christ is the result of acts of obedience to the Word of God and therefore to God himself.

Thus, when Ward concludes that Derrida's *différance* provides to "Barth's theology of the Word a coherence for what otherwise has been seen as a contradiction which logically flaws his Christology and the soteriological operation of the Trinity,"[92] the claim could not appear more inappropriate, especially since Barth has been working with a logic of grace and personal faith that Ward has not taken into account. No doubt Derrida's strategies of interpretation bring contradiction into a kind of alignment that is both a breaking and a joining and thus the formation of a new form of logic, but it hardly serves what Barth is doing. Because the composite of Barth's project includes the dynamic dimension of participation in God by faith, there is more taking place than his often-referred-to "unveiling and veiling" of God in his revelation. Ward is attentive on the centrality of Jesus Christ in Barth and therefore the intractability of this center to the difference decentered by bonded unities in the postmodernist thinker. Most curiously, to finalize his vision of the connection between Barth and Derrida, Ward correlates Jesus Christ with *différance* itself in a move he calls *"analogia Christi."* But this is the riskiest and most limiting claim of all: "'The God of God' in the human Jesus has been reduced, not merely to a sign but to the intersection of signs, the

90. *CD* II/1:250–51.
91. Ibid.
92. Ward, *Barth, Derrida and the Language of Theology,* 247.

resistance to meaning and the creation of new meaning in a continuous cycle of making and unmaking. I would agree that the nature of theological discourse is . . . inseparable from the doctrine of Christ."[93] At this point, however, the regrettable failure of Ward is to miss one other vital negation: The nature of theological discourse is both inseparable and *irreversible* from the doctrine of Christ. Theological discourse is shaped by the revelation and grace of God in Christ, but theological discourse does not shape God. This is the great test of the appropriateness of all theological discourse, whether it betrays a yielding to divine initiative or not. The greatest danger for theology in this vein is precisely at the point where it perceives the Word in the words—something that the Word and the faith created by that the Word enables. But this cannot be reversed without committing new acts of *analogia entis* in self-sufficient acts of perceiving our words in any way determinative of that Word.[94] This could hardly be more tellingly expressed than in the statement "Theological discourse articulates the theology of discourse itself"—not that it makes theology of discourse derived from revelation possible, but that something about discourse itself is theological on its own terms. And to seal its fate: "The economy of signification *is* this economy of faith." Ward wants to dampen the implications of this for theology and for faith, acknowledging only fleetingly at the very end of his discourse that the latter is both "gift and personal commitment." And yet his contention that *différance* as "a law of textuality, cannot provide grounds for a natural theology" begs the question, since the perceived trace of divine Otherness in this law is the instantiation of yet another variety of the same.

We cannot here look further into postmodernist readings of Barth, but some of the most inventive uses of him are to be found on this path. There are traces of evidence that such a move is not entirely wrongheaded. Although postmodernism in many ways is a kind of ethos that rejects a variously interpreted modern ethos, certainly Barth's early rejection of what was quintessentially modern, liberal theology, cannot help but be interpreted as postmodern in some basic sense. Barth's recovery of premodern theological language, along with his radical attack on the presumptions of critical judgment and system building, all resonate deeply with postmoderns. In adopting his theological dialectic, the asymmetrical relation between God's address and our response, one fundamental claim by Barth is that before we can begin speaking about God, we must renounce our speaking about him. Only insofar as we have repented of speaking about God can we begin to hear God on God's terms and by his Spirit begin to speak about him on the basis of revelation alone.

93. Ibid.

94. This happens, surprisingly, even where we might least expect it, e.g., Vanhoozer, *Is There a Meaning in This Text?* 426, where in defining "the relation between Word and Spirit," he uses speech-act theory to do so and equates this to the theology of the Reformers. In the interest of finding divine authority for shoring up losses to the authority of the biblical authors, Vanhoozer develops a theory defending the authority of all authors, which invariably is read back into his notion of authorial communication in Scripture, whether by God or divinely inspired humans.

This is not to say that "revelation alone" will mean without the aid of human conventions and conceptual forms but that there will be no reversal of the relation between God and his prerogatives, and humans speak about him always as a form of response. The postmodern linkage with Barth is the divine silencing of the human.

In dialectical terms, the silencing of the human (cf. Deut. 27:9; Job 6:24; Isa. 47:5; 53:7; Lam. 2:10; Hab. 2:20; Zeph. 1:7; Zech. 2:13; Matt. 26:63) is a firstfruit of the Spirit's gift of faith. Consider such choice passages as the following:

> When you are disturbed, do not sin; ponder it on your beds, and be silent [דֹמּוּ].
>
> Psalm 4:4

> For God alone my soul waits in silence [דוּמִיָּה]; from him comes my salvation. . . . For God alone my soul waits in silence [דֹומִּי], for my hope is from him.
>
> Psalm 62:1, 5

> If you would only keep silent [הַחֲרֵשׁ], that would be your wisdom!
>
> Job 13:5

> . . . to sit alone in silence [יִדֹּם] when the Lord has imposed it.
>
> Lamentations 3:28

But then of course, there is also the command to speak: "One night the Lord said to Paul in a vision, 'Do not be afraid, but speak and do not be silent [μὴ σιωπήσῃς]'" (Acts 18:9).

Much of this reflection is a recovery of the truth that on our own we can say nothing true about God. This will also be a part of Barth's assault on religion as such. In apophatic theology, or theology by negation, the "unknown God" (ἄγνωστος θεός; Acts 17:23) is known not through what religion knows and constructs but through denying these things. What would be done by Ward in connecting Barth's apophatic elements with Derrida's deconstructive strategies is matched by other postmodern approaches.[95]

---

95. Cf. Walter James Lowe, *Theology and Difference: The Wound of Reason* (Bloomington, Ind.: Indiana University Press, 1993); and Brian D. Ingraffia, *Postmodern Theory and Biblical Theology: Vanquishing God's Shadow* (Cambridge: Cambridge University Press, 1996). Importantly, postmodernism in theology need not work with Barth as exemplar; see, e.g., Stanley J. Grenz and John R. Franke, *Beyond Foundationalism: Shaping Theology in a Postmodern Context* (Louisville: Westminster John Knox, 2000).

2

READINGS FROM AN AMERICAN PERSPECTIVE

Since Douglas Horton introduced Barth's work to American Protestant theologians in the late 1920s,[1] the spectrum of responses has been great and changing throughout the twentieth century and into the twenty-first century. I prefer to regard Barth as the leading twentieth-century Christian theologian, who for contemporary purposes cannot be labeled conservative or liberal.[2] Some would regard him as liberal, others even as revolutionary because of his social democratic sympathies, some as evangelical but rebuffed by many American evangelicals, and yet others as the founder of postliberal theology. Many from other theological traditions, particularly Orthodox and Roman Catholic, read Barth for ecumenical and even deeply catholic reasons. I read Barth because his work is such a turning point for Christian theology. His work is not merely a great intellectual and conceptual achievement; most importantly, it changes the way that "faith seeks understanding," both for its own sake and for the sake of the proclamation of the gospel for the salvation of the nations.

This chapter reviews a number of key readings of Barth in North America. To appreciate the deeply held objections and suspicions, we begin with "prob-

---

1. This unheralded Harvard theologian was responsible for the translation of Barth's *Word of God and the Word of Man* in 1928. For the first complete biography, cf. Theodore Louis Trost, *Douglas Horton and the Ecumenical Impulse in American Religion* (Cambridge: Harvard University Press, 2003).

2. Hunsinger describes Barth's theology as a "uniquely innovative blend of modernism and traditionalism." See George Hunsinger, *Disruptive Grace: Studies in the Theology of Karl Barth* (Grand Rapids: Eerdmans, 2000), 253.

lematic readings" and note where Barth has collided with patterns of theological thought and habit. Then we move on to Barth-friendly readings as we try to ascertain things typical for a general appreciation of Barth. A number of positive receptions are delineated according to schools and then in the broad Protestant movement of America known as evangelicalism, as it emerged in the last decades of the twentieth century. Barth has had a particular influence on the two historic theological institutions that retained some version of their Reformed roots, Yale and Princeton theological schools. His influence touched even the early work of those who, like Gordon Kaufman, would later abandon him, crystallized in the postliberal movement in theology, and deeply affected the central theological institution of the Reformed tradition in America, Princeton Seminary. After the liberal and pluralist rejection of Barth, evangelicalism became a natural home for Barth, even if only in certain segments of it. This chapter also includes some necessary reflections on Catholic and Orthodox positive receptions as well as appreciation for Barth globally, particularly in Asian contexts. "American readings" is about tracing tendencies, not providing a book-by-book account of how Barth has been interpreted or misinterpreted by American theologians.

Problematic Readings

There have always been problems with Barth. The fact that he began his professorial career in Germany did not impact his reception as a Swiss theologian since he emerged before World War II. But the fact that he was a Reformed theologian meant that Lutherans and Episcopalians would have some predispositions to overcome if they were to receive him. The fact that the fundamentalist-modernist controversy had been largely fought over theological education meant that his standing as a university theologian would plague American evangelicalism's[3] reception of him for several generations. What characterizes an evangelical reception is the degree to which the movement overcomes some of its fundamentalist roots—something that Carl F. H. Henry and Harold J. Ockenga had heralded about neoevangelicalism. In general, since the scholarship of Westminster Seminary (near Philadelphia) was founded on theological separatism, Barth represented, at best, an inadequate reaction against liberalism and so would have to be rejected. A generation later, with the founding of Fuller Seminary by those trying to overcome the tradition of separatism, Barth would be regarded generally as an ally and in the passing of time even as an immense theological figure shaping many other segments of global Protestantism. Crucial to reception by evangelicals and especially

---

3. By far the most penetrating study of the reception of Barth by American evangelical theologians is Phillip R. Thorne, *Evangelicalism and Karl Barth: His Reception and Influence in North American Evangelical Theology* (Allison Park, Pa.: Pickwick, 1995).

by the Roman Catholic and Eastern Orthodox communions would be the degree to which Barth captured the countercultural nature of the church and theologically achieved the kind of sovereignty of knowledge that the prophetic word endows in the theological tradition. As such, the reception of Barth would be largely determined by whether a particular community of theologians and church saw him as sufficiently wed to revelation and to the norms of Christian community.

Below are several approaches to the problematic readings, which were not necessarily complete rejections, although there were numerous objections. Some objections were based on tradition, inter-Protestant differences. Others were based in theological method, particularly the nature and role of Scripture. Still others were rooted in theological interpretation itself, tendencies in the nature of revelation and history, the doctrine of the Trinity, election, the personhood of Christ, atonement, the scope of salvation—these and others have been sources of polemical attack on Barth.

Traditions against Barth

Karl Barth was part of his Swiss German Reformed world, with his father as pastor and professor of church history at the University of Bern, the wider Germanic world of Lutheran and Reformed and United churches, and the combined theological faculties throughout the universities. By the end of the nineteenth century, awakening movements, biblicism, liberalism, and cultural Protantism had embraced in so many ways an anti- or postdogmatic stance. At both ends of the spectrum, highly differentiated dogmatic systems had simply lost their currency for a variety of reasons. Upon taking up his first post at Göttingen, Barth had made his postliberal move and was intent on recovering the riches of orthodox dogmatics. He assigned himself Heinrich Heppe's *Dogmatics* textbook—a collection of commonplaces from post-Reformation (sixteenth- to eighteenth-century) Reformed dogmaticians. To the extent that Barth used these same theologians for his own orientation, whether to affirm or criticize, he became particularly susceptible to the attacks of traditionalist Reformed theologians. This would be typified by the unfailing negative reception of Barth by one leading historical theologian, Richard Muller. Eventually, seeing Barth as one who would twist Calvin's formulations to serve modern ends, Muller challenged Barth on the same dogmatic territory, with the same dogmaticians.[4] Parallels could be multiplied with Lutherans, to the extent that

---

4. Muller's articles in *Westminster Theological Journal* are consistently denunciatory. See Richard A. Muller, "Directions in the Study of Barth's Christology," *Westminster Theological Journal* 48, no. 1 (1986): 119–34; idem, "The Place and Importance of Karl Barth in the Twentieth Century: A Review Essay," *Westminster Theological Journal* 50, no. 1 (1988): 127–56; idem, "Karl Barth and the Path of Theology into the Twentieth Century: Historical Observations," *Westminster Theological Journal* 51, no. 1 (1989): 25–50. To understand his perspective

Barth interacted profoundly with Lutheran orthodoxy as well, from Luther[5] to Johann Gerhard and down to the biblicists of the nineteenth century.

The first, then, would be reflected in the tragic division between the Lutheran and the Reformed. Although Barth evidences an immense indebtedness to Luther, he is clearly situated within the Zwingli and Calvin axis of Reformed interpretation, and one must thus be alert to confessional Lutheran motives for rejection. Probably the greatest point of tension is in the area of the sacraments of baptism and the Lord's Supper and the christological and pneumatological implications connected with them.

The derisively named *"extra-Calvinisticum," "finitum non capax infiniti"* (the finite cannot comprehend the infinite), appeared in the ongoing debate regarding the risen Christ's two natures and his relation to the Eucharist. From the Lutheran perspective, this theological axiom denies what it affirms about the "exchange of attributes" in the resurrection of Christ so that the risen body is "everywhere" present where the divine Son is present in creation.[6] Believing that the Eucharist is the quintessential moment when Christ is truly present, when "two or three are gathered in my name" (Matt. 18:20), Lutherans reject a notion of a disembodied Christ present to creation. Indeed, a whole set of uniquely Lutheran sacramental notions derives from their christological doctrine of exchange of attributes.[7] By

---

on Reformed orthodoxy and his commitment to its continuing authority, cf. Richard A. Muller, *After Calvin: Studies in the Development of a Theological Tradition* (New York: Oxford University Press, 2003). His massive historical theological textbook has grown to four volumes: *Post-Reformation Reformed Dogmatics: The Rise and Development of Reformed Orthodoxy, ca. 1520 to ca. 1725,* 4 vols. (Grand Rapids: Baker, 2003). One should review the more positive assessment of Barth's relation to Calvin and the Reformed tradition in Matthias Freudenberg, *Karl Barth und die reformierte Theologie: Die Auseinandersetzung mit Calvin, Zwingli und den reformierten Bekenntnisschriften während seiner Göttinger Lehrtätigkeit* (Neukirchen-Vluyn: Neukirchener Verlag, 1997); and Hans Scholl, ed., *Karl Barth und Johannes Calvin: Karl Barths Göttinger Calvin-Vorlesung von 1922* (Neukirchen-Vluyn: Neukirchener Verlag, 1995).

5. Cf., Joachim Heubach, ed., *Luther und Barth* (Erlangen: Martin-Luther-Verlag, 1989).

6. Cf. *CD* I/2:163–65.

7. Very early Luther makes his opinion known in "That This Word of Christ (This Is My Body, etc.) Stand Fast against the Fanatics," meaning, e.g., Zwingli. See Martin Luther, *Das diese Wort Christi (Das ist mein Leib etce) noch fest stehen widder die Schwermgeister* (Wittemberg: Michael Lotther, 1527). This is greatly expanded on by Martin Chemnitz, *De duabus naturis in Christo* (Jenae: Ritzenhainus, 1570). See Martin Chemnitz, *The Two Natures in Christ: A Monograph Concerning the Two Natures in Christ, Their Hypostatic Union, the Communication of Their Attributes, and Related Questions, Recently Prepared and Revised on the Basis of Scripture and the Witnesses of the Ancient Church,* trans. J. A. O. Preus (St. Louis: Concordia, 1971); and more recently, Hermann Sasse, *This Is My Body: Luther's Contention for the Real Presence in the Sacrament of the Altar* (Minneapolis, Augsburg, 1959). On the Reformed side, see Edward David Willis, *Calvin's Catholic Christology: The Function of the So-called Extra Calvinisticum in Calvin's Theology* (Leiden, E. J. Brill, 1966). For the outstanding historical theology on the matter, cf. Helmut Gollwitzer, *Coena Domini: Die altlutherische Abendmahlslehre in ihrer Auseinandersetzung mit dem Calvinismus, dargestellt an der lutherischen Frühorthodoxie* (München: Chr. Kaiser, 1988). For the most interesting problem of Luther's associate and his views, cf. Ralph W. Quere,

contrast, Barth's sacramental views become virtually Zwinglian and Baptist by the end of the *CD*.[8]

At mid-career, Barth as a Reformed theologian was representative on the sacrament of baptism as a sign of the mediatory identity of Jesus Christ as God and man for us.[9] Even then, as consistently Reformed, Barth did not believe that anything salvific took place in water baptism other than a visible signification of the word and work of Christ. But he was not to remain convinced of this approach largely due to the careful exegetical work of his son, Markus Barth.[10] In true biblical-theological fashion, Markus had unflinchingly and with overwhelming evidence pressed for a set of conclusions that would ultimately be represented in the last volume of the *CD* (IV/4). Everything that Karl Barth had been developing regarding the doctrine of the Holy Spirit was now coming together, first, in the abandonment of the entire notion of sacrament as a means or instrument of grace. Already quite Zwinglian in his view of the Lord's Supper, together with baptism, Barth regarded these two as essential to the unique ethical life of the Christian. Second, water baptism was to be understood as response or answer to the regenerating action of the Holy Spirit, which is the actual baptism into the life of God in Christ. For Barth, since the sign of water baptism conveyed the meaning of the free work of the Holy Spirit, there can be nothing sacramental about it: Baptism is not an instrument of the church whereby the presence and power of the Holy Spirit is in any way at its disposal *(ex opere operato)*. Penetrating deeply into the Reformation understanding of the justifying work of the Spirit, Barth was emphasizing what the Augsburg Confession (1530) had so early declared

---

Melanchthon's Christum Cognoscere: Christ's Efficacious Presence in the Eucharistic Theology of Melanchthon (Nieuwkoop: B. de Graaf, 1977).

8. The compelling arguments used by the later Barth to sustain his basically ethical view of the sacraments, as the life of new obedience or sanctification, is unmistakable, not in the least inconsistent with Scripture, and not some kind of gnostic interpretation. Barth is keenly aware of the linkage between the christological disputes of the Reformation and those over the sacraments. Indeed, because of the uniqueness of Christ's incarnation, he calls it "the one and only sacrament" and says even more pointedly, "We can only say that the true *unio sacramentalis* is the *unio personalis* in Jesus Christ" (*CD* IV/2:55). For his distinction between baptism of the Spirit producing faith and the obediential nature of the rite of baptism, see nearly the entirety of *CD* IV/4. Most interestingly, Barth keeps exercising a restriction of theological analogy and correspondence rather than engaging in it as a unifying principle. In the prior section, Barth rejects Baillie's newly constructed thesis that Galatians 2:20, "Not I, but Christ lives in me," is schematic for the God-human relation.

9. Cf. Karl Barth, *Die kirchliche Lehre von der Taufe* (München: C. Kaiser, 1947).

10. Cf. the massive reworked dissertation by Markus Barth, *Die Taufe—ein Sakrament? Ein exegetischer Beitrag zum Gespräch über die kirchliche Taufe* (Zollikon-Zürich: Evangelischer Verlag, 1951), which ran to nearly six hundred pages of careful argumentation. Markus's exegetical/theological approach extended to the other "ordinance" of Christ, the Lord's Supper, as a κοινωνία (fellowship) that includes Christians and Jews; cf. Markus Barth, *Das Mahl des Herrn: Gemeinschaft mit Israel, mit Christus und unter den Gästen* (Neukirchen-Vluyn: Neukirchener Verlag, 1987); and also idem, *The People of God* (Sheffield: JSOT Press, 1983).

about the Spirit, "who works faith; where and when it pleases God, in them that hear the Gospel" *(qui fidem efficit, ubi et quando visum est deo, in iis, qui audiunt evangelium)* (art. V).

Barth felt obligated to count baptism as the great sign of the gracious application of Christ's saving work by the Holy Spirit, who works faith in hearers of the gospel who in turn make the good confession.[11] Far from being instruments of grace, baptism and the Lord's Supper are instruments of the Word of God and when performed, particularly in the case of baptism, are first steps of Christian obedience. As uncomfortable and church-politically problematic as this development was in the *CD*,[12] no less than the likes of Eberhard Jüngel would acknowledge its essential trueness to the gospel.[13] Curiously, Jüngel's two key essays found in his collection of writings on Barth and his own position in developing Barth's views on sacrament and baptism were not translated for inclusion in the English edition of this volume.[14] But considering the strong advocacy for Jüngel's theology among some Anglicans, this controversial point is perhaps not surprising. Timothy Gorringe tellingly calls Barth's view of baptism nothing less than "a very distinctive theology of rebellion," and he quotes Dieter Schellong's conclusion:

> In my view *KD* IV/4, with the denial of infant baptism, is the test whether or not one has understood or has a clue about what it is that Barth is up to and what Barth intended, and which way it was he sought.

To this Gorringe adds, "I agree. It implies a devastating comment on much Anglo-Saxon reception of Barth."[15] But that Schellong's argument-turning, thesis-determining statement and Gorringe's comment on it should be relegated to a footnote in the latter's highly significant recent book on Barth is also telling. Without any problem, one can detect that Barth has had and continues

11. As Paul writes in Romans 10:9–10, "Because if you confess with your lips that Jesus is Lord and believe in your heart that God raised him from the dead, you will be saved. For one believes with the heart and so is justified, and one confesses with the mouth and so is saved."

12. T. F. Torrance takes great exception to it.

13. Cf. Eberhard Jüngel, *Karl Barths Lehre von der Taufe: Ein Hinweis auf ihre Probleme* (Zürich: EVZ-Verlag, 1968); see also his contribution to Fritz Viering, ed., *Zu Karl Barths Lehre von der Taufe* (Gütersloh: G. Mohn, 1971).

14. The extended essay is reprinted in Eberhard Jüngel, *Barth-Studien* (Zürich: Benziger, 1982), 246–96. Note its conspicuous absence in Eberhard Jüngel, *Karl Barth: A Theological Legacy,* trans. Garrett E. Paul (Philadelphia: Westminster John Knox, 1986); trans. of *Barth-Studien* (Zürich: Benziger, 1982).

15. D. Schellong, "Karl Barth als Theologe der Neuzeit," in *Karl Barth und die Neuzeit,* by K. G. Steck and D. Schellong, Theologische Existenz heute, N.F., 173 (München: C. Kaiser, 1973), 72, quoted and commented on in Timothy Gorringe, *Karl Barth: Against Hegemony* (New York: Oxford University Press, 1999), 262 n. 265. Schellong is notable for his theological leadership with respect to the problem of radically diminishing inclinations by Christian parents to have their infants baptized. See Dieter Schellong, ed., *Warum Christen ihre Kinder nicht mehr taufen lassen* (Frankfurt a. M.: Stimme-Verlag, 1969).

to have immense influence in English theology, particularly among postliberals and the radical orthodox. Thus, it is simply amazing that the significance of *CD* IV/4 has not shaped the discussion more.

Jüngel's two articles lay out the full implications of interpreting Barth in the most thoroughgoing way and of answering critical questions raised by his reading of the final work of Barth in *CD* IV/4. Jüngel reminds us that the context of baptism is his discussion of the Christian life of active obedience, lived in the way of sanctification. Barth distinguishes between what is entirely God's prerogative in baptism, namely, "baptism in the Spirit," and what is the believer's part out of obedience to the Word of God, together with their special signification in "baptism in water." Like prayer and the Word of God, like faith and the same Word, the relation between the two is irreversible. Baptism in the Spirit necessarily calls for baptism in water but not the reverse because baptism in the Spirit is an exclusively divine act. In Spirit baptism only is Jesus Christ himself to be found. Water baptism is exclusively a human act following upon and corresponding to that prior act of God. As such, it is the basis for the living of the Christian life. Neither the church nor the individual can make a Christian; only this divine act does. "In no way does water baptism have any instrumental power. It does not mediate grace; instead, it answers grace. As an act of human answering, water baptism belongs to the foundation of the Christian life; as such it is required."[16] Baptism belongs to the ethical dimension of dogmatics. In view of this, infant baptism can only be "demythologized" and therefore rejected "as a deeply disordered practice of baptism."[17] Jüngel writes, "One could formulate pointedly, that the necessity of becoming like children [in baptism, cf. Matt. 18:3 et par.] excludes the baptism of children."[18]

In his first essay on Barth, Jüngel's task was to clarify Barth's position and to point out hermeneutical problems in his "unsacramental" doctrine—eclipsed by the sacramentality of the person of Christ. Jüngel perceptively mentions that Barth only late in the *CD* appropriates *in nobis* theological reasoning together with the classic *pro nobis* formula,[19] thus raising the expansion of understanding from what Christians are *in Christ* to the reality of Christ *in the Christian*. As late as 1962 Barth for the first time declares the formula *"Extra nos—pro nobis—in nobis"* (outside us—for us—in us).[20] This in itself is indicative of a change late in life: Barth embraces an element of the Pietism that he had for so long kept at a distance. Now the subjective experience of inner transformation by baptism in the Spirit finds its analogue in the purely human work of water baptism, as testimony to God's prior work in the heart. Theologically, Barth

16. Jüngel, *Barth-Studien,* 259.
17. *CD* IV/4:116, 213; and Jüngel, *Barth-Studien,* 261.
18. Jüngel, *Barth-Studien,* 261.
19. Ibid., 270.
20. Karl Barth, "Extra nos—pro nobis—in nobis," in *Hören und handeln: Festschrift für Ernst Wolf zum 60. Geburtstag,* ed. H. Gollwitzer and H. Traub (München: C. Kaiser, 1962), 15–27.

could not be clearer about the fundamental distinction between the two acts: The first is decisively the work of God; the second is decisively the work of human beings in correspondence to the first, in the same way that proclamation and prayer correspond to the Word of God and are in obedience to the Word that we have heard and believed.[21] Baptism is based on faithful correspondence, then. Like the church's proclamation and prayer, which answer the Word of God through preaching and praying, baptism answers in the form of petition, and the Lord's Supper answers in the form of thanksgiving.[22] Jüngel is emphatic at this point that Barth has, with utmost consistency, brought baptism into line with the classic Reformation understanding of "*solo verbo*" and "*sola fide*" (Word alone and faith alone): The human act of water baptism is the "answering act," like the faith that corresponds to the sole saving act of God alone in Jesus Christ for us.

One must also point out that Barth does not speak of two baptisms but of a single event with two subjects in two acts. Together they witness to the same reality: Water baptism corresponds to Spirit baptism. In this way, like all other ethical acts in the Christian life, baptism is not the result of an independent moral decision but is grounded in a prior act of God recognized by the individual believer within the context of the believing community. Jüngel acknowledges that the doctrine of baptism is not an appendix to churchly dogmatics but rather a kind of exemplary test—like Schellong's comment—that can be traced directly back to Barth's doctrine of predestination/election. In Barth's doctrine of baptism, we see even more clearly how his theology is a theology of "God himself for men": "As God proves his own divine being through his actions, so also man proves his own human being through his actions. That he can do this is thanks to God. That he ought to do this God himself demands. Insofar as he does this, he corresponds to God. But in this way, man is himself."[23] Jüngel goes on to lay out his own corrective theses for a doctrine of baptism as an act of response, like faith itself, to the justifying, reconciling grace of Christ, rather than a sacramental instantiation of it. Indeed, as a "necessary precept" rather than a "necessary medium," baptism is "only possible and meaningful for the believer."[24] This chapter is an exposition of his most eloquent and sharpest argumentation on how this more truly evangelical correction of baptism can and must overcome the limitations of both Lutheran and Reformed theological traditions. Ultimately, Barth's doctrine of baptism is the expression of the ethics of reconciliation—this is where it falls within the *CD*. As such, it

---

21. Jüngel, *Barth-Studien*, 275–77.

22. Ibid., 281.

23. Interestingly, at this very point, Jüngel is fully aware of all the congenial voices that have categorized Barth either as neoorthodox in the sense of "revelatory positivist" or as a "church father," a protector of the churchly status quo. Jüngel, *Barth-Studien*, 288.

24. Ibid., 308, developing in the following chapter "Zur Kritik des Sakramentalen Verständnisses der Taufe" (Toward a Critique of the Sacramental Understanding of Baptism), 295–314.

is a correction in church doctrine that is consistent with his entire dogmatic project and with the Reformation itself. Barth's own testimony regarding *CD* IV/4 is most telling as well:

> I can foresee that with this book [IV/4], which by human reckoning will be my last considerable publication, I shall once again find myself in a position of some loneliness in the theological and ecclesiastical scene, which I first entered almost fifty years ago. I am conscious of making a bad exit with it. So be it! The day will come when people will do me justice on this question, too.[25]

While so many are doing Barth great justice in the advancement of his counsel in the *CD*, perhaps there will be those like Jüngel who will do him justice in advancing a more consistent reformational and above all Christian doctrine of baptism.

Many theologians of the major Protestant churches have conspicuously avoided Barth's doctrine of baptism, even though many of the most notable New Testament scholars of the twentieth century have lent credence to his position.[26] The traditional Lutheran theologians would have some difficulty with Barth anyway since baptism is one of the breaking points with the Reformed.[27] But neither could Barth's position be well received by the Reformed.[28] Nevertheless, Barth was never deterred from his best attempts always to follow what the Word of God teaches at every point and to perceive how each point

25. In this preface, Barth declares, "I have had to abandon the 'sacramental' understanding of baptism, which I still maintained fundamentally in 1943." Acknowledging his debt to his son's 1951 monograph, largely spurned by biblical scholars and theologians, Barth continues, "Without following him [my son] closely, without cashing in to a large extent on his work, I could hardly have made the reorientation in my own doctrine of baptism." Barth calls his move on baptism his "*aggiornamento*" (reorientation), although he does "not expect the full healing of the Church from advances in the matter of infant baptism. But how can the Church be or become again, as is said today on many sides (and very definitely by the Second Vatican Council), an essentially missionary and mature rather than immature Church, so long as it obstinately, against all better judgment and conscience, continues to dispense the water of baptism with the same undiscriminating generosity as it has now done for centuries? How can it be credible to the rest of the world so long as it persists in thinking that it can pacify its concern for recruitment of personnel in this way which is responsible neither to God, to its own message, nor to those who live either externally or internally *extra muros?* Of what help will the best ecclesiology be to us so long as there is obstinate evasion of long overdue reform at this small but practically decisive point?" (*CD* IV/4:x–xii). Indeed, my tendency throughout the present work is to take *CD* IV/4 along the lines Schellong has indicated, as something of a lens through which to view the entire *CD*. This is justified, I believe, by Barth's final little word: "long overdue reform at this small but practically decisive point."

26. Jüngel frequently cites the work of Bultmann and Conzelmann, as in his treatment here.

27. Cf. Edmund Schlink, *The Doctrine of Baptism* (St. Louis: Concordia, 1972).

28. One of the great Reformed exponents of Barth's theology in North America takes pointed issue with him on this point: George Hunsinger, "Baptism and the Soteriology of Forgiveness," *International Journal of Systematic Theology* 2 (2000): 247–69.

is integral to every other. The history of this doctrine is a curious one, ranging from including infants in the early church as a hoped-for way of securing their salvation in the face of high mortality rates and a belief in the damnation of the unbaptized, to the pressure of a level of reform that the Catholic Church and popular piety would not accept in the sixteenth century, to a multitude of approaches that cancel one another out in view of Pauline teaching. All acknowledge that Barth was still venturing beyond a safety zone in the last segments of what he could produce in the *CD,* but this was as true of him as ever in his understanding of faithful attention to the task of theology.

The Catholic traditions of Eastern Orthodoxy and Roman Catholicism must also be mentioned. Barth has been read with respect, when not dismissed out of hand, by a broad spectrum of theologians who represent the traditions of the ancient churches. With respect to the latter, the immense, multiauthored dogmatics of post–Vatican II, to which the likes of Karl Rahner contributed, owes much of its orientation to the impact of Barth's exegetical reasoning.[29] But covering everything with their judgments against Protestantism were the Canons of Trent and the pronouncements of Vatican I. Among American readers, before the release of the documents of Vatican II regarding Barth from a Roman Catholic perspective, little was positive if mentioning Barth at all. Although invited, Barth had not been able to attend the last sessions of Vatican II for health reasons; yet he was able to accept an invitation to the Vatican in 1966. Familiarizing himself with the conciliar documents, he fixed on the repeated reference to Protestants as *"fratres sejuncti"* (disjoined brethren) rather than the official Vatican translation of "separated brethren," which without the underlying Latin adjective *separati* was not justified and connoted a highly pejorative sense. But Barth's difficulty with Catholicism would be at the point of its dogmatics and the nature of theological reasoning in a dispute over *analogia entis* (analogy of being).

Barth came to identify the conflict between Catholic and Reformation understandings of soteriology as derived from Thomas Aquinas's doctrine of *analogia entis.*[30] But this doctrine had ancient roots, as in Augustine's employment of the metaphysical notion of an essential similarity between God and the human being. He had made this connection through reflection on the biblical doctrine of the *imago Dei* (image of God) in the human creature. A number of other early Christian theologians had associated it with vestiges of divinity that ancient philosophy speculated were the substantial derivation of human reason (e.g., as in Justin Martyr's *logos spermatikos* [generative word] and much of Origen's anthropological reflections). By the time of the medieval theologians, mystical theology was predicated on this notion of essential similarity rooted in a metaphysic of a divine-human continuum of being.

---

29. Johannes Feiner and Magnus Löhrer, eds., *Mysterium Salutis: Grundriss heilsgeschichtlicher Dogmatik,* 5 vols. (Einsiedeln: Benziger, 1965–1975).

30. Cf. Aquinas, *Summa theologiae* I.13.1.

Since the human mind participated in the divine mind by virtue of its nature, necessary grace imparted by the Holy Spirit enabled the performance of spiritual exercises to overcome the "noetic" effects of sin. Through this practice of utilizing an infused grace to awaken the mind's capacity for divine knowledge, noetic experience would realize a *visio Dei* (vision of God) and ultimately an *unio mystica* (mystical union). This is the great tradition of mystical ascent through the hierarchy of being, beyond the imperfections of the lower rungs of that hierarchy to the soul's true home in God. Indeed, at the highest level of Christian mystical practice eternal salvation would be attained. By contemplating Christ and indeed by imitating him, this liberation of the soul could take place. The Reformers had opposed this as a synergistic soteriology whereby gracious assistance from God to perform these disciplines relativizes the reality of sin and the completed work of Christ. Luther had interpreted the Pauline statement "Christ is the end of the law" as meaning that Christ was the end of human work, particularly mystical labors, since their motivation suffered under the delusion that they participated in or contributed to the work of Christ on the cross. Barth tried to penetrate into the heart of the foundational mystical theology and bring its metaphysic of a divine-human continuum under radical criticism and reform.

During Barth's early professorial career, he had occasion to converse with and to debate the great Jesuit theologian Erich Przywara (1889–1972), whose influential work on religious philosophy[31] had included a set of arguments for *analogia entis.* Barth in *CD* I/1 and I/2 challenges Przywara's modern defense of the *analogia entis* and counters it with *analogia fidei* (analogy of faith). In ancient and medieval hermeneutics, analogy was a way of reasoning between two objects of knowing perceived to have a proportional relation to one another. An analogy of being between God (eternal being) and humanity (temporal being) connotes an essential relation between a greater and a lesser species of being. The two are essentially the same but manifest themselves differently on account of different attributes. Barth perceived in this form of analogy a dual claim that conflicted with essential truth of revelation: (1) the Creator/creature distinction constituted a fundamental difference of being in the human that *analogia entis* obscured, and (2) it supported the related claim of the divine status of the human institution known as the Roman Catholic Church. Because of *analogia entis,* Barth felt led to declare:

> Our fellowship with this faith is broken by the way in which grace here becomes nature, the action of God immediately disappears and is taken up into the action

---

31. Erich Przywara, *Religionsphilosophie katholischer Theologie* (München: Oldenbourg, 1926); cf. also idem, *Analogia entis,* Bd. 3 of *Schriften* (Einsiedeln: Johannes-Verlag, 1962). Some of the interaction with Barth is reported in the recent treatment by Thomas F. O'Meara and Michael A. Fahey, *Erich Przywara, S.J.: His Theology and His World* (Notre Dame, Ind.: University of Notre Dame Press, 2002).

of the recipient of grace, that which is beyond all human possibilities changes at once into that which is enclosed within the reality of the Church, and the personal act of divine address becomes a constantly available relationship [i.e., a transmitted material condition]. Roman Catholic faith believes this transformation. It can recognise itself and God's revelation in this constantly available relationship between God and man, in this revealedness. It affirms an *analogia entis*, the presence of a divine likeness of the creature even in the fallen world, and consequently the possibility of applying the secular "There is" to God and the things of God as the presupposition, again ontological, of that change or transformation, of that depriving of revelation and faith of their character as decision by evasion and neutralisation.[32]

Barth's reference to "decision" here entails God's gracious decision, both to reveal himself and to grant the gift of faith to sinners.

Late in life Przywara would have occasion to comment on his reading of Barth. In an immensely broad-ranging work, he writes:

> Then there is the appearance as if that Reformation dynamism intended Luther's accentuation of "becoming" and Calvin's defensive obedience before the divine majesty to be foundational. The great *Church Dogmatics* of Karl Barth can answer this question. For on the one hand, the style of this dogmatics introduces an entirely great Catholic style, not only in the unabridged historical sweep from Scripture to the Fathers to the Scholastics in viewing the content of revelation, but also in being truly speculative in its finest differentiated distinctions. On the other hand, never has a reformational dogmatics so sharply opposed Catholic dogmatics with the "ancient Church" in view only as "heresy" (*CD* I/1:33), indeed, in its basic structure of *analogia entis* as "the invention of the Anti-christ." But both of these tend ever more toward a single point.[33]

He goes on to quote extensively from *CD*. So Barth makes things difficult early on, in spite of his famous statement that if he had to choose between the liberalism of "cultural Protestantism" in Germany and Roman Catholicism, he would choose the latter. But Barth's declaration of the "fact of heresy" heads in two directions, against sixteenth-century Roman Catholicism (as above) and, quoting Barth, the

> pietistic and rationalistic Modernism as rooted in mediaeval mysticism and the humanistic Renaissance. The fact of the modern denial of revelation, etc., is quite irrelevant compared with this twofold fact. For here, in its antithesis to Roman Catholicism and Protestant Modernism, the Evangelical faith stands in conflict with itself. For these two things are not irrelevant paganisms, nor do they seek to be such. If we take them for what they purport to be, they en-

---

32. *CD* I/1:41.
33. Erich Przywara, *Humanitas: Der Mensch gestern und morgen* (Nürnberg: Glock und Lutz, 1952), 172–73.

counter us as possibilities of faith, and therefore of our own faith, within and not without the Church.[34]

Methodologies against Barth's

Method in theology is a far more individualized matter than how a theologian represents a major theological tradition. Here we are recognizing some of the notable theological voices that have shaped the reception of Barth in North America and beyond. Theological method is often identifiable not so much through a monograph in hermeneutics but in the writing of a theological text itself. Method becomes apparent often through critical review and contrasting statement rather than an explicit treatise on method alone. Classically, early church biblicism and apologetic; creedal exposition and the contravention of heresy; Origenist, Augustinian, and Dionysian speculations; as well as dogmatic-practical formulations that are Irenaean, Athanasian, Cyprianic, and Gregorian all typify premedieval methodologies. As the medieval theologians appear, much of what they do methodologically is determined by their rather limited intellectual resources. Nevertheless, whether Isidore of Seville's encyclopedia, John Scotus Eriugena's metaphysics, Peter Lombard's *Sentences,* Anselmian theo-logic, Ockhamist voluntarism, Duns Scotus's metaphysical ethic, Abelardian dialectic, (Christian) Bernhardian spiritualism, Thomas's *summae* reflections on *theologia* as *scientia,* or the realism and biblicism of Wycliffe and other pre-Reformers, method in theology was constantly evolving. With the epistemological revolution of the early Enlightenment stemming in large degree from implications of reformational hermeneutics, theology attentive to this revolution began to embody its implications in various ways from Semler to Schleiermacher to Ritschl, Troeltsch, and Bultmann. In many respects, methodologies that sought to resist this revolution tended either toward forms of biblicism or naive realism, leading to great alienation among Protestant theologians depending on their view of Enlightenment principles of critical reason and its authority in making truth and knowledge claims. In many respects, the postmodern breakdown of the ideal of universally valid knowledge claims was anticipated by the Protestant theological schisms of the nineteenth and twentieth centuries.

Barth's work beginning with *Romans* and continuing through the *CD* is a massive effort not at a mediating theology but at a modern intensification of Christian knowledge claims and the recovery of the differentiated theological method of traditional dogmatics of the late sixteenth and seventeenth centuries. But not everyone could perceive the radical nature of his project. Barth's great teacher, Adolph von Harnack, would regard him as having fallen backward into a naive biblicism and dogmatic Scholasticism. Possessing many of the

---

34. *CD* I/1:34.

existential assumptions of Barth's theological teacher, Wilhelm Herrmann, Harnack's theology was a construct of religious psychological and ethical notions. He had fully excised the necessity of any detailed correspondence between the doctrinal and historical content of Scripture and modern faith.[35] Barth's theology was already (by 1924) profoundly disturbing to this sensibility. Harnack was convinced that Barth's theology separated God from culture, and that in doing so it would not be able to withstand the forces of barbarism and atheism. These very forces of a theology that united God and culture forced Barth out of his professorship and the German state in 1934.

In his interactions with Rudolf Bultmann, Barth appeared to be hopelessly wedded to a naive supernaturalism and biblical literalism that disregarded settled knowledge of the world of nature and religion. Indeed, many would fault him for having isolated his theology from critical judgment, something that made his claim to "scientific, objectivist theology" appear oxymoronic. Beyond all this, Barth's christological commitments to the miracles of virginal conception and bodily resurrection—however qualified by respect for the limits of historical evidence in the case of unique, unrepeatable events of divine causation—have been regarded by ever so many inside and outside the theological academy as grounds for intellectual disqualification.

The most acute survey of Barth's American critics is to be found in the recent work by Gary Dorrien.[36] Probably the most stirring initial methodological charge against Barth was that of Dietrich Bonhoeffer in the form of "revelatory positivism" (the standard translation of *Offenbarungspositivismus,* which might just as easily and perhaps more clearly be "positivism of revelation"). At first sight this might come across as a critical point on theological substance, where Bonhoeffer actually had deep agreement with Barth; but as the masterly study of Simon Fisher shows, it is primarily about theological method.[37]

In the fundamentalist and evangelical camps, we begin with Cornelius Van Til. This great conservative Reformed apologist professor of Westminster Theological Seminary was an ardent polemicist for a "presuppositionalist" approach: All correct knowledge stems from the knowledge of the sovereign God. Any reliance on autonomous human processes is fatally flawed. His animus toward Barth spans three decades, and his bibliography shows that he made himself into the watchdog of evangelicalism against Barth.[38] We

35. Cf. H. Martin Rumscheidt, *Revelation and Theology: An Analysis of the Barth-Harnack Correspondence of 1923* (Cambridge: Cambridge University Press, 1996).

36. Gary J. Dorrien, The *Barthian Revolt in Modern Theology: Theology without Weapons* (Philadelphia: Westminster John Knox, 1999).

37. Simon Fisher, *Revelatory Positivism? Barth's Earliest Theology and the Marburg School* (Oxford: Oxford University Press, 1988).

38. A cross section of works by Cornelius Van Til (but by no means all) cited in Thorne, *Evangelicalism and Karl Barth:* "Karl Barth: His Message to Us," *Banner* 104 (July 4, 1969): 4–5; *Karl Barth and Evangelicalism* (Philadelphia: Presbyterian & Reformed, 1964); *Christianity and Barthianism* (Philadelphia: Presbyterian & Reformed, 1962); *Barth's Christology* (Philadelphia:

should not be surprised that such extensive output would result in something like what Bernard Ramm expressed, that it became "the official Evangelical interpretation of neo-orthodoxy."[39] Contrary to Barth's own direction and the preponderance of those who both accepted and rejected his program, Van Til accused Barth of being essentially Schleiermacherian. For Van Til, there is no difference between the liberalism attacked by his mentor, J. G. Machen, and the theological product of Karl Barth.

At the core of Van Til's attack is Barth's rejection of the claim that revelation supplies the direct knowledge of God. He lays the blame for Barth's failure in this partly on the use of dialectic method, in which the divine and human poles of revealed knowledge interact and the creature is included in the self-knowledge of God. In addition, Van Til rejects Barth's emphasis on the divine gift of freedom in Christ, which grants a kind of bounded autonomy. He saw both of these aspects as an accommodation to the philosophical presuppositions of Hegel and Kant. This seemed to him simply a subtler liberal theology dressed up in biblical exegesis and traditional language. For Van Til, these philosophical sources had had primary influence in breeding a culture of despair and moral fragmentation. Unfortunately, Van Til could not seem to recognize that Barth absolutely rejected theology held captive to anything but revelation. He could not appreciate that language of theological description could borrow from any philosophical tradition to critique these very philosophies. Indeed, the theologians of "cultural Protestantism," in which theology had accommodated to Kantian and Hegelian principles, rejected Barth's theology. Whether Van Til was aware that Barth rejected a Hegelian process of divine self-actualization in nature or a Kantian bifurcation of knowledge is not in evidence. The overarching determination of Barth to show that God was in no way limited by or dependent on creation went unacknowledged in Van Til's determination to find fault with him.

An important further development in the evangelical reception of Barth is the approach of Gordon Clark and Carl F. H. Henry. Clark, while acknowledging great agreement, faults Barth for an irrationalism in his dialectical method and a biblical fallibilism, which in the end cannot affirm Scripture as God's Word. Because Barth was not working out a system of theology as it had come to be practiced in the eighteenth and nineteenth centuries according to a set of metaphysical and logical presuppositions—indeed, Barth did not believe

Presbyterian & Reformed, 1962); review of *Kirchliche Dogmatik* IV/1 and 3, *Westminster Theological Journal* 22 (1959): 64–69; "Has Karl Barth Become Orthodox?" *Westminster Theological Journal* 16 (1954): 135–81; *The New Modernism: An Appraisal of the Theology of Barth and Brunner* (Philadelphia: Presbyterian & Reformed, 1946); "More Barthianism at Princeton," review of *Christianity in America: A Crisis,* by Elmer Homrighausen, *Presbyterian Guardian* 5 (February 1938): 26–27; review of *Karl Barth's Theology,* by A. S. Zerbe, *Christ Today: A Presbyterian Journal* 1, no. 10 (February 1931): 13.

39. Bernard Ramm, *After Fundamentalism: The Future of Evangelical Theology* (San Francisco: Harper & Row, 1983), 23, quoted in Thorne, *Evangelicalism and Karl Barth,* 35.

one was possible—those who wanted such systems were disappointed. By this time, however, that system in theology had collapsed entirely into a question of epistemology. Systematic development of one's theological knowledge claims was all the rage, and whether one was defending plenary inspiration of Scripture or demythologization, one guiding systematic interest was subsuming all theological topics: the possibility and actuality of the knowledge or any knowledge of God. Of course, any Christian theology is a negotiation between the text of Scripture and the topical expositions of theological tradition. But as Barth expounded Scripture in terms of the classic themes of doctrine instead of using one systematic orientation, here in the nature of revelation, he found many themes from which to ask questions about the truth of God. Each doctrine in the classic representation of Christian faith, when explored according to itself, brought out different facets and emphases in the richness of revelation. Then there is ever the struggle of the theologian just to bring this richness to expression. These two factors in themselves are enough to frustrate specialists of single-minded systematic interest.

The indictment of biblical fallibilism was and is a more problematic issue for traditionalist interpreters. By Barth's time, much ink had already been spilt trying to defend Scripture's infallibility in scientific and philosophical terms. One must be clear here, however. Although evangelicals tend to utilize "propositional truth" as the preferred term for reality beliefs, obviously Scripture itself does not know of such a term. While Barth preferred to regard Scripture as the providentially and graciously appointed "witness" to revelation, which "becomes the Word of God" when the Holy Spirit effectuates it as such, this does not mean that he taught that the Bible was either full of errors or that it was not inspired. Instead, in the clinch of rampant apologetic concerns in theology in the twentieth century, both conservative and liberal, Barth simply could not agree that Scripture could be verified or experientially confirmed on universally agreeable foundations of truth. Since he had rejected natural theology as incompatible with the revelation of God in his Word, there could be no independent ground whereby Scripture could be substantiated as truthful or even counted as the unique and only saving truth of God.

Modern theology is very much a prescientific way of knowing religiously and has undergone as much alteration and revolution as any of the human disciplines. Indeed, for many the very appendage "modern" is a signal of what is to be rejected either as what could never have been attempted or what should never have been attempted. Because epistemology became the great philosophical project of the modern period, theology likewise sent itself into many multiple contortions in attempting to find its own best epistemic norm. Barth is not antimodern in the strict sense. He probably did not believe one could avoid being modern (living with and by the communication and culture in which one has found oneself). This would have the impact of respecting contemporary culture's analyses of culture and communication, including those surrounding the Scriptures in their original as well as their much-transmitted forms. Barth was not opposed to the modern, but he was resolutely opposed to the adoption of multiple sources for his *Church Dogmatics*. To the extent, however, that liberal and conservative perspectives had for long adopted different stances toward the sources of theology, methodological issues with Barth would reflect another problematic.

Barth-Friendly Readings

Yale Reflections

One of the earliest and most significant locations of reception for Karl Barth in the United States has been Yale Divinity School. By the 1960s, Barth had become a part of the working theological imagination of the place. By the late 1980s, its leading lights—Hans Frei, Paul Holmer, David Kelsey, and George Lindbeck—held Barth in common in a way they esteemed no other theologian.[40]

Frei had embraced Barth on one front for his rejection of a relational model of revelation since revelation is divine self-communication, not a consequence of religious anthropology. Frei recognized in Barth a divine freedom. Divine freedom asymmetrically related to the human maintains revelation in covenant:

> Fundamental in . . . [Barth's] concern is the acknowledgment of the freedom and Lordship of God. These qualities God affirms in his condescending grace. They are not restricted by creation or grace. It is the greatest perversion, therefore, to tie God "relationally" to any preconceived method, supposedly the echo of a "symmetrical" relation between divine revelation and an independently gained concept of religion. Instead, one must insist that grace is sheer miracle which we can only "*ac*-knowledge."[41]

> It is quite apparent that the restlessness which underlies Niebuhr's continuous dialectic and necessitates it is due to the fact that in and through all other relations man is fundamentally related to an ultimate "Other" who confronts him at once as the haunting enemy of his natural religion and as the bestower of grace.[42]

Frei's *Eclipse of Biblical Narrative*[43] is an attempt to recover not just revelation but also Scripture. This recovery of Scripture had to take place to deliver it from its apologetic usages, attempts to make the Bible believable.

40. Cf. Mark I. Wallace, "The New Yale Theology," *Christian Scholar's Review* 17 (1987): 154–70.

41. Hans W. Frei, "Niebuhr's Theological Background," in *Faith and Ethics: The Theology of H. Richard Niebuhr*, ed. P. Ramsey (New York: Harper, 1957), 9–64, quoting 41.

42. Ibid., 66.

43. Hans Frei, *The Eclipse of Biblical Narrative: A Study in Eighteenth and Nineteenth Century Hermeneutics* (New Haven: Yale University Press, 1974).

Barth tells us that theology is a function of the Church; specifically, it arises because the Church is accountable to God for its discourse about God. . . . Barth says that the criterion of Christian discourse is the being of the Church, and the being of the Church for him is Jesus Christ, God in his presence or turning to humanity.[44]

Relying as well on the hermeneutical contributions of Erich Auerbach and Gilbert Ryle, Frei appropriated Barth in the deepest possible way by making Scripture the fundamental source of meaning in theology. Particularly with Auerbach's great work *Mimesis*,[45] the unique realism and dominance of Scripture on the reader come to the fore. Reading Scripture causes a world of reality and meaning to be fashioned in the soul of the reader. Frei regarded this as what in fact Barth was doing in the *CD*. In addition, the influence of Ryle[46] illuminates the narratival sources of self-formation. Scripture describes the only world for the believer such that all other accounts must be absorbed into it—which classic theology has always done. Again, this is what Frei regarded Barth as having accomplished so masterfully: The world of the Bible is identical with the world in which we live.[47]

George Lindbeck, as a Lutheran theologian preoccupied throughout his career with the ecumenical movement and relations with Roman Catholicism, nevertheless drew on the postcritical reputation of Barth since he possessed so much currency in his Protestant theological world. Lindbeck related his work in *The Nature of Doctrine* this way: "Karl Barth's exegetical emphasis on narrative has been at second hand a chief source of my notion of intratextuality as an appropriate way of doing theology in a fashion consistent with a cultural-linguistic understanding of religion and a regulative view of doctrine." No doubt the secondhand reference hints at his dependence on Frei.

But in his own right, Lindbeck was acutely sensitive to the unique contribution Barth had made and echoed Barth's program in his own:

> In order to fully hear the Word of God in Scripture, theologians and the Christian community at large are called upon to engage in close reading of the entire canon in its entire typological and Christological narrative unity in ways which are imaginatively rich, conceptually exact, argumentatively rigorous, and forever open to the freedom of the Word, to new understanding.[48]

In the same article, Lindbeck indeed highlights the universal metaphysics that will result from the theological exposition of Scripture that narrates the

---

44. George Hunsinger and W. Placher, eds., *Types of Christian Theology* (New Haven: Yale, 1992), 39.

45. Erich Auerbach, *Mimesis* (Bern: Francke, 1945); idem, *Mimesis: The Representation of Reality in Western Literature*, trans. W. R. Trask (New York: Doubleday, 1953).

46. Gilbert Ryle, *The Concept of Mind* (New York: Barnes & Noble, 1962).

47. Frei, *Eclipse*, 161–62.

48. George Lindbeck, "Barth and Textuality," *Theology Today* (1986): 362.

whole: "It is the religion instantiated in Scripture which defines being, truth, goodness, and beauty."[49] Thus, even the mediating theologies of modernity (cf. Ronald Thiemann and John Thiel below), epitomized in Schleiermacher, cannot help but fail to do justice to the gospel. In each case, one cannot work by finding common ground between the secular or nonbiblical narratives and the biblical narrative.

But in the end Lindbeck's contribution is ambiguous. While rejecting the foundationalism of modern thought, he does not adopt the critical realism of Barth. Instead, he adopts Scripture as merely religiously and notionally regulative and not corresponding to reality as it is. This is his own demurring along lines initiated by Frei, where the dismissal of apologetics in theology amounts to granting some truth to those who perceive Scripture as nothing other than religious fiction. There is a kind of rational legitimacy in religious unbelief for those whose criteria for belief are factual matters. One wonders, then, if the motive to do theology of Barth's type could have been done merely on a regulative and fiduciary basis.

Nevertheless, Lindbeck can claim, "Scripture textualizes everything, including theologians and the work they do. When this is expressly realized, the God unsubstitutably identified and characterized in the text, supremely in the story of Jesus, becomes, as Barth says, 'the basic text.'"[50] But contrary to the expectations of the above quote, this means that issues of metaphysical and historical truth are not primarily to be faced. Scripture will do what it does and nothing more, and theologians indeed are to eschew doing anything more. But more is at stake in terms of reference. Scripture does make historical, existential, and metaphysical claims, if only all its own. Carl F. H. Henry made an important point that narrative theology à la Frei and Lindbeck "set aside the ultimacy of narrated occurrence as historical revelation."[51]

At this point, Ronald Thiemann's critique may be most helpful by reminding narrative theologians of Barth's insistence on revelation as God's self-interpretation:

> Barth is interested in Scripture as self-interpreting text, because he sees Scripture as the vehicle of the self-interpreting triune God. . . . It is Barth's view of revelation that warrants his intratextual view of theology. Without that doctrine of revelation, or its functional equivalent, textuality, intratextuality, and self-interpreting texts have no theological force.[52]

49. Ibid.
50. Ibid., 374.
51. Carl F. H. Henry, "Narrative Theology: An Evangelical Appraisal," *Trinity Journal*, n.s., 8 (1987): 3–19; cf. Bruce L. McCormack, "Revelation and History in Transfoundationalist Perspective," *Journal of Religion* 78 (1998): 18–37; Mark I. Wallace, "Karl Barth's Hermeneutic," *Journal of Religion* 68 (1988): 396–410; and George Hunsinger, "Beyond Literalism and Expressivism," *Modern Theology* 3 (1987): 209–23.
52. Ronald Thiemann, "Response to George Lindbeck," *Theology Today* 43 (1986): 378.

Bruce McCormack, echoing something of Thiemann's outlook, critiques the
Frei and Lindbeck approach as a "conflicted Barthian apology for construing
all reality through the template of the Bible without Barth's robust confidence
in the prevenient reality of God's speaking and acting in the world as the
guarantor of Christian truth-claims."[53]

Evangelical Reflections

Paul Louis Metzger has probably performed the greatest service in the area
of critically assessing the main American evangelical reviewers of Barth.[54]
Writing with attention to his missionary context of Japan and its political
theology, Metzger tracks the ways in which Barth distinguished himself from
his liberal environment and offered his constructive alternative to Christian
faith in the world. Metzger highlights the profound tension Barth allows for in
his juxtaposing of "theonomy" and human "autonomy" in the world.[55] This is
the case since all things, including human freedom, are brought about through
the creative agency of Christ himself. The world has been endowed with its
freedom. Its "worldliness" is only sinful when sins are committed; otherwise,
its being testifies to its not being God. Displaying a deep acquaintance with
a wide range of Barthian scholarship, Metzger also brings out the importance
of the simultaneous veiling and unveiling of God in his revelation, thereby
virtually determining that a world "without God" would be just as likely in
human perception as the world with God.[56] Even where God's presence and
truth are veiled, God is still present and the source of all truth. Thus, God's
ways in Christ are utterly obscured by the human will to perceive and to
construct its own ways of knowing. Yet in knowing the ways of the world
through the Word of Christ, one's face is unveiled not only to God but also
to the world. The darkness of the world that is still light to God becomes
light to the knowledge of faith in Christ (cf. Gen. 1:18; Job 12:22; 29:3; Ps.
139:11–12; Eccles. 2:13; Isa. 9:2; 42:16; John 8:12; Eph. 5:8; 1 Peter 2:9).

53. Bruce McCormack, "Beyond Foundationalism and Postmodern Reading of Barth,"
Zeitschrift für dialektische Theologie 13 (1997): 94–95; cf. idem, "Revelation and History in
Transfoundationalist Perspective."
54. Paul Louis Metzger, *The Word of Christ and the World of Culture: Sacred and Secular through
the Theology of Karl Barth* (Grand Rapids: Eerdmans, 2003), based on a doctoral thesis in King's
College, London. Unfortunately, some odd terms plague the discussion, such as *dedivinization,*
as well as some inattention to matters otherwise of importance to the topic in terms of the religious influence on political theory in the modern West and critical theory. Also, in discussing
the Promethian in culture, Metzger might have made special reference to Barth's great student
and next-generation Basel theologian Jan Milíč Lochman, in his *Christ and Prometheus? A Quest
for Theological Identity* (Geneva: WCC Publications, 1988).
55. Metzger, *Word of Christ and World of Culture,* 90–93.
56. Ibid., 124.

Catholic and Orthodox Reflections

During Barth's lifetime, the Catholic theologian who shared the greatest affinity with him was the Swiss Hans Urs von Balthasar, whose study of Barth influenced an entire generation of interpreters. He was particularly attracted through his reflection on Barth's engagement with Erich Przywara over *analogia entis* in favor of Barth's own category, *analogia fidei*.[57] Although his historical schema of an early dialectical Barth and a later analogical Barth has been shown to be too facile, it is Balthasar among the Catholics who early on recognized an exceedingly special theological witness in his colleague. "We have in Barth," Balthasar writes, "two crucial features: the most thorough and penetrating display of the Protestant view and the closest rapprochement with the Catholic. Theology attains a breadth of subject matter and historical range."[58]

Global Reports

Some of the most important new readers of Barth are to be found in Asian theological contexts. The *Church Dogmatics* have been translated into Japanese, Korean, and Chinese for some time.

One interesting development is a work by Heup Young Kim investigating connections between the modern Confucian thinker Wang Yang-Ming and Barth.[59] Kim is particularly interested in how Barth's and Wang's anthropologies find resonance with each other, even at points of the humanity of Christ, sin, and the work of the Holy Spirit in discipleship, love, and *imago Dei*. With the understanding that the practical philosophies of Confucianism serve as an existential orientation for many East Asian Christians, especially Korean, Kim presents a thoroughgoing investigation of ways in which a meshing with Barth takes place.

After opening up classic Confucian categories, especially that of public virtue through self-cultivation, Kim compares the reforming work of Martin Luther through *sola fide* (faith alone) with Wing's "*hsin chi li*" (self-realization in the mind-and-heart alone).[60] In both cases, Kim contends, the matter of becoming human lies at the root of essential concern. Indeed, through the concentration of all concerns in one chief concern, this is what is at stake, whether through receiving the saving work of Christ by faith or by holding fast to the uniting of heart and mind. The upshot of the former in humanization translates into the Christian doctrine of sanctification, which Kim picks up in his discussion of Barth in the second half of his book.

57. Hans Urs von Balthasar, *The Theology of Karl Barth,* trans. Edward T. Oakes (New York: Ignatius Press, 1997), 86–167.

58. Ibid., 98.

59. Heup Young Kim, *Wang Yang-Ming and Karl Barth: A Confucian-Christian Dialogue* (Lanham, Md.: University Press of America, 1996).

60. Ibid., 25.

Defending Barth against the misplaced charges of obfuscating interreligious encounter, Kim points out that the later Barth had much more room for a wider religious apologetic in recognizing degrees of truth in the world's religions.[61] But through Barth's anthropology, Kim pushes beyond merely discussing sanctification. By moving in this direction, he recognizes that the humanity of Christ in incarnation, death, and resurrection embodies the whole of humanity for its reconciliation. In this way, what is to be done is self-realization in Christ. Through dialogue with the Confucian tradition as expressed by Wang, Kim aligns the two paradigms of becoming human. They are not symmetrical in that Christ forms one into a humanity ready for the resurrection, but in terms of a vision of the human in this life, there are interesting parallels.[62] Kim is alert to the fundamental difference, however: "the Confucian anthropocosmic mode of thinking versus the Christian theohistorical mode of thinking."[63] Kim is most interested in showing how certain aspects of Christ's humanity can absorb essential affirmations of Confucianism that are integral to it while allowing for Christianity to assert the unique truths it embodies. This develops into a "Confucian Christianity," which is not syncretistic but instead provides a "novel paradigm of radical humanity in a new context, the eschatological theanthropocosmic vision in the new aeon."[64]

61. Ibid., 64, citing *CD* IV/3.1:110, 114, 136–37, and the great phrases "true words . . . *extra muros ecclesia*," "lights in the world," "parables of the kingdom of heaven."
62. Ibid., 142, where "mind and heart" match "Word of God," "selfish desires" connect with "sloth," and "*cheng*" (sincerity) connects with "*agape.*"
63. Ibid., 176.
64. Ibid., 185.

3

THEOLOGIA AMERICANA, THEOLOGIA VIATORUM

This chapter presents a kind of index of cultural characteristics shaping and shaped by Christian faith and theology in North America,[1] particularly the United States. Such an index could be expanded but not easily reduced, and certainly any single item could receive extensive treatment. But theses are dimensions of religious and cultural sensibility that present themselves particularly for the doing of theology in this region of the world and at this time in the life of the churches. Running throughout the present book

---

1. American theology is a vast spectrum of approaches coming into view in the twentieth century from Protestant evangelical to liberal to postliberal, postconservative, and ultimately particularist approaches (e.g., Hispanic and immigrant) to Roman Catholic. The most significant development in evangelical theology is its most recent tendencies toward defining a new mainline in American Protestant theology. Some helpful points of reference from this broad spectrum include Mark G. Toulouse and James O. Duke, eds., *Makers of Christian Theology in America: A Handbook* (Nashville: Abingdon, 1997); Richard John Neuhaus, ed., *American Apostasy: The Triumph of "Other" Gospels* (Grand Rapids: Eerdmans, 1994); Robert Horton Gundry, *Jesus the Word according to John the Sectarian: A Paleofundamentalist Manifesto for Contemporary Evangelicalism, Especially Its Elites, in North America* (Grand Rapids: Eerdmans, 2001); Gary J. Dorrien, *The Remaking of Evangelical Theology* (Louisville: Westminster John Knox, 1998); Stanley J. Grenz, *Renewing the Center: Evangelical Theology in a Post-Theological Era* (Grand Rapids: Baker, 2000); idem, *Revisioning Evangelical Theology: A Fresh Agenda for the Twenty-First Century* (Downers Grove, Ill.: InterVarsity, 1993); Millard J. Erickson, *Christian Theology* (Grand Rapids: Baker, 1998); Donald G. Bloesch, *Christian Foundations* (Downers Grove, Ill.: InterVarsity, 1992); idem, *Essentials of Evangelical Theology,* 2 vols. (San Francisco: HarperCollins, 1978, 1982); John G. Stackhouse Jr., ed., *Evangelical Futures: A Conversation on Theological Method* (Grand Rapids: Baker, 2000); Veli-Matti Kärkkäinen, *Toward a Pneumatological Theology: Pentecostal*

is the sense of theology in each generation as a part of the great pilgrim-age to the "better country, . . . the city prepared by God" in the kingdom of his beloved Son (cf. Heb. 11:16). Theology is an imperfect and partial task, which Barth characterized thus: "*Unser Theologie is bestenfalls theologia viatorum*" (at best, our theology is theology on the way, theology for pil-grims).[2] *Theologia viatorum* must always be "theology for the way" because it strives to be "theology of the Way" (in the theological sense of ὁδός [Way] as the preaching of Christ for salvation; cf. Acts 9:2; 18:25–26; 19:9, 23; 24:14, 22).

Pilgrim theology—treated in the last chapter of this book—understands itself in the humility of human faith and thus dependent on the grace of God. It testifies to grace that is the bridge between God's self-knowing and our knowing of him, a bridge not only of being but also of time—"*Theologie zwischen den Zeiten*" (theology between the times), as living through the tension between the now and the not yet of the coming of Christ and the kingdom of

---

and Ecumenical Perspectives on Ecclesiology, Soteriology, and Theology of Mission, ed. Amos Young (Washington, D.C.: University Press of America, 2002); Daniel E. Albrecht, *Rites in the Spirit: A Ritual Approach to Pentecostal/Charismatic Spirituality* (Sheffield: Sheffield Academic Press, 2000); Gordon D. Fee, *Gospel and Spirit: Issues in New Testament Hermeneutics* (Peabody, Mass.: Hendrickson, 1991); James Patrick Callahan, Donald W. Dayton, and Kenneth E. Rowe, eds., *Primitivist Piety: The Ecclesiology of the Early Plymouth Brethren* (Lanham, Md.: Scarecrow Press, 1996); Bernard L. Ramm, *After Fundamentalism: The Future of Evangelical Theology* (San Fran-cisco: Harper, 1983); Michael J. Oleksa, *Orthodox Alaska: A Theology of Mission* (Crestwood, N.Y.: St. Vladimir's Seminary Press, 1992); Alexander Schmemann, *Church, World, Mission: Reflections on Orthodoxy in the West* (Crestwood, N.Y.: St. Vladimir's Seminary Press, 1979); Donald L. Gelpi, *Gracing of Human Experience: Rethinking the Relationship between Nature and Grace* (Collegeville, Minn.: Liturgical Press, 2001); Orlando E. Costas, *Liberating News: A Theology of Contextual Evangelization* (Grand Rapids: Eerdmans, 1994); Gabriel J. Fackre, *Ecu-menical Faith in Evangelical Perspective* (Grand Rapids: Eerdmans, 1994); Anthony B. Pinn and Benjamin Valentin, eds., *The Ties That Bind: African American and Hispanic American/Latino/a Theology in Dialogue* (New York : Continuum, 2001); Gary J. Dorrien, *The Making of American Liberal Theology: Idealism, Realism, and Modernity, 1900–1950* (Louisville: Westminster John Knox, 2003); Clara Sue Kidwell, *A Native American Theology* (Maryknoll, N.Y.: Orbis, 2001); and Peter C. Phan, *Christianity with an Asian Face: Asian American Theology in the Making* (Maryknoll, N.Y.: Orbis, 2003).

2. See *CD* II/1:209, where Barth, in discussing God's objectivity in the revelation of Christ also in terms of the biblical understanding of "truth . . . in itself proper, and permanent, valid and right as such, which can become the content and order of man's language and action. But this possibility is not an independent possibility which man himself can control. It is a possibil-ity which is imparted to him by the speaking and acting of God" (208). Barth asserts that the very nature of our being creatures makes our knowledge of God always "on the way" and the product of grace even after we meet God face-to-face in eternity. Only God's self-knowledge is complete, a true *theologia comprehensorum,* in spite of the "older theologies'" use of this term about the nearer presence of God in the new creation. But Barth is particularly referring to the knowledge of God in theology here and now as ever "inadequate" by comparison to the then and there of face-to-face knowledge of God. Until then, we humbly accept what the "light of grace" provides: "the fully satisfactory form, here and now, of the true knowledge which corresponds to its object and is thus of saving power" (III/4:34).

God. Yet Christ is the fullness and therefore over all things, just as all things have their being through him:

ἐστὲ ἐν αὐτῷ πεπληρωμένοι, ὅς ἐστιν ἡ κεφαλὴ πάσης ἀρχῆς καὶ ἐξουσίας.

You have come to fullness in him, who is the head of every ruler and authority.

Colossians 2:10

Our theology is always coming to this fullness and therefore is "theology on the way." There is a painful awareness in this:

ἐκ μέρους γὰρ γινώσκομεν καὶ ἐκ μέρους προφητεύομεν· ὅταν δὲ ἔλθῃ τὸ τέλειον, τὸ ἐκ μέρους καταργηθήσεται. . . . βλέπομεν γὰρ ἄρτι δι᾽ ἐσόπτρου ἐν αἰνίγματι, τότε δὲ πρόσωπον πρὸς πρόσωπον· ἄρτι γινώσκω ἐκ μέρους, τότε δὲ ἐπιγνώσομαι καθὼς καὶ ἐπεγνώσθην.

For we know only in part, and we prophesy only in part; but when the complete comes, the partial will come to an end. . . . For now we see in a mirror, dimly, but then we will see face to face. Now I know only in part; then I will know fully, even as I have been fully known.

1 Corinthians 13:9–10, 12

Short of the arrival of this fulfillment (τέλειος), theology through the preaching and teaching of the Word can "know only in part, and . . . prophesy only in part." In comparison to that eschatological face-to-face knowing, for which we wait, our present and historical knowledge is dim or enigmatic[3]—indeed, if knowledge is memory, then the dimness is profound. The knowledge of God and his works are known now only through a mirror (ἔσοπτρον)—a classic signifier of our theological knowledge as always reflection. Together with the ever-partial (μέρος) knowledge of theology, mediated and not-yet-whole knowledge, theology corresponds to faith, which cannot know via the directness of face-to-face encounter, even in the experiences of the Spirit. And yet the hope of this completeness beckons us to that place beyond this time, where our knowledge corresponds with God's knowledge, "even as I have been fully known."

Yet another text will fill out the sense of what is meant by pilgrim theology:

Οὐχ ὅτι ἤδη ἔλαβον ἢ ἤδη τετελείωμαι, διώκω δὲ εἰ καὶ καταλάβω, ἐφ᾽ ᾧ καὶ κατελήμφθην ὑπὸ Χριστοῦ [Ἰησοῦ]. ἀδελφοί, ἐγὼ ἐμαυτὸν οὐ λογίζομαι κατειληφέναι· ἐν

---

3. Only here in the entire New Testament do we find αἴνιγμα itself a noun that is taken adverbially: "dimly" to modify "mirror."

δέ, τὰ μὲν ὀπίσω ἐπιλανθανόμενος τοῖς δὲ ἔμπροσθεν ἐπεκτεινόμενος, κατὰ σκοπὸν διώκω εἰς τὸ βραβεῖον τῆς ἄνω κλήσεως τοῦ θεοῦ ἐν Χριστῷ Ἰησοῦ.

Not that I have already obtained this or have already reached the goal; but I press on to make it my own, because Christ Jesus has made me his own. Beloved, I do not consider that I have made it my own; but this one thing I do: forgetting what lies behind and straining forward to what lies ahead, I press on toward the goal for the prize of the heavenly call of God in Christ Jesus.

Philippians 3:12–14

The apostle must confess faith as a faith on the way. He is pressing on, like that corresponding knowledge of faith and of God in the text just cited, but now to mutually own what Christ already owns in him or to apprehend as one has been apprehended by Christ. This will be "fulfillment" or "perfection" (τετελείωμαι) in the future, which is very much "not yet" (οὐχ ὅτι). Theology is nothing other than the "striving" (διώκω) toward the "goal" (σκοπός) and "victor's crown" (βραβεῖον; cf. 1 Cor. 9:24). Of secondary yet nevertheless great significance here for the exercise of faith is the practice of "forgetting" (ἐπιλανθανόμενος)—a unique reference in Paul and the rest of the New Testament.[4] Forgetting "what lies behind" (τὰ . . . ὀπίσω), Paul is called to undertake that for which he has been called into a life of service of the gospel.

Pilgrim theology has a particular poignancy within the North American context since at its earliest stage it was populated by European Protestant, Catholic, and Orthodox immigrants seeking refuge in a new world, which would become a "new world order" *(novus ordo saeculorum)*. Into this world relatively free and oppressed persons migrated. Their settlements led to both displacements of aboriginal peoples and their conversion and, indeed, whole hosts of new churches and denominations and organizations birthed on this soil. North American Christianity extended the Reformation search for an original experience of faith while at the same time seeking to transplant and to preserve its Old World forms of faith. What marks its destiny is not so much the success of a transplanted church but ecclesial innovation. Christianity keeps proliferating, and much of this innovation and proliferation is driven by ever imagining a New Testament community. This religious ethos has achieved a dominance that defines the sense of church and polity. The following are exceptional forms of religious experience that inform the way theology is done in America.

---

4. And in surprising contrast to James (1:24), who in his own special use of the mirror analogy warns against forgetting—in this case, not things past but the present self presented in the Word, which reflects the self's true and corrigible image.

An Awakening Faith: Reality and Experience

One of the effects of the Reformation has been the migration of theological knowledge from clerical center to lay periphery. Part of what brought this about was the relocating of the Word of grace from being a word uttered externally and authoritatively by the priestly and ordained intermediary to a word uttered internally and authoritatively by the experience of the Holy Spirit in conversion. Indeed, it is difficult to reconstruct the radical importance for the Reformation that preaching and publishing had on Christian experience. The cultural significance of the gospel as something to be heard and memorized had revolutionary effects that would eclipse the social effects of the sacramental memorials of baptism and Eucharist. Indeed, proclamation attained sacramental status in Reformation theology largely because the time was ripe for a radical application of the Pauline text of Romans 10:8–15:

> ἀλλὰ τί λέγει; Ἐγγύς σου τὸ ῥῆμά ἐστιν ἐν τῷ στόματί σου καὶ ἐν τῇ καρδίᾳ σου, τοῦτ᾽ ἔστιν τὸ ῥῆμα τῆς πίστεως ὃ κηρύσσομεν. ὅτι ἐὰν ὁμολογήσῃς ἐν τῷ στόματί σου κύριον Ἰησοῦν καὶ πιστεύσῃς ἐν τῇ καρδίᾳ σου ὅτι ὁ θεὸς αὐτὸν ἤγειρεν ἐκ νεκρῶν, σωθήσῃ· καρδίᾳ γὰρ πιστεύεται εἰς δικαιοσύνην, στόματι δὲ ὁμολογεῖται εἰς σωτηρίαν. λέγει γὰρ ἡ γραφή, Πᾶς ὁ πιστεύων ἐπ᾽ αὐτῷ οὐ καταισχυνθήσεται. οὐ γάρ ἐστιν διαστολὴ Ἰουδαίου τε καὶ Ἕλληνος, ὁ γὰρ αὐτὸς κύριος πάντων, πλουτῶν εἰς πάντας τοὺς ἐπικαλουμένους αὐτόν· Πᾶς γὰρ ὃς ἂν ἐπικαλέσηται τὸ ὄνομα κυρίου σωθήσεται.
>
> Πῶς οὖν ἐπικαλέσωνται εἰς ὃν οὐκ ἐπίστευσαν; πῶς δὲ πιστεύσωσιν οὗ οὐκ ἤκουσαν; πῶς δὲ ἀκούσωσιν χωρὶς κηρύσσοντος; πῶς δὲ κηρύξωσιν ἐὰν μὴ ἀποσταλῶσιν; καθὼς γέγραπται, Ὡς ὡραῖοι οἱ πόδες τῶν εὐαγγελιζομένων [τὰ] ἀγαθά.

But what does it say? "The word is near you, on your lips and in your heart" (that is, the word of faith that we proclaim); because if you confess with your lips that Jesus is Lord and believe in your heart that God raised him from the dead, you will be saved. For one believes with the heart and so is justified, and one confesses with the mouth and so is saved. The Scripture says, "No one who believes in him will be put to shame." For there is no distinction between Jew and Greek; the same Lord is Lord of all and is generous to all who call on him. For, "Everyone who calls on the name of the Lord shall be saved."

But how are they to call on one in whom they have not believed? And how are they to believe in one of whom they have never heard? And how are they to hear without someone to proclaim him? And how are they to proclaim him unless they are sent? As it is written, "How beautiful are the feet of those who bring good news!"

This text encapsulates what the reforming programs of the sixteenth century were after, even beyond their institutional intentions. The closest tie is made among three distinct Christian truths in just 10:8 as throughout the passage: faith (ἐν τῷ στόματί σου καὶ ἐν τῇ καρδίᾳ σου), proclamation (τὸ ῥῆμα τῆς πίστεως ὃ κηρύσσομεν), and media of salvation (ἐγγύς σου τὸ ῥῆμά ἐστιν). Indeed, 10:10 essentially declares that the receiving of grace is a self-administered practice, where internal (καρδίᾳ . . . πιστεύεται) and external (στόματι . . . ὁμολογεῖται) action eventuate in justification (εἰς δικαιοσύνην) and in salvation (εἰς σωτηρίαν). Massive changes for ordination are implied here, but we focus on the sacramental ones with respect to the means of grace.

Conversion

Conversion[5] signifies the transformation from what we are "naturally," as creatures, sinners, members of a human community, into a new kind of humanity in Christ. As an event of faith dependent upon the work of God by the Holy Spirit, conversion is closely associated with the act of repentance, turning away from sin and turning toward God in Christ, with internal as well as external effects. Conversion is an active, conscious embrace of Christ through the gospel, and as such it indicates that Christian identity is never acquired merely by birth or inculturation but by a volitional act in response to the promise and power of God. Indeed, it is the volitional characteristic that leads to the definition of the Christian community and by inference all religious communities as "voluntary associations." For the purposes of Christian theology, however, voluntary association applies to all religions by virtue of the possibility that one is truly free before God to convert to the truth in Christ (cf. Isa. 6:10; 31:6; Jer. 3:10, 12, 14, 22; Amos 4:6, 8, 10; Zech. 1:2–4; Luke 24:44–47; Acts 3:19; 9:35; 11:21; 14:15; 15:3, 19; 26:20; 1 Thess. 1:9–10).

Ordo Salutis

This doctrine of conversion has often been defined according to a sense of the process of becoming a Christian, entering the *ordo salutis* (order of salvation). Although there is no precise agreement in Protestant theology about this order or whether to think of these components as a graduated process or simultaneous, the listing appears something like the following:

- *vocatio* ("calling" by the Holy Spirit to Christ)
- *illuminatio* ("illumination" by the Holy Spirit to understand)
- *conversio* ("conversion" by the Holy Spirit to a new disposition)

5. Conversion is not at all absent from Barth's theology. He devotes a significant portion of chapter 66 to the topic, where discipleship and the new obedience of the Christian is predicated upon this experience (*CD* IV/2:553–84). But see also his discussion under the rubric of the Son's work of liberating individuals for conversion, indeed, for freedom itself in him (ibid., 305–6). Cf. Stephen R. Yarbrough and John C. Adams, *Delightful Conviction: Jonathan Edwards and the Rhetoric of Conversion* (Westport, Conn.: Greenwood Publishing, 1993).

- *fides iustificatio* ("justifying faith" by the Holy Spirit, through which we are accepted)
- *renovatio* ("regeneration" by the Holy Spirit to new life)
- *unio mystica* ("mystical union" by the Holy Spirit through faith alone)
- *sanctificatio, nova oboedientia* ("sanctification," "new obedience")

Throughout the nineteenth century, the tendency in Protestant theology was to streamline such a list to the essentials of repentance, regeneration, and faith, but always under the sovereign influence of the Holy Spirit representing God the Father and God the Son to the sinner-become-believer.

But what has happened in the understanding of conversion in the past two centuries requires appreciating a significant supplement to the theocentric perspective of the traditional *ordo salutis*. Already from the Great Awakening of the eighteenth century and then through the revivalism and mass evangelism of the twentieth century, a personalizing and psychologizing dimension enters in. No one is more on their guard and yet no one more advances this supplement than Jonathan Edwards himself. On the one hand, Edwards's theology of the conversion experience is part of the larger movement known as Pietism, but he uniquely develops its theology at a much more sophisticated level both in terms of Reformed Orthodoxy and the utilization of Lockean psychology. The "conversion" of conversion reflects the exploration of the autobiographical nature of apostolic testimony on Scripture and, indeed, the requirement of every Christian to testify to the "hope that lies within."[6] Edwards's work, which many regard as the first psychology in America, was not merely individualistic but truly communitarian in the sense of concern not only for one's own salvation but also for that of others.[7] What is important about Edwards's theology of revival and religious affections is that it unites the various strands of objective and subjective truth by which converting faith is communicated and acquired.

---

6. First Peter 1:3, 13, 21; and especially 3:15: "But in your hearts sanctify Christ as Lord. Always be ready to make your defense to anyone who demands from you an accounting for the hope that is in you."

7. Jonathan Edwards, *A Treatise Concerning Religious Affections* (Boston: S. Kneeland and T. Green, 1746), part 3, section 2, www.jonathanedwards.com/text/RA/RAPart3–2.htm, states: "True saints have their minds, in the first place, inexpressibly pleased and delighted with the sweet ideas of the glorious and amiable nature of the things of God. And this is the spring of all their delights, and the cream of all their pleasures: it is the joy of their joy. This sweet and ravishing entertainment they have in the view of the beautiful and delightful nature of divine things, is the foundation of the joy that they have afterwards, in the consideration of their being theirs." He develops this further in part 3, section 12, www.jonathanedwards.com/text/RA/RAPart3–12.htm: "Indeed the power of godliness is exerted in the first place within the soul, in the sensible, lively exercise of gracious affections there. Yet the principal evidence of this power of godliness, is in those exercises of holy affections that are practical, and in their being practical; in conquering the will, and conquering the lusts and corruptions of men, and carrying men on in the way of holiness, through all temptations, difficulty, and opposition."

A kind of "liturgy of awakening" or "liturgy of renewal" forms itself where the search for and realization of salvation in Christ unites the various dimensions of Christian faith: representing the truth of the redeeming, Triune God of the gospel, the complex of desires and emotions associated with both pre-Christian and Christian psychology of faith, the duties of faith and obedience, participation in the community of Christians who guide others and one another through the process of conversation and maturation in Christ. Over the past three centuries, much of the publishing in evangelical circles would constitute liturgies and rituals of awakening, employing powerful symbols and methods by which conversion becomes a highly personal and generalized possibility.

The power of awakening doctrines and rituals are not only positive in terms of conversion but also negative in terms of resisting secularization. One of the confusions over interpreting Christian fundamentalism is at this very point. Too often, fundamentalism is interpreted as antimodernism, only to be rendered meaningless by a thousand qualifications since fundamentalists do not generally withdraw from everyday affairs of social, political, and economic life. The reason for this misinterpretation is to be found in the so-called secularization thesis, which essentially claims that modernization renders religion implausible at best and sociologically dangerous at worst. Even though the point is secularization, the polemic is a certain optimism and valorization of modernization. But then one must account for the resurgence of religion coupled with the social phenomena often classified as postmodern. The point here is that fundamentalists (less successfully) as well as evangelicals and Catholics (perhaps more successfully) actually are resolute antisecularists.[8] This comports with an important dimension of postmodernity as well in the form of post-secularity. Multicultural pluralism is not in the first instance hostile to religious believing—only to any one religion acquiring political and therefore coercive dominance. Indeed, religious pluralism is originally a subset of the Christian pluralism of early modern laws of religious liberty.

Resistance to secularization or to secularity has many dimensions to it in the Christian outlook. In the first instance, being oriented to the voluntary nature of conversion and to religious liberty, Christians recognize that secularity, particularly of the agnostic or irreligious type, is an option. Indeed, the culture of "*etsi Deus non daretur*" (as if God did not exist) of Barth and Bonhoeffer's generation took the advancing secularity of civil society as an inevitable aspect of its "coming of age."[9] This proved disastrous in the face of fascism and com-

8. Cf. Peter L. Berger, ed., *The Desecularization of the World: Resurgent Religion and World Politics* (Grand Rapids: Eerdmans, 1999); but this essential insight was announced years earlier and strikingly prescient of the important elements of postmodernism in Harvey Gallagher Cox, *Religion in the Secular City: Toward a Postmodern Theology* (New York: Simon & Schuster, 1984).

9. Cf. John W. de Gruchy, ed., *The Cambridge Companion to Dietrich Bonhoeffer* (Cambridge: Cambridge University Press, 1999), 226–45.

munism since the forces of religious resistance were too diminished or even compromised to accomplish much.

But awakening and reform do not engage secularism in the same way it engages democratic culture. As we consider below, it is the undemocratic dominance of secular reasoning to the exclusion of religious reasoning in public discourse that is so vehemently opposed. One cannot live with the principles of religious liberty installed within modern states, aware of the presence of multiple religious communities and denominations, without caring about peaceful coexistence of them all. At the root of early-twentieth-century concerns for secularity on the part of theologians, including Barth, is the recognition of the profound sense of the voluntary nature of religious belief. Barth argues consistently for the inner compulsion of revelation and faith while rejecting the coercion of religion and religious institutions.[10] Indeed, at a number of major points in the *CD*, the antireligiousness of Barth is a radical critique of the idolatrous and self-justifying nature of *homo religiosus* (religious humanity) and in some way funds the bent toward secularization of the wider social and political order for the sake of the gospel. Anti-Constantinianism is quite consistent with Barth's program.

Charismata

Several years ago a most disturbing pneumatology appeared, written by Ephraim Radner,[11] an American Episcopal who contended that the disunity of the churches was fundamental evidence of the absence of the Holy Spirit as their living reality. The great apostle in writing to the Corinthians and to Timothy also experienced disunity such that one might question not the questioning but the conclusions of this work. But certainly the lack of evidence of the gifting Spirit in the gathered community of Christians should raise great alarm. With the great disruption of church authority since the Reformation, its Constantinian supports ever waning and ultimately disappearing—for the sake of a Spirit-filled church—there is no doubt that a great sense of loss and disorientation has resulted. But what the marriage of church and state could never do, their separation and the reconstruction of church authority along the lines of charismatic and congregational rather than of office and institution will be, in the long run, a superlative blessing. Indeed, although disunity is a grievous scandal, the growing phenomenon of increased participation in and conferring of spiritual authority to the faithful is perhaps an important step along the way toward unity.

10. This is certainly part of what Timothy J. Gorringe is after in his work *Karl Barth: Against Hegemony* (Oxford: Oxford University Press, 1999).

11. Ephraim Radner, *End of the Church: A Pneumatology of Christian Division in the West* (Grand Rapids: Eerdmans, 1998).

In the ancient churches, the charismatic reality is often embodied in its mysteries or sacraments and also charisms, which emphasize the mediation of salvation in varying degrees to the whole church. The Holy Spirit is said to spirate, pour out, or infuse the faithful with divine power and grace, enabling the works by which faith participates in the work of Christ. From evangelical perspectives this spiration is seen more in terms of divine calling to a holy life and missional action. The Holy Spirit pours out *pneumatikoi,* and as embodied they are realized in vocations that mobilize potentially all of the faithful. In terms of Barth's third dimension of God's work now—"*in nobis*"—this is participation in the testimony and mission of the Spirit through us, enabling the faithful with callings to call those ready to hear to faith and obedience.

In the great movement toward evangelism in the global church's agenda in the last decades of the twentieth century and into the twenty-first century, the necessary multiplication of Christian communities is finding its enablement through the massive dissemination of spiritual gifts and leadership functions. This is a time of great soul-searching regarding, particularly, ordination. The great Lima Document of the WCC, "Baptism, Eucharist and Ministry" (1981), was a first step in endeavoring to acknowledge this crisis. The building up of community in Christ through the increase in charismatic participation in this mission initially puts great stress on giftedness over office. The two are not mutually exclusive, but one is prior to the other. For the charismatic community to know a bond and way of following "*en pneumati*" (in the Spirit), it is no surprise that, with increased congregational authority stemming from this movement, there would be an insistence upon charismatic experience in leadership. Indeed, the tendency toward a bottom-up, grassroots appeal for leadership rather than a top-down almost "aristocratic model" is quite understandable.

What counts, however, are the increasing commonalities of experience that have appeared in global Christianity as a result of movements of awakening, conversion, and the widening experience of the Holy Spirit. Indeed, this more than institutionalized missionary activity has promoted the expansion of Christian communities in the developing world. Over 50 percent of the world's Christians, over half a billion, testify to charismatic experience. This overwhelming fact outstrips by far any other common experience in the otherwise dizzying multiplicity of churches and factions that we could account as Christian.

Ecumenical Awakening

The theological orientation of awakening faith links with Barth and ecumenical truth at the point of centering on Christ and Christ's work. For all of the claims to experience of the Holy Spirit, the characteristic of the conversionist message is the gospel *pro nobis, pro me.* In the centuries since the Reformation—whose remarkable success is due to the new measure of its populism and the clarity of its gospel message—the question of the degree to which Barth is christocentric has been raised when reading him from the perspective either of his doctrine of revelation or of his doctrine of the Trinity. The irony of such a charge is that others found him "christomonistic" as they read the later volumes of the *CD*. One must remember that Barth's constant attention to the act of God in revelation as gracious and salvific, stressing that revelation is found only in God's revelation in Jesus Christ, is fundamental to the tradition of Reformation theology. In light of defining revelation in terms of God's gracious self-revealing, "This is eternal life, . . . [to] know you . . . and Jesus Christ whom you have sent" (John 17:3) is immediately also trinitarian, since God's saving work is God's triune work.

It must be emphasized that the center of trinitarian faith as enunciated in the Nicene-Constantinopolitan Creed is not an expression of Christian accommodation to Hellenistic categories. The content of the creed is controlled by the narrative flow of the creating and saving work of God as Father, Son, and Holy Spirit. While the Johannine sense in seeking to honor Christ aright in "God of God, Light of Light" (cf. John 1:1, 4, 9) is further defined by the two terms *homoousios* and *hypostasis,* the center of the confession is the christological *pro nobis*. The constructive nature of Reformation theology as a theology of awakening stems from what I regard as Luther's insistence on an implicit *pro me* in the creedal affirmation.

As a result of the burgeoning pneumatology of the charismata, realignments in theology are also emerging. Overwhelmingly, this is a blessing. The charismatic movements of the globe show amenability to seek orthodox resolutions to innovations in the life of the church. Trinitarian, synergistic, and ethical challenges are met with careful study and the search for spiritual maturity. Large minorities of the students at Protestant, Catholic, and Orthodox graduate schools and seminaries claim charismatic experience and insight.

But one must be careful that realignment not be confused with recasting of doctrine. Pneumatology is always trinitarian, and trinitarian theology is always pursuing scriptural and evangelical and ultimately catholic and orthodox forms of expression. The tendency to claim a work of the Spirit that somehow leaves Scripture behind, reformulating doctrine, indeed, introducing new doctrine, jeopardizes the ecumenical realities of the faith as it is known and practiced among the historic churches. Of course, to pursue this triadic determination of doctrinal identity—evangelical, Orthodox, Catholic—is not to speak institutionally in the first instance but to speak biblically and attributively. Even ecclesial identity can be a matter of striving after these attributes in personal and corporate faith without immediate reference to hierarchies or denominations. The fact that the great traditions of the church are the common property and source of instruction for all Christians everywhere is enough to begin bringing millions of new believers and their churches into doctrinal relation and maturation with the historic churches. Out of a fading memory of a unity of beliefs and values between church community and political community, we must guard against thinking that a bald pneumatology is the solution to maintaining that unity.

What I have been discussing are the great households of Christian faith and mission that have come to exist in the world and are the substance of ecumenical reality. The North American context is a harbor and a launching pad for multitudes of these communities united by Christ and liberated to self-expression by the history of its religious liberty and revivalism.

A Fallibilist Faith

American fallibilism in the first instance is born of the practical realities of accommodating difference and a divergence of beliefs and viewpoints. Out of this reality has grown a practical philosophy known as pragmatism, which tends to focus on the function of ideas rather than demonstrations of their correspondence to universal truths and realities. A humble admission of limitation of perception and judgment in matters universal insists on a philosophy of limits and deeds. Even its metaphysics asks for functional relations in terms of language, symbols, and social meaning. Rooted in the practical concerns of immigrants to a perceived wilderness in the seventeenth century, the provisionality of institutions and yet the successes in building community life have all suggested even a virtue in fallibilist self-understanding. From the biblical-psychological tests of religious experience of Edwards to the voluntarist faith of Finney, to the semiotics of Peirce and the democratic constructivism of John Dewey and Reinhold Niebuhr, fallibilism is at its deepest level shaped by the duties of personal conversion: repentance, personal study, prayer, and vocation.

Agreements That Divide

Human beings are aggressive and contentious creatures. Indeed, in their sin they fall into acting out such deeds of selfishness, injustice, and cruelty that one cannot exempt the mind from this reality. All human goodness and excellence are marred by human fallenness. And fallenness manifests noetic effects as much as moral effects such that our capacities to reason are always flawed. Reckoning with sin is not merely a matter of honesty about our finitude but is fundamental to understanding the gospel of Christ's atoning death. Indeed, sin is a subtext to Paul's arguments about salvation and moral anthropology throughout the Epistle to the Romans (esp. chaps. 1–8). In the chapter most descriptive of the struggle of the mind and sin, Romans 7 (esp. vv. 20–25), Paul presents the internal operative power of ἕτερον νόμον, "another law," as our entrapment "ἐν τῷ νόμῳ τῆς ἁμαρτίας" (in the law of sin) (v. 23). Paul testifies to a delight in "τῷ νόμῳ τοῦ θεοῦ κατὰ τὸν ἔσω ἄνθρωπον" (the law of God according to my inner humanity) (v. 22),[12] expressing the biblical understanding of the law written on the heart.[13] But on account of the "other law," every act of goodness is exercised in conflict with it. While Paul esteems the law of God, "ἐμοὶ τὸ κακὸν παράκειται" (evil is present with me) (v. 21).[14] He confesses, "ὃ οὐ θέλω [ἐγὼ] τοῦτο ποιῶ" (I do what I do not want) (v. 20), because this other law gets the upper hand in his conduct, "αἰχμαλωτίζοντά με ἐν τῷ νόμῳ τῆς ἁμαρτίας τῷ ὄντι ἐν τοῖς μέλεσίν μου" (making me captive to the law of sin that dwells in my members) (v. 23). Of course, every act of the intellect has moral dimensions in terms of truth-telling and the representation of other people's words in debate and citation. Unfortunately, but realistically, the subtlety of human falsehood and prevarication, particularly at the level of relationship and community goods, exhibits the radical flaws of human reasoning as well as moral action.

Paul's metaphors of internal conflict can be applied to human communities as well. Deeply imbedded in the consciousness of North Americans is their sense of origin as refugees from religious conflict in former homelands. Embedded within the economic interests driving colonization are the cultural spaces removed from the contested ground of the homeland. With the rejection of the Puritan model of civil authority in North America in favor of religious liberty, the agglomeration first of rival Christian theologies meant the strained willingness to live with fallibility while at the same time affirming the God of Jesus Christ. Over time, the cultural space of religious liberty and the fallibilism it entails make room for all kinds of refugees of conscience as virtually religious. In a world such as ours, the utopian dream of a humanly constructed empire of unitary truth is one of the primary reasons why hermeneutics of suspicion are practiced.

But fallibilism does not have relativism as its consequence. A vision of unitary truth persists, and approximations of truth ring true to experience and perception; indeed, most acts of communication ride on and successfully convey meaning because truth is abundant. But the greater the value, the more contested the object of truth. Rival versions of truth therefore require a kind of *critical realism* in interpretive practice. Enduring rivalries, particularly in theology, are indicative of the capacity for traditions to modify themselves on account of both new generations of practitioners as well as adapting to the existence of the other. Fallibilism within a tradition instills a degree of humility

12. Author's translation; NRSV renders ἄνθρωπον here as "self" but loses too much of its sense as "humanity" or "man."

13. Cf. Rom. 2:15. This is usually expressed as a divine act, an act of grace, but can also be an act of devotion by the self. Cf. Gen. 20:6; Deut. 30:6; Ps. 51:10; Prov. 3:3; 7:3; Ezek. 11:19; 18:31; 36:26; 2 Esd. 14:25.

14. Author's translation; again, the NRSV "evil lies close at hand" misses the first-person pronoun and even suggests an externalized evil rather than its deep embeddedness within the human being.

in its exponents. Representatives of a tradition as well as eclectics and contrarians live by acts of belief and commitment and, to the degree that they find ways of respecting the other in their rival beliefs, eschew claims of certainty. This is not to say that definite truth could not exist eschatologically but that under the conditions of rival claims, human beings do not find it in very large communities of knowers of the truth.

As a result of fallibilism and its ramifications, science is no longer viewed as a collective effort toward a single truth. Only revelation can provide such single truths that speak to the whole of existence. Truth for the human is always a formulation, a best interpretation of a particular state of affairs in nature or in communication, and therefore a cultural construction that has persuaded its adherents that it adequately reflects reality at its point of description. The very fact that truth is communicated at best in adequate formulations is indicative of what is meant here. When an interpreter of Scripture offers formulations of a best understanding, those formulations are both from their time and place and for their time and place. To the extent that the formulation is a close exegesis of particular texts of Scripture, historical theological meaning is removed from the demands of its application in a particular contemporary context. But how one is to bridge the hermeneutical gap between the historic past and the coming present is a matter of much greater fallibility. The specific demands of contemporary sermon and theological statement, wherever this is being done globally, is—even after diligent attention to sound rules of exegesis and the study of traditions—a matter of great faith.

There can be no better theological rule of fallibilism than "*semper reformandum*" (always reforming). Hidden within this rule is the other concerning the believer himself or herself: "*simul iustus et peccator*" (at once righteous and sinner). These rules imply that error is constitutive of human beings and human community, no matter how clearly the truth of revelation is grasped, no matter how virtuously human beings comport themselves with respect to it. The church and the believer are ever in need of reform because their best forms and testimonies are at once righteous and sinful.

Sinful Interpreters

Christian theology faces moral and noetic impairments in the practice of interpretation at points beyond those of other interpretive traditions. Christian interpretation is more than literary criticism, more than poetic understanding. Faithful interpretation, however much it may employ critical skills, must be constantly concerned that in the end its statements are not a falling away from faith. This is reflected in the ways in which apostasy is described at various points in the New Testament. Rooted in the classic text on exorcism (Matt. 12:22–45) is the parable of the self as a house from which one demon has been removed. The failure to make it the habitation of the divine Spirit results in the "rehabilitation" of the demonic, now sevenfold, so that "the last state of that person is worse than the first"[15] (Matt. 12:45; Luke 11:26). Jesus' ominous words concerning his betrayer, "better for that one not to have been born" (Matt. 26:24; Mark 14:21), are indicative that there are courses of action instantiated by Christian truth that either fulfill it or offend against it. These are the contexts in which theological speech must be companioned by theological virtue, and yet even then "we have these truths in earthen vessels" (cf. 2 Cor. 4:7). Even if our lives overflow with truth, we are still no better than useful, never truly adequate to the task, let alone being embodiments equal to their content. As something of a motto, Barth took the words of Jesus: "So you also, when you have done all that you were ordered to do, say, 'We are worthless slaves; we have done only what we ought to have done!'" (Luke 17:10). And we often fail to do even that.

Throughout the *CD* we are reminded that theology is an act of obedience as much it is an act of worship and proclamation. But the inadequacy of our statements, whatever their degree of godliness and precision, is always the lesser truth about all theology. Augustine's great musings on the work of the theologian come to mind: We cannot in ourselves say anything appropriate to God, but we are commanded to do so, and therefore we speak and write. Paul likens apostles to the incense of Christ's victory: "to the one a fragrance from death to death, to the other a fragrance from life to life. Who is sufficient for these things? For we are not peddlers of God's word like so many; but in Christ we speak as persons of sincerity, as persons sent from God and standing in his presence" (2 Cor. 2:16–17). Paul's sense of inadequacy and yet his confidence in the calling and message of Christ press him into obedient action. One detects Barth's view of theology as a spiritual discipline, action in obedience, from the preface of *CD* IV; no matter how habituated Barth might have become to his own project, he practices a daily renewal of his concentration on his subject matter, not in his work but in the way of Christ. Barth's chief concern is that he attempt not to err against the truth knowingly since to do so would corrupt the entire project of the *CD*.

Barth does not pursue this from belief in the perfectability of theology; instead, he accepts its fallibility as utility for the divine purpose. One must recognize how significant the fallibilist position is in Christian theology. The history of theology is replete with references to the inadequacy of human language to achieve the truth of God. Thomas's reflection on analogy, that every degree of similarity between human and divine speech is engulfed by infinitely greater dissimilarity, expresses well something of this dilemma of theology. Nevertheless, under the conditions of historical consciousness in the last two centuries, theology was forced to come more fully to grips with its fallibility.

Perhaps the most interesting such case in the nineteenth century is that of John Henry Cardinal Newman and his great theological treatise of 1845, *An*

15. Cf. 1 Cor. 11:17; 1 Tim. 5:8; Heb. 10:29.

Essay on the Development of Doctrine.[16] Although the "unreformable" papal infallibility doctrine of Vatican I was not yet formulated, the infallibility of the church's settled theology in the form of dogma was fundamental to Newman's theological situation as a member of the Roman Catholic hierarchy. Only gingerly did Newman introduce a theology of "development" in his theology. Drawing on the classic formula of Vincent of Lerins identifying dogma as what the church has believed "everywhere, always, and by everyone" (principles of ecumenicity, antiquity, and agreement), Newman was walking a tightrope between immutability and change. Can there be "development" without change? To make such an assertion, he introduced what he called the church's "illative sense" as the characteristic means of development in its theological formulations over time. In the course of the church's life, the official adoption of doctrine was based on a dynamic impulse that bridged probability and certainty. Emergent beliefs and practices, which over time appear to have persuaded and permeated the entire faithful of the church, take on a kind of doctrinal sense; they come to possess a dogmatic sensibility, and the magisterium responds to this sense, taken as the direction of the Holy Spirit, by dogmatizing a particular belief. This supposedly does not indicate change but rather makes more explicit what had only been dimly perceived in the early history of the church but was truly latent in the revelation all along. In this way, ultimately, one could even embrace papal infallibility.

Divine infallibility is promulgated by the ancient churches in their dogmas and, indeed, by the Reformation churches, particularly the Reformed branch in giving special credence to the work of the Holy Spirit to secure correct interpretation and statements of doctrine. Hence, to alter this belief from the truth claims of Christian theology constitutes a highly questionable "reform." The challenge of balancing the claim of the infallible God in his revelation on the one hand and the actual knowledge of highly fallible knowers on the other raises the question of the status of the knowledge claims. From the ancient perspective, through Thomas and beyond, that grace is viewed as perfecting nature. In special cases, already in this world, it would mean that there always are perfected witnesses in history: first prophets and apostles, next hosts of preachers and teachers whose lives are progressively embodying this perfecting grace, and finally historical moments in the life of the church, primarily in councils, where infallible doctrine would be secured. But from the perspective of the Reformation and the free churches of the last five centuries, the view of divine grace is that perfection remains solely attributed to the divine. An infallible declaration of pardon and the infallible work of the Holy Spirit enabling the believer to persevere through the trials and death of this world mean that the believer shares in the infallibility of the divine nature only in the consummation of the resurrection. Until then, the *simul iustus et peccator*

16. Cf. John Henry Cardinal Newman, *An Essay on the Development of Christian Doctrine* (South Bend, Ind.: University of Notre Dame Press, 1990).

nature of human knowing and action qualifies every doctrine and mission of Christianity.

What then of the presence of divinely infallible communication in Scripture? In every case, the Christian tradition testifies to the miracle of inspired authorship for the texts of Scripture and also for their preservation through time. The fact of their late collection or canonization as Holy Scripture means that the canonical listing of book titles comes from sources other than the prophetic and apostolic writings of Scripture. Quite apart from the conflict over whether the church is the source of Scripture or the Scripture is the source of the church, the listing of authoritative books and the existence of differing lists—some including what we now call apocryphal writings—cannot help but raise the question of the fallibility of the institutional processes that offered the various lists or even produced a preferred list. A great deal of thought has been given to this matter. Recently, there has appeared a shift to analyzing Scripture in terms of speech-act theory, derived from the philosophical writings of William Alston and applied most impressively by Nicholas Wolterstorff. Avoiding the burden of establishing philosophically where a foundation exists that could substantiate a revelatory claim, Wolterstorff simply reflects on the nature of speaking or writing on another person's behalf, at the behest of that person. Thus, in the case of the prophets and the apostles in their relation to God, their writings effectively become divine speech. Rather than attempting to justify claims of divine revelation, the intent is to provide a philosophical account of what is meant by the liturgical affirmation "Thus says the Lord" whenever Scripture is read to the faithful. The question of the infallibility of Scripture, like the authorship of Scripture, would then be accounted for in the same way. To hear and believe this word as from the Lord is then to take it as infallible as much as it is authoritative.

To take Scripture as infallible does not mean that the reception of its communications takes place infallibly. Indeed, for those who acknowledge it, the very principle *semper reformandum* means by definition that no formulation or act of the church or the believer can be infallible. "Ever reforming" means the full embrace of theological and missiological fallibility as the truth about our believing and ecclesial condition, everywhere, at all times, for everyone. Something akin to Karl Popper's principle of falsifiability is at work in the history of theology when one attends strictly to the nature of theology as a human work. In this case, the falsifiability of doctrine does not mean that the truth of doctrine is dispensed with if a particular theological formulation has been falsified. Indeed, the very reason that doctrine is being constantly worked on is that the truth to which it refers has successfully won commitment over time. Falsifiability is a way of accounting for the modification of doctrinal formulation such that the core truths endure, while comprehension and application of them achieve greater success. Indeed, there is reflected a kind of "failing toward success." But all of this takes place under divine grace.

Grace is original to revelation and our understanding of it. Unlike the doctrine that views grace as perfecting nature, grace never does anything more than to make use of human faculties of moral, intellectual, and aesthetic judgment. Since God makes gracious use of the creation on behalf of the creature, revelation is always an act of grace making possible understanding and experience of God. A gracious logic is at work here, linking believers with the Word of God uniquely and solely incarnate in Jesus, whose faithful obedience unto death gives rise to faithful and obedient reading-hearing of this Word for adequate understanding. This event is unlike our reading of other texts, from poetry to newspaper: None of them commands faithfulness and obedience in God's name, and none offers itself to us as the Word of God. The question of understanding Scripture according to divine intention goes beyond the demands of understanding any other text.[17]

Pragmatics of Faith

The story of religious and political liberty in America, while filled with too many injustices to recount, is still one of such ineluctable success that in the nineteenth-century, Americanism was often judged to be a kind of heresy. Indeed, throughout Barth's own life, a kind of European skepticism toward things American characterized his attitude while visiting his American friends only once and late in his life, in 1962. In the CD, among the few Americans mentioned are Mary Baker Eddy and her Christian Science and John Foster Dulles, John Eliot, Benjamin Franklin, John Mott, and Wilhelm Pauck. Barth does not mention a range of theologians from Edwards to Niebuhr. Indeed, few theologians of the British tradition are reflected other than John Wesley. Because of his Gifford Lectures, Barth has more positive theological interaction with the Scots Confession than with any other English reference.

How are North American theologians to read a theologian who did not read their own local sources? At the primary level, of course, it is the theological reading of Scripture that unites them to Barth and allows for Barth to be incorporated fully into their own reading of Scripture. To do so, a translation has to be made. Early twenty-first-century theologians of the Western Hemisphere will inevitably read Barth in terms of the practicalities of their situations. In North America, attention to these practicalities is so basic because of the life projects to which its culture subjects its citizens. Since the principle of religious liberty disallows the official privileging of a single religious tradition in the culture, and the principle of self-governance defines the deeper social condition of each of its citizens, cultural construction and identity formation are unavoidable tasks in this context. The settlement of this hemisphere as

---

17. At this point we will not consider similarities in the ways in which interpreters in other Scripture-based religions often call for similar, extraordinary routines by which understanding is adequately achieved.

an ongoing reality of immigration and integration precludes the possibility of a "settled" cultural mind-set. The Puritan, separatist, and eighteenth-century liberal roots of American beginnings can still be felt through the impact of its founding documents. And yet the procedural openness of its political and economic ways of life and the constant founding of new associations and institutions that make sense of the possibility for ever-new relationships and organizations make for unavoidable pragmatics of culture.

The pragmatics of this culture are derived from the democratic relations that determine only the outcome of peaceful coexistence imposed upon its citizens. Tremendous attention is given to Protestant and most often to varieties of evangelical Christianity, but we also recognize the immensely influential presence of Catholicism as well as the branches of Orthodoxy, and beyond this new religions such as Mormonism along with Judaism, Islam, and many Asian religions. This situation simply means that calls to a common religious root are not possible. Indeed, the experience of democratic pluralism in Europe and the procedural conventions by which democratic culture comes to be practiced have led to only the most general reference to religion in the new Constitution of the European Union.[18]

But the pragmatics began with the development of a theology of conscientious conviction in the Reformation itself. Nonconformity, religious toleration, and finally religious liberty were all supported by evangelical Protestants to varying degrees because institutional divisions provided one way out of religious wars of the sixteenth and seventeenth centuries. The resulting constitutional polities mirrored the ecclesial polities that found ways of coexistence, sometimes with a state church attempting to adjudicate on religious liberty but finally with procedural democracy and judiciary oversight limiting or eliminating religious privilege.

On the ecclesial level, by the beginning of the twentieth century, certain procedural relations had come to qualify internal ecclesial relations. This is the case with the Swiss Reformed Churches: To avoid conflict between liberals and conservatives, minimal denominational affiliation requirements were instituted. This left local congregations to determine the nature of doctrine and the limits of theology. In a much more complex way, with the mass of Christian denominations in America existing in a laissez-faire environment, procedural democracy will not resolve disputes among or within Christian communities or other religious communities, for that matter. The one area

18. The proposed preamble to the constitution of the EU contains the particular words, "Drawing inspiration from the cultural, religious and humanist inheritance of Europe, which, nourished first by the civilisations of Greece and Rome, characterised by spiritual impulse always present in its heritage and later by the philosophical currents of the Enlightenment, has embedded within the life of society its perception of the central role of the human person and his inviolable and inalienable rights, and of respect for law" (news.bbc.co.uk/1/hi/uk_politics/2938272.stm). Interestingly, the fundamental values expressed in the working document include "human dignity," which is drawn largely from Roman Catholic natural-law tradition.

where hierarchical doctrinal authority persists in American Protestant Christianity is in its denominational staffs (e.g., administrators, missionaries, and seminary professors). For the most part, however, theological authority is a reality corporately shared among local congregations themselves. Finally, conscientious believers participate with the ordained, who interpret Scripture in light of the particular confessional and dogmatic traditions of their respective denominations.

But the wider reality of differing and even rival Christian communities, united by their own theologically authoritative traditions, puts the churches in the position of working out pragmatics of peaceful coexistence and, where possible, cooperation. Working out of the democratic social orders of public life, with coexistence precluding destructive legal privileges of any religious perspective, but also encouraging internally guided cooperation, the pragmatics of the situation is not an indication of philosophical relativism but a coping strategy of multiple claims to a share in public cultural space. As Jean Bethke-Elshtain has pointed out, the cultural situation of democracy means that this public space will always be a place of contest in which rivals are protected and their ideas find freedom of expression. Along with the likes of Stephen Carter, commitments to authoritative Christian doctrine are not precluded in the least, but neither are they legally imposed or privileged. The voluntary nature of Christian faith in the experience of responding to the gospel, under the guidance of the Holy Spirit, has as its correlate social relations and the constructive minimalism of pragmatist philosophy.

The pragmatist tradition, beginning with Charles S. Peirce, William James, and John Dewey, and continuing through Richard Rorty, displays a common set of procedures for thought. Although the phenomenological and analytical traditions in philosophy have large followings in North America, they do not capture or embody political and social imaginations like the versions of pragmatism. Concerned neither with proofs for metaphysical claims nor with the relation between knowledge and language, pragmatism opts for detecting the function of ideas in human action—from the linguistic all the way to the legal and even religious levels. Although American pragmatism can be blamed for what is viewed as the characteristic lack of conceptual depth in American culture, the preoccupation with procedure and function reflects the immense degree to which notions of popular sovereignty and self-governance are rooted in the culture itself. What the liberality of thought did in terms of critical philosophy on the Continent, political liberty does for pragmatist philosophy in America.

The American tradition took a different road from the Continental and Anglo-Saxon traditions. A postcolonial sensibility emerged already at the end of the eighteenth century and was still concerned to be colonial on its own terms; American pragmatism became an eclectic method of reasoning. The nineteenth century was a time in North America for resolving internal conflicts—slavery above all—and not one of experimentation with revolutions and democratic reforms. This experience placed at an advantage what has only recently become the evolution of democratic polities. Although pragmatism developed in a context of a successful model of scientific reasoning, there was recognition that the scientific was not the sole arbiter of what constituted human knowledge. Pragmatism can be a vehicle for moderating both secular and theological forms of discourse within a given social and political context simply because of their rivalries. But this does not grant to pragmatism the superiority of its own philosophical accounts of truth. They are and will be contested as well.

Barth's profound elucidation of the freedom in Christ that God's grace brings to sinful humanity[19] simultaneously acknowledges the impossibility of imposing this faith on anyone. Liberal theological perspectives that resisted his ideas might have succeeded in shutting him down had he lived under less-liberal conditions. Of course, he was shut down momentarily when a conservative ideology in the form of Nazism gained the upper hand and imposed its monolithic program on the German people. Is it any wonder that Barth, although deeply grieving the tyranny in Germany during the war, reveled in the degree to which Swiss democracy afforded him the space to make his voice heard? The pragmatics of democratic culture in no way supplied Christianity with its message or its church dogmatics with their related truth claims, but they do allow for the debate of and voluntary adherence to those claims. The most the churches can do is bear their testimony to the redeeming truth of Christ and exhibit that testimony in works of charity and words of wisdom to an exceedingly fallible world.

Scriptural Faith

The capacity of the printing press to publish mass quantities of Bibles impacted the destiny of Christianity. It meant that the reforming impulse would one day win out in the events that make up the epoch known as the Reformation. The "always reforming" *(semper reformandum)* character of Christianity is largely a function of the continuing spread of the published Bible and of faithfulness to this text, eschewing the spiritual urges to rewrite, abbreviate, or add to its canonical shape and content. This is true even at the theological level, although the historical-critical study of Scripture includes bracketing out attempts to make contemporary theological statements and formulation. Reading Scripture may or may not be critically informed, but reading invariably connects ancient and contemporary frames of reference. As such, Scripture trumps theology. And it does so first in a traditional sense and second in a radical sense.

19. E.g., *CD* III/1:265–300; III/2:92–181.

In the first sense, Scripture trumps theology because of the Reformation principle of its objective authority and function as "norming norm" *(norma normans)* over and above the "normed norms" *(norma normata)* of tradition, primarily in terms of creed and confession. This principle means that no matter how convincing church consensus might be about a particular articulation of doctrine in creedal form, these articulations are always open to the church's own judgment and possible revision. Scripture is the "norming norm" of doctrine because it alone is taken as divinely authoritative. Whatever authority tradition has—much in the way the ministry has its authority—is derived from the truth of Scripture. It might be sufficient simply to quote Scripture, but Scripture's own demand for testimony, both corporate and personal, means that restatements and interpretive applications will always be forthcoming. This means that although consensus is an immensely powerful and oftentimes correct source of "normed norms," individual testimony can be correct against a powerful majority. Under such circumstances, the consensus that was once opposed by someone may ultimately agree with the dissenter and in turn must in some way find a reformed expression of the church's testimony. Thus, a theologian like Luther or Calvin or Simons, or a host of others, can call the church to conform its doctrine more fully to Scripture; then ever so slowly, if they are correct, tradition finds some degree of conformity to their testimony.

In the second sense, Scripture trumps theology, not through the reform of doctrine but through the empowerment of the believer to fulfill its commands through the authorization that comes by the Scripture as it addresses every reader. Although it is preferable for lay ministry to be exercised under proper institutional conditions, the Spirit moves the believer "where it chooses" (John 3:8), extending the mission of Christ far beyond the capacities of institutional management. But the regulative principle is present through faithfulness to Scripture. In this case, the faithfulness is expressed simply in a conformity to its message, truths about the Triune God and salvation in Christ and the commission of Christ to preach to all nations. This is quite literally the primary origin of the massive growth of global Christianity in the second half of the twentieth century. The so-called new churches of this phenomenon have depended on a Scripture principle of lay empowerment and the sufficiency of its simple reading. Although simple readings of Scripture are often scorned for lack of theological sophistication and inadequate check against heresy, they nevertheless tap into ancient Christian practices of simplicity, which are not lacking in virtue. Indeed, Bonhoeffer's meaning in his direct phrase *"einfältige Gehorsam"* (simple obedience) is close to the sense of something scripturally authorized that comes by simple reading and elicits action commanded by Christ.[20]

---

20. His *Nachfolge* from 1937 (München: Kaiser) continues to be Bonhoeffer's great contribution to the twentieth-century history of theology. See Dietrich Bonhoeffer, *Discipleship,* trans. Barbara Green and Reinhard Krauss (Minneapolis: Fortress, 2001).

The reading of Scripture does not mean that incorrect interpretation will be avoided or that it will not become a misused resource for manipulation. But instead of the old ecclesiastical sense of regulating and protecting society and church against outbreaks of blasphemy and heresy, the churches that pursue ordering in doctrine and life, learning from the scripturally normed norms of tradition, will exercise their own cautionary means of guarding the faith and the faithful. The history of Christianity is always the history of the interpretation of Scripture. Yet at the levels of its spread and influence since the eighteenth century, it is largely along the lines elaborated here that it can be said that Scripture has its own history through all of its faithful readers. This is what Barth means by the "history of Holy Scripture, . . . its origin and transmission, and its exegesis and influence in the course of history generally."[21] In the same section, not surprisingly, Barth ascribes to the Scriptures "that, quite irrespective of the way in which they were humanly and historically conditioned, its authors were objectively true, reliable and trustworthy witnesses. . . . It pleased God the King of Israel, to whom the power of their witness is pledged as to the Lord, to raise up these true witnesses by His Word and work."[22] Here the dynamism and inclusivity of Barth's thinking is remarkable:

> There can be no doubt at least that we shall always see in that history a history of their own self-exegesis. And this means that we shall never look upon the prophets and apostles as merely objects for the study and assessment of later readers; they will always be living, acting and speaking subjects on their own account. The fact that they have spoken once does not mean that they have now ceased to speak. On the contrary, they take up and deliver the Word afresh in every age and to every people, at every cultural level and to every individual. And they do it in such a way that what they have to say is far more acute and relevant than what may be said or thought about them. What are all the commentaries and other expositions of the Bible but a strong or feeble echo of their voice? If we are in that direct relationship to the Bible, then in the last and decisive analysis we shall not consider the history of biblical exegesis in the light of what took place outwardly. On the contrary, we shall consider the history of its outward experiences in the light of its own continually renewed and for that reason always surprising action, as a history of its self-declaration and self-explanation.[23]

Strikingly, the real question of scriptural faith is the identity of those whom the Scripture has enlisted for faithful reading. Scripture—in its continual vivification by the Holy Spirit, who has gone out into the whole world to illumine all who receive God's Word—has a pneumatological agency of its own: As the believer exegetes, Scripture self-exegetes, self-declares, and self-explains for the benefit of a new generation of churches and readers. This certainly is the

---

21. *CD* III/3:200.
22. Ibid., 201.
23. Ibid., 202.

case with Christianity in the Western Hemisphere. Scripture interpretation is so varied and so ubiquitous and ecclesial authorities display such immense ambiguities, potencies, and impotencies of colonialism and the demographics of religious politics that there simply cannot be a central ecclesial authority to which interpreters are accountable.

While there is justifiably great concern over diminished guidance from the reading of Scripture because of legitimate ecclesial authority and compelling liturgical forms, we must acknowledge that Scripture is constantly acquiring its own readership for the formation of faith and community. It attracts readers through what a theology of the Word would describe as Scripture's "perspicuity." As the medium of the Word of God, as the textual form of the Word of God, it is the medium of God's speaking, the medium of announcing the once-and-for-all salvation that is in Christ. To receive this salvation is to receive the mandate that not only includes one in the spiritual body of Christ that is the church but also begins to constitute one in the church and often in the formation of new churches. The fact of this and the authority to do this is inherent within Scripture:

> In order to be proclaimed and heard again and again both in the Church and the world, Holy Scripture requires to be explained. As the Word of God it needs no explanation, of course, since as such it is clear in itself. The Holy Ghost knows very well what He has said to the prophets and apostles and what through them He wills also to say to us. This clarity which Scripture has in itself as God's Word, this objective *perspicuitas* which it possesses, is subject to no human responsibility or care. On the contrary, it is the presupposition of all human responsibility in this matter. All the explanation of Scripture for which we are responsible can be undertaken only on the presupposition that Scripture is clear in itself as God's Word; otherwise it will at once disintegrate.[24]

Reading Scripture does not necessarily produce explanations, but, as Barth is indicating, it does produce understanding and action. This is a primary function of Scripture's being "clear in itself as God's Word."

There is the question here, however, as to whether Scripture as agent interprets itself properly and stands in practical and critical relation to the church's proclamation or vice versa. In practice, when Scripture is set over against the church, is not some kind of rationalistic argument being made, albeit with respect to the context of adhering to Scripture in understanding and faith?[25] Barth writes:

---

24. *CD* I/2:712. Cf. Bernhard Rothen, *Die Klarheit der Schrift* (Göttingen: Vandenhoeck & Ruprecht, 1990), 87. In the critical sections of Rothen's book, he is particularly anxious to point out the tension between Barth's declaration that theology is done according to the faith and teaching of the church and Barth's declaration that Scripture can be read faithfully on its own terms. Rothen does not analyze whether he is working with a prior understanding of an ecclesial reading of Scripture that might be different from anything Barth intends.

25. This certainly is Rothen's concern.

The Word of God is the judgment in virtue of which alone proclamation can be real proclamation. Proclamation is also asked whether it is true. . . . If there is to be any assessment at all of Church proclamation as such it must be from another angle. It is this fundamentally different aspect of the judgment to be made on Church proclamation that we have in view and describe when we acknowledge it to be the Word of God. We are not denying thereby that proclamation is subject to other criteria too. . . . This criterion which is recollected and expected, though not at our disposal in our own or any present, is the Word of God. We cannot "handle" this criterion. It is the criterion which handles itself and is in no other hands. We can handle the other criteria in recollection and expectation of this criterion. But its judgment alone is absolutely binding and inviolable. Proclamation becomes real proclamation when it is endorsed by this judgment. Real proclamation, therefore, is the Word of God preached.[26]

The church is not removed from the process of establishing criteria for the truth of proclamation, but it can do so only because of the Word of God and Scripture. Barth is emphatic:

We must begin exegetically, conscious that what we pursue is Evangelical and Reformation exegesis of the reality of the Church. The Church . . . is not referred to itself or consequently to self-reflection [as in Platonic *anamnēsis* (remembrance)]. It has not the confidence to appeal to itself as the source of the divine Word in support of the venture of proclamation. . . . Holy Scripture . . . is the past revelation of God that we have to recollect . . . ; it is the Canon . . . consisting of specific texts. [The word of the prophets and the apostles] constitutes the working instructions or marching orders by which not just the Church's proclamation but the very Church itself stands or falls. . . . The exegesis of the Bible should be . . . left open on all sides, not for the sake of free thought, as Liberalism would demand, but for the sake of a free Bible. Here as everywhere the defence against possible violence to the text must be left to the text itself, which in fact has always succeeded in doing something a purely spiritual and oral tradition cannot do, namely, maintaining its own life against the encroachments of individual or total periods and tendencies in the Church, victoriously asserting this life in ever new developments, and thus creating recognition for itself as a norm.[27]

But Barth adds a crucial distinction:

In Holy Scripture . . . the writing is obviously not primary, but secondary. It is itself the deposit of what was once proclamation by human lips. . . . Scripture [is] the commencement and present-day preaching [is] the continuation of one and the same event, Jeremiah and Paul at the beginning and the modern preacher of the Gospel at the end of one and the same series. . . . In this similarity as phenomena, however, there is also to be found between Holy Scripture and

26. *CD* I/1:92–93.
27. Ibid., 100–106.

present-day proclamation a dissimilarity in order, namely the supremacy, the absolutely constitutive significance of the former for the latter, the determination of the reality of present-day proclamation by its foundation upon Holy Scripture and its relation to this, the basic singling out of the written word of the prophets and apostles over all the later words of men which have been spoken and are to be spoken to-day in the Church.[28]

Again, the theology of Scripture, Barth's bibliology, is accented according to the agency of this text under and with the dynamic Word of God that is inseparably united with it. As such, the Scripture advances itself, imposes itself, defends itself, and promotes itself in the central activity of the church, which is proclamation of the Word of God. This is why the connection between proclamation and exegesis is so fundamental; this is why the connection between the traditions of the church and Scripture as their norm is so vital and unalterable. In Barth's determination to believe in the living and active Word of God, which creates ever new a present proclamation for itself, he says of Scripture:

> The fact that God's own address becomes an event in the human word of the Bible is, however, God's affair and not ours. This is what we mean when we call the Bible God's Word. . . . But this is precisely the faith which in this way sees and reaches beyond itself and all related or unrelated experiences to God's action, namely, to the fact that God's action on man has become an event, and not therefore that man has grasped at the Bible but that the Bible has grasped at man. The Bible, then, becomes God's Word in this event, and in the statement that the Bible is God's Word the little word "is" refers to its being in this becoming. It does not become God's Word because we accord it faith but in the fact that it becomes revelation to us. But the fact that it becomes revelation to us beyond all our faith, that it is God's Word even in spite of our lack of faith, is something we can accept and confess as true to us and for us only in faith, . . . and therefore precisely not in abstraction from the act of God in virtue of which the Bible must become again and again His Word to us.[29]

Although many have stumbled over Barth's use of "event" and "becoming" with respect to Scripture, the best way to understand his use is not so much as an accommodation to historical criticism or a philosophy of religion but as a focus on the actual events of divine revelation in divine speech and action. What Barth wants to declare is that whenever the sinner enacts faith in Christ, this takes place as a result of the Holy Spirit making revelation as much of a reality as the historical revelatory act of God in Christ. This does not mean that completely new and unknown expressions of the Word of God are ever forthcoming beyond the prophetic and apostolic testimonies of canonical Scripture. But to have faith in Christ by the grace of God, one is receiving this

28. Ibid., 102.
29. Ibid., 109–10.

faith on account of the gracious revealing work of the Holy Spirit. "Revelation engenders the Scripture which attests it,"[30] and revelation also continuously engenders faith in Christ and obedience to him when we obey his commands as found in Scripture.

The role of the Holy Spirit in Barth's exposition cannot be overestimated, particularly with reference to receiving revelation in the canonical Scriptures. The Holy Spirit convicts and sets the reader/hearer free (Gal. 5) for revelation such that *"homo peccator"* becomes *"capax verbi divini"*[31] (sinful humanity becomes able to comprehend the Word of God). This freedom is a divine enablement both to be children of God and to receive revelation of God beyond that which is natural within them. The "πνεῦμα υἱοθεσίας" (Spirit of adoption)—adoption being virtually synonymous with election of Jew and Gentile in Christ (cf. Rom. 8:15, 23; 9:4; Gal. 4:5; Eph. 1:5)—means in some sense to share "sonship" with Christ and to be bearers of revelation as its recipients. Barth's frame of reference is theologically objectivist:

> And so this freedom, ability and capacity for God can be understood only as the power of the resurrection of Christ, not as an immanent freedom of his own, but as that which is conferred on him by God, which he can neither manipulate nor understand, which can only be understood as factual, and factual indeed only as the fact of God. In this fact God makes us sure of Him and makes Himself sure of us, and He teaches us what we are to say as His witnesses. All statements about the Holy Spirit, like all statements about the Son of God, can relate only to this divine fact. For us as in the New Testament itself, they are comprehensible or incomprehensible only in the light of it.[32]

All of this falls under what Barth repeatedly calls the *"regnum gratiae"* (reign of grace), which is always behind the revelatory action of God making knowledge of himself both possible and actual and, in this case, both factual and certain. Barth's objectivism and realism here could hardly be more explicit. And yet the objectivism and realism are not conceived in terms of natural ability or genius; this would be to make an independent claim upon God in willful human terms. The "understanding" referred to here is based on these human terms. The reorientation of understanding comes only through our obedience to the Holy Spirit's influence in our following the commands of Christ in Scripture.

What about Barth's theology of Scripture? In reflecting on Scripture, which for Protestants at least cannot by its very nature be infallible and which was completed only in the fourth century after Christ and was in many respects still not settled until the fifteenth or sixteenth century in the enduring Protestant confessional lists, we can understand why Barth could not consider the text in

---

30. Ibid., 115.
31. Ibid., 456ff.
32. Ibid., 458.

hand as infallible. Barth paid close attention to what Scripture actually claimed for itself in relation to its divine "inspiredness," namely, its unique usefulness for faith and life (2 Tim. 3:16). Most important, Barth wanted his readers to focus on the active revelation of God's Word, which God is constantly accomplishing through Scripture, and the preaching of Scripture by the power of the Holy Spirit. Barth was not expounding a message of religious subjectivity in the guise of Christian orthodoxy. He was too concerned with objectivity, actuality, particularity, and specificity, and also with divine communication, to allow for the reduction of what he meant by revelation to some prearticulate boundary experience of the holy or of absolute dependence. Religious subjectivity is just not there.

At the same time, one must acknowledge that Barth resisted what is otherwise the agreement of the overwhelming majority of theologians and confessions in Catholic, Orthodox, and evangelical traditions, that Scripture in its entirety is without error—because Scripture in its entirety teaches with absolute faithfulness the truth of God concerning salvation. As in the canons of the Second Vatican Council, Scripture does not pose itself as a textbook in science or history, but it must be read in all its particulars according to genre type and actual claims that are being made. Having affirmed that God is the author of Scripture "acting in and through" the human authors of the texts of Scripture, the basic Vatican II affirmation is as follows: "Since everything asserted by the inspired authors or sacred writers must be held to be asserted by the Holy Spirit, it follows that the books of Scripture must be acknowledged as teaching firmly, faithfully, and without error that truth which God wanted put into the sacred writings for the sake of our salvation."[33]

But even the majority of churches make a clear distinction between inspiration and revelation in their theologies of Scripture. Divine-human authorship of the whole of Scripture is not an affirmation that every passage or every statement of Scripture is a revelation of God. Indeed, the vast majority of Scripture is the inspired account of the responses to revelation in the forms of narrative, instruction, parable, hymn, prayer, and so on. For Barth, the word of Scripture is always pointing toward the Word that became flesh and communicated and communicates itself by the Holy Spirit. There is no vehicle other than Scripture and the preaching of Scripture by which we know this Word that is always the self-revelation of God.

33. In addition, it is noted that Aquinas taught that only those things that teach salvation "belong to inspiration," and that Augustine paid the same attention to saving and moral truth. But inspiration is not a partial thing: It is not quantitative but encompasses the entire text of Scripture. Scripture's own affirmations are these, not other kinds of truths. The edition of Vatican II documents here cites Augustine, *Gen Litt.* 2.9.20; *Epistle* 82.3; Aquinas, *On Truth* Q. 12, A. 2, C; "Dogmatic Constitution on Divine Revelation," *The Documents of Vatican II,* ed. Walter M. Abbott, S.J. (New York: Guild Press, 1966), 118–19.

Pluriform Faith

One of the primary reasons for stressing the fallibility of theology is the pluriformity of theological traditions and methods. Although Catholics and evangelicals often cite their tensions and frustrations, the most fundamental frustration existed long before the Reformation in the great schism between Eastern and Western churches, and of course before that between Byzantine and non-Byzantine Eastern churches after Chalcedon (451). Beginning with problems of language, political rivalries, and ultimately in the search for correct doctrine, the tendencies of division among the churches of the ancient world became a reality in the medieval one. Among evangelicals, the Lutheran and Reformed condemnations of Baptists, the dissociation among free and charismatic churches, and the formal ecumenical bodies make theological unity a present impossibility and only the remotest plausibility. This means that all faithful theological reflection must by definition be ecumenical, recognizing a vast body of church organizations, each existing under separate structures of authority and doctrine but all under Jesus Christ.

The pluriformity of theology reminds us that beyond heresy and apostasy there exist unresolved differences of doctrine and practice that are only overcome through perceiving the "family resemblance" among all of them. Pluriformity in theology reminds us that there is a distance between God and us, between ourselves and the scriptural norm of theology, God's Word. This distance is not a Kantian one determined entirely by a phenomenology of epistemic possibilities and limits; instead, we have confidence that God's gracious self-giving makes knowing God an actuality. But as sinful, perspectival, interested, and situated believers, our reception of what is communicated to us of God results, at best, in the pluriformity of theologies and Christian traditions. Yet disunity, especially divisiveness, is evidence of resistance to God's Spirit, who would lead the churches into a single communion (Eph. 2:18; 4:3–6; Phil. 1:27; 1 Peter 3:8).[34]

Positively construed, pluriformity manifested itself in the freedom of the reformations of the sixteenth century with the proliferation of books and publishing itself. Although these churches were at times accused of becoming a Babel of theology, the freedom of the Holy Spirit in the multiple testimonies on the part of those who studied Scripture and preached its message at great risk of persecution and death from all sides points to the possibility of the Spirit's will for pluriformity of faith. To become a published theologian came to mean that reform, dissent, and heresy would be ongoing to a degree

34. Although there are serious divisions throughout global Christianity, Ephraim Radner, *End of the Church: A Pneumatology of Christian Division in the West* (Grand Rapids: Eerdmans, 1998), charts the seriousness of division as a mark of deadness in the Spirit, or "pneumatic abandonment." Radner calls for "ecclesial repentance" as the only way to break the negative forces constricting the church.

beyond the institutional capacities of official church bodies to make adequate judgments of whether many texts were acceptable or unacceptable. Only the most celebrated cases could be dealt with. By the time Christianity became established in North America, the possibility of regulating theological diversity was rendered moot by the demands of personal faith and public peace.[35] The history of religious toleration and finally religious liberty, however shaken by secularism as a domineering public ideology, meant that simple demonstrations of religious identity and community cohesion produced a permanent religious plurality defined by Christian Scripture and heritage within the democracies of the world. In this world, with its lay Christian theologies following hard on the heels of the multiplying theologians, the possibility of achieving anything like a single voice is perhaps not even desirable. Indeed, to the extent that theology is at its best when it is an intellectual exercise of faith, with self-critical testimony that tends toward humble but confident proclamation, pluriformity will always be with us, and it is a good and wholesome reality.[36]

We are of course discussing here Christian plurality, along with its denominational forms. This does not include interreligious Christian theology in which Christianity is placed alongside other religions as a coequal member of a universe of religions, after which theology begins. Theologies that suggest some kind of incarnation of Christ in all religions,[37] or simply the critical reduction of Christianity to religious symbol systems that typify all religions,[38] are not functional for constructive theological truth claims. But there are constructive tendencies within recent theology to recognize the value of plural witnesses to the truth of Christ even within a particular denomination.[39]

35. Cf. Jon Butler, *Awash in a Sea of Faith: Christianizing the American People* (Cambridge: Harvard University Press, 1992). On the debate as to how religious voices might make themselves heard, cf. Robert Audi and Nicholas Wolterstorff, *Religion in the Public Square: Convictions in Political Debate* (Lanham, Md.: Rowman & Littlefield, 1996).

36. One of the fine examples tending toward this is John G. Stackhouse Jr., *Humble Apologetics: Defending the Faith Today* (New York: Oxford University Press, 2002). In its humility and orientation to the spirit of the Gospels, the book actually proposes the end of apologetics in favor of the positive engagement of theological dialogue and evangelization.

37. As in Marjorie Hewitt Suchocki, *Divinity and Diversity* (Nashville: Abingdon, 2003). Something along the lines of both recognizing partial religious truths but measured according to the fullness of truth in Christ is in order. Cf. Vinoth Ramachandra, *Recovery of Mission: Beyond the Pluralist Paradigm* (Eugene, Ore.: Wipf & Stock, 2002); and Russell F. Aldwinckle, *Jesus: A Savior or the Savior? Religious Pluralism in Christian Perspective* (Macon, Ga.: Mercer University Press, 1982). Unfortunately, the massive treatment of theological pluralism in D. A. Carson, *The Gagging of God* (Grand Rapids: Zondervan, 2002), suffers from far too much reliance on American evangelical identity markers and inadequate theological argumentation.

38. As in Beverly J. Lanzetta, *Other Side of Nothingness: Toward a Theology of Radical Openness* (Albany, N.Y.: State University of New York Press, 2001); and Gordon D. Kaufman, *God, Mystery, Diversity: Christian Theology in a Pluralistic World* (Minneapolis: Augsburg, 1996).

39. Catholic theologians have done some of the best work in this area, e.g., Thomas G. Guarino, *Revelation and Truth: Unity and Plurality in Contemporary Theology* (Scranton, Pa.: University of Scranton Press, 1993); Robert W. McElroy, *Search for an American Public Theology:*

Theological plurality can be a confusing thing, especially when it becomes a source of combativeness among fellow believers who are only denominationally apart from one another. Theological plurality under the common trinitarian confession of Christ as Savior and Lord can be something to receive along the lines of "in an abundance of counselors there is safety" (Prov. 11:14) and "in abundance of counselors there is victory" (24:6). It is instructive that this sapiential repetition assures both safety and victory in the sense of our warfare doctrinally and spiritually. At best, our doctrine is wholesome and sound. It is never free from error, nor does it perfectly direct us to everything God wills for us to know and to do. In our spiritual warfare, we do not take up arms for the cause of the church or Jesus Christ, and yet victory is promised to us. Through the community of believers and the community of theologians, Christian traditions old and new are maintained and generated. It seems that the Holy Spirit has willed this diversity through a unity only spiritually appraised and only occasionally realized. Barth recognized that, while being an evangelical in the sense of the Reformation heritage as it had come down to him in his own day, he nevertheless had to be Reformed in the sense of the Calvinist tradition. He was as immensely dedicated to this tradition as he was evangelical. And yet out of such a theological position and tradition, the theologian works ecumenically at a dogmatics that is for the whole church. Of other evangelical or Protestant churches, Barth writes:

> We must say of them what in view of their doctrine may seem strange and difficult to approve, that in another form they are the one Church of Jesus Christ just as much as is the Reformed Church. The grounds of objection and division are not heresies but specific errors, specific theological notions, badly, misleadingly, erroneously and arbitrarily construed, of a type which may easily arise within the Reformed Confession itself without necessitating disruption.[40]

These are crucial distinctions. The plurality of theological voices reminds us that there are multiple traditions and participants representing and giving new shape to those traditions. Human error is unavoidable, and yet fundamental error is being avoided in terms of the only foundation, which is Christ and the trinitarian and scriptural form and trajectories of many-sided orthodox

---

The Contribution of John Courtney Murray (Mahwah, N.J.: Paulist Press, 1989); and above all, Hans Urs von Balthasar, *Truth Is Symphonic: Aspects of Christian Pluralism*, trans. Graham Harrison (Ft. Collins, Colo.: Ignatius Press, 1987). Catholicism is also having to deal with diversity in contexts that were once politically Catholic. Cf. R. Andrew Chesnut, *Competitive Spirits: Latin America's New Religious Economy* (New York: Oxford University Press, 2003). We are not referring to religious pluralism, which is an entirely different matter. Among Jewish thinkers, perhaps the best recent treatment of intrareligious plurality is David Hartman, *Heart of Many Rooms: Celebrating the Many Voices within Judaism* (Woodstock, Vt.: LongHill Partners, 2001).

40. *CD* I/2:831–32.

Christianity. Barth was sensitive to this even while he was deeply convinced that the Calvinist Reformed tradition was the best theological path.

But Barth's ecumenism was also very real. He understood that to be a theologian writing out of a particular tradition meant that one wrote to the entire *Ökumene,* arguing the position of that tradition for the sake of general reform. In the case of theology, a disciplined expression of Christian truth, reversibility is never possible in terms of following revelation and then legitimately reading theology back into revelation. Yet reversal can be legitimate at the level of rival traditions and the one church of Jesus Christ. Barth makes this reversal directly before the comments just cited above:

> Again, in the last resort it can only be a question of practising Church dogmatics in the form of Reformed dogmatics, that is, Evangelical and therefore ecumenical Church dogmatics, not the dogmatics of a particular branch of the Church distinguished by and proudly emphasising certain historical peculiarities. And, again, for this reason, Reformed dogmatics cannot be, nor can it wish to be called, "Reformed" but only Church dogmatics, or dogmatics pure and simple.[41]

Barth knows he can do nothing other than work ecumenically out of the theological tradition he has embraced so deeply. At the same time, this is not an embrace simply for historical reasons. He is convinced that the Reformed tradition is most correct among its rivals and therefore holds the greatest benefit for the ecumenical goal of all.

All of this attention to plurality changes its tenor when one looks at an entire culture or social grouping in which particular expressions of the church find themselves. Reading Barth on this matter takes on its own angle of approach. We must remember that Barth also perceived a branch of the church fully shaped by the liberal theology he had so vehemently rejected, known as neo-Protestantism or *"Kulturprotestantismus"* (cultural Protestantism). Since Schleiermacher, various strategies had been tried to maintain a *Volkskirche* (a church of the people), in which citizenship and church membership were coterminus, constituting a unified social culture inclusive of an official and therefore legally privileged religion. By the mid-nineteenth century, the national churches of Germany—Lutheran, Roman Catholic, Reformed, and United—were all vying, not so much against one another as against the forces of free thought and secularity. As a result, by the turn of the twentieth century, many of the theologians of neo-Protestantism were grappling with a cultural theology that could be inclusive of the secular outlook summed up in the Latin phrase *"etsi Deus non daretur"* (as though God were not given).[42] The program of including the secular paradigm could be embraced by an adaptation of *theologia crucis* (God has revealed himself [apophatically] in his

41. Ibid., 831.
42. Dietrich Bonhoeffer, *Letters and Papers from Prison* (New York: Macmillan, 1972), 360–61.

opposite, or where he appears to be absent, as in the dereliction of the cross, rather than in the "godlessness" of secularism and naturalism). Barth, however, was utterly unwilling, for the gospel's sake, to submit to this cultural-religious project, which in many respects continues today, since it invariably reduces theology to apologetics.

4

OVERCOMING *PROLEGOMENA* WITH THE *PRO-LEGOMENON*

Barth had far more than a rhetorical strategy for his theology—by not having a strategy at all. Rhetoric serves the *CD,* but this is not the source of what we might call its "newness," not in the sense of radical innovation or new revelation but in the sense of a new manifestation of promised grace. "The *Church Dogmatics* . . . tries and tries again in the *ever new* attempt to start at the beginning."[1] As with each generation of theologians, Barth was bearing witness to the reality of knowing the living and Triune God.

> The object of theology is God in his self-presentation—for everyone first in Scripture under the guidance of the Holy Spirit and then as the truth which is ours in the mind of the Spirit, the internalized truth of this objective self-presentation. This is the basis for the unity of content and event in Christian theology. The subject-matter . . . of Christian faith, which is disclosed in the event of the self-objectification of the Trinitarian God in revelation, is also the content . . . of faith. The task of theology is therefore the explication of the content and event of the self-presentation of God as the ground of created reality and as the realization of its reconciliation.[2]

The systematic structure of the *Church Dogmatics* is the resolution of the dilemma posed early in Barth's career: As theologians, we must speak of God,

---

1. Christoph Schwöbel, "Theology," in *The Cambridge Companion to Karl Barth,* ed. John Webster (Cambridge: Cambridge University Press, 2000), 19.
2. Ibid., 26.

but as human beings, we cannot. The resolution of this dilemma lies not in a third option that could somehow transcend the contradiction between must and cannot. It is to be found in God's free action and can be expressed only in sentences about God's free action. At the same time, coming to a knowledge of God's action in Christ by means of the Word of God brings the possibility of freeing our task in theology to become a true following of this action so rooted in the Word of God. This word is always the first Word, the *pro-legomenon,* the word addressed to us *prior to* anything we have to say. It is the word that takes priority in the sovereignty of God so that our words can approximate the truth of God's Word, and this first word is our own word of testimony to the church and to the world concerning our knowledge of God and the reality that all things stand in created relation to him.

When Theology Is Proclamation: Theology as First-Order Narrative

Barth's determination to let theology be the full testimony to faith in Jesus Christ certainly is part of what had originally shocked his theological world. The retreat from testimony before the face of apologetical approaches to theology as it had come to dominate theological discourse after Ritschl was to be radically disturbed by an unapologetic commitment to the nature of prophetic and apostolic texts of the Bible: proclamation of the Word of God to God's people and to the world.

> The man who so hears their word [of prophets and apostles] that he grasps and accepts its promise, believes. And this grasping and accepting of the promise: Immanuel with us sinners, in the word of the prophets and apostles, this is the faith of the Church. In this faith it recollects the past revelation of God and in this faith it expects the future revelation that has yet to come.[3]

At this point in the *CD,* Barth is acutely conscious of the ancient historical contexts of the scriptural corpus. The purpose of Scripture under the work of the Holy Spirit, who teaches us in and through it, is to establish the recollection of the foundational acts and communications of God in historic revelation. This is the historical realism of Barth's theology, that through the faith given to us by the Holy Spirit, we are invited again and again to participate in the "anamnetic" (cf. "*anamnēsis*" [remembrance]) act of recollection, as at the Lord's Supper (Luke 22:19; 1 Cor. 11:24–25). This is nothing less than our sacramental relation to Jesus Christ, the "one and only true sacrament"[4]

---

3. *CD* I/1:108.
4. *CD* IV/2:55, where Barth perceives "that the true *unio sacramentalis* [sacramental union] is the *unio personalis* [personal union] in Jesus Christ."

in every present act of faith eliciting an actual and active knowledge of him and his Word.

According to Barth, the Holy Spirit aids the theologian and the listening church in receiving Scripture anamnetically for what it actually is, the Word of God (cf. 1 Thess. 2:13). Yet more must happen for full theological reasoning and statement to be achieved. The knowledge of *Christus praesens* (present), indeed, of *Deus praesens,* must be the reality of the knowledge that theology conveys; if not, it fails to do more than inspire the heretical misnomer of "historical faith." The problem is one of connecting the persons, time, and space of the original revelation as conveyed in Scripture and those of our own.

> The problem has indeed this temporal and spatial aspect. . . . That there is this distance cannot be denied. "Jesus Christ for us," the incarnation and the crucifixion, do not exist or take place in an abstract always and everywhere in which our here and now are included, but in a concrete and singular then and there which cannot be taken away or exchanged—outside our here and now and opposed to it. In this respect the greatness of the historical remove does not greatly matter. It may exceed 1,900 years or it may not. . . . It is enough that the connexion between the here and the there, the now and then, can apparently take only the form of recollection, that it can apparently be only indirect or historical, mediated by the report and tradition and proclamation of others, bound up with their truthfulness and credibility, with whether we are able to trust them, to accept the truth of what they say, to make the connexion in this roundabout way as recollection. And if everything does finally hang by this thread, it is obviously a very disturbing fact. . . . If it is really to be received, can it come to us or be received by us in any but a direct way, removing the distance altogether, establishing between the one remembered and our recollection a contemporaneity which has to be explained but which is real, enabling that distant event to become and to be true to us directly and therefore incontrovertibly? But what is the mediation in which recollection becomes presence, indirect speech direct, history present-day event, the *Christus pro nobis tunc* [Christ for us then] the *Christus pro nobis nunc* [Christ for us now] the Christ who meets us, the Christ who is our Saviour not only as He is known and remembered historically, but as He Himself saves us to-day? The genuineness of this question cannot be disputed.[5]

Theology must be about that movement of the Holy Spirit that brings a knowledge of Christ that bears the contemporaneity of his reality in the life of his witness (cf. Luke 12:12; John 14:26). This stands in profound contrast to the task of theology as Barth had inherited it from the neo-Protestant theologies of the nineteenth century. Faith in Jesus Christ had been based on assiduous attempts at historical reconstruction of his life, as supposedly appropriate to a disciplined attentiveness to the ethical form and content of his teaching.[6] But

---

5. *CD* IV/1:288.
6. Cf. Robert Jenson, "Karl Barth," in *Modern Theologians,* ed. David F. Ford (Cambridge, Mass.: Blackwell, 1997), 21–36.

this is not at all what Christian theology must do if it is to appropriate the
Word of God on its own terms, in the richness and fullness of its claims.

The quote immediately above arises in the context of Barth's discussion of
the atonement, and this raises the question of the presence of the crucified and
risen Christ personally present to the believer, the church, and the world.

> But we ought not to stand, as it were, rooted to this one spot, trying to find
> and remove the difficulty only in this spot. The well-known offence in the fact
> of atonement does not exhaust itself in this problem of distance. We ought to
> be warned against too great or exclusive a preoccupation with this aspect by the
> fact that this problem which has become so acute within more recent Protes-
> tantism has, all things considered, more the character of a technical difficulty
> in thinking than that of a spiritual or a genuine theological problem. . . . It is
> a methodological question. . . . May it not be that the real scandal is grounded
> in the fact, in the Christi-occurrence, in the event of the atonement itself? . . .
> How can this our Judge be judged for us? . . . What can His being and activity
> mean in our sphere? . . . How are we going to apprehend Jesus Christ? . . . How
> are we going to apprehend ourselves in relation to Him, ourselves as those for
> whom that has taken place which has taken place in Him? What does it mean
> to live as His fellow? . . . [cf. Luke 5:8; Isa. 6:5; Mal. 3:2; Exod. 33:20]. . . .
> This is obviously the underlying form of our problem. . . . On the one hand it
> is God for man, on the other man against God.
>
> Supposing our contemporaneity with the Word of God made flesh, with the
> Judge judged in our place, is already an event? Supposing the *Christus pro nobis
> nunc* is already *Christus pro nobis praesens nunc*, here and now present with us?
> . . . It is obvious that we do not want this, that we do not want to accept the fact
> that our evil case is done away and ourselves with it, that we do not therefore
> want to accept the coming of the Son of God in our place, His being and activ-
> ity in contemporaneity with us, and our being in contemporaneity with Him.
> The assault this makes on us is too violent and incisive. If all this is true and
> actual, it is clear that we have good reason to close our eyes to it, to keep as far
> from us as we can the knowledge of this truth and actuality. . . . As long as we
> can question and discuss the presence of that once and for all event . . . —so
> long we are obviously protected against the catastrophe which the knowledge
> of the content, the knowledge of the *Christus pro nobis praesens,* would mean
> for us. We do not then have to notice that we are in exactly the same position
> as Peter in the boat and the women at the empty tomb and the shepherds of
> Bethlehem. . . .We find ourselves in a relatively sheltered corner where we can
> dream that we are still in some way existing *ante Christum* since He is not there
> for us . . . and all because we think that we are excused and safeguarded by the
> gaping and wide chasm of temporal distance; all because of the existence of
> Lessing's question . . . of historical distance.[7]

In this, Barth fundamentally and critically asked how historical facts (if
they were historical) could possibly convey universal truth. He is clear that

7. *CD* IV/1:288–92.

the presence of the Christ who made atonement for us is a methodological issue. And yet it connects with the entire issue of theological method, the task of accounting for the Christian faith in the living presence of Christ and Christ's living presence to us. Theology is an act of trembling, fearful faith because of the actual reality with which it has to do. This is a matter not only of the experience of the Holy Spirit as a present enlightening, empowering influence[8] but also of the direct encounter with Jesus Christ mediated by this Spirit. Barth counts Lessing's question as a genuine one but regards it as not reflective of a genuine problem to theology. It merely asks about the relation between the past and the present. The much greater problem is our confrontation with the presence of Christ. In this methodological problem for theology, faithful receiving of the grace of God and systematic questions of formulating theological statements are inseparable. Barth's answer to bridging the distance is through the actuality of the living Jesus Christ.

> The resurrection of Jesus Christ from the dead was the exclusive act of God, a pure divine revelation, a free act of divine grace. It is of this that we speak when we say: "Jesus lives," and when we deduce and continue: "and I with Him." The statement has this deduction and continuation. For Jesus lives as the One who was put to death for me, as the One in whom I am put to death, so that necessarily His life is the promise of my life. But with His life, my life too, the life of man who is not himself Jesus Christ but only His younger brother, is an exclusive act of God, a pure divine revelation, a free act of divine grace. . . . As such it is "hid with Christ in God" (Col. 3:3) in a way that we cannot comprehend or control. . . . More important for us is the positive side that as such, as that which is created and revealed in that divine act of sovereignty, our life, the life of man in and with Jesus Christ, is promised from the place whose sureness and unequivocal transcendence gives to the promise a clarity and certainty which are beyond comparison or compromise. It is a matter only of the act of God, the self-revelation of God, the free grace of God. The free act and self-revelation of God cannot be called in question. They are there. And that gives an unsurpassable clarity and an axiomatic certainty. The Yes of God, which

---

8. In his extraordinary book, Gary Dorrien emphasizes Barth's "commitment to the primacy of the Spirit-illuminated Word" as more important than a mere demonstration of the coherence of Barth's entire project. Dorrien comes close to Barth's sense regarding the role of the Spirit-illuminated Word, which "subverts and transcends the authority of all theoretical systems, philosophical categories, and historical judgments." But he does so to advance an unlikely thesis, that Barth was merely "reworking" themes he had learned from his Marburg teacher, Wilhelm Herrmann—which of course flies directly in the face of all of Barth's own declarations. See Gary Dorrien, *The Barthian Revolt in Modern Theology: Theology without Weapons* (Louisville: Westminster John Knox, 2000), 5. Dorrien, possibly taking a cue from the fact the Herrmann had also rejected natural theology and apologetics (cf. Bruce L. McCormack, *Karl Barth's Critically Realistic Dialectical Theology: Its Genesis and Development, 1909–1936* [Oxford: Clarendon, 1995], 466), is unconvincingly insistent about Herrmann's influence, in spite of the fact that the entire *CD* makes reference to Herrmann only once and that to indicate Barth's continuing distance from the old liberalism.

cannot be disputed by any conceivable No, has been pronounced and has to be received. . . . He has spoken and speaks and will speak it in His Son; and on earth with the same sovereignty in which He is God in heaven.[9]

The methodological stakes could not have been raised higher. The inseparability of revelation and anything theological could not be more definite. The status of the claims "unsurpassable clarity and axiomatic certainty" could not have been more realistic, concrete, or eschatological in the always contemporaneous speaking of God through his Son. If we miss Barth's emphasis on the presence of Christ in the life of the theologian as in the life of the Christian community and the integral relation of this reality to every theological utterance, we miss the reason why Barth dares to be so clear and axiomatic in his theological statements. Under the conditions of hermeneutical reticence and measured metaphysical gravity, what are we to do theologically?

Christocentric Objectivity of Reality: Theology's Universal Metaphysic

Barth's answer, effectively, is to allow theology its own metaphysic and consign the rest of the options to inadequacy and negation in the histories of obsolescent systems.

In some respects, the *CD* inaugurates the "postmetaphysical" movement in Christian theology, not so much because there are no metaphysics that continue to be tried, but because Scripture demonstrates and generates its own. The prophetic and apostolic testimonies can be gathered together to formulate an entire schema of God-human-world relations. Here, the centrality of Christ issuing in the knowledge of the trinitarian life of God is fundamental. The mode of possibilities and order in the world and the metaphysics of revelation in Christ then come into view.

> The triumph of God's freedom in immanence is seen precisely in this hierarchy of his being and action as it operates in relation to the being which is distinct from Himself. Yet it is not the case . . . that we stand confronted by this richness of divine being as by an unfathomable ocean of possibilities. . . . They have their basis and their consummation, their meaning, the norm and their law in Jesus Christ. In the first place, the fulfilled union of the divine and the human in Jesus Christ is . . . in its once-for-all and unique aspect, . . . the possibility of all other possibilities. For the Son of God who became flesh in Jesus Christ is, as an eternal mode of the divine being, nothing more nor less than the principle and basis of all divine immanence.
>
> We have seen that the freedom of God, as His freedom in Himself, . . . has its truth and reality in the inner Trinitarian life of the Father with the Son by the Holy Spirit. . . . [In] spite of the almost confusing richness of the forms of

9. *CD* IV/1:356–57.

divine immanence we are led to recognize a hierarchy, a sacred order, in which God is present to the world. We have only to grasp the fact that Jesus Christ is the focus and crown, and not merely the focus and the crown of all relationship and fellowship between God and the world, but also their basic principle, their possibility and presupposition in the life of the Godhead. . . . God's freedom . . . does so as the one work of one unvarying wisdom, which excludes the fortuitous and the contradictory, which does not will at random or juxtapose incompatible elements, but which in the abundance of its effects will only one thing, namely itself, and which orders all things to its own glory but also to the life and the healing of the other which has its being by it and in it. Thus, everything for which God is free and in which God is free will be understood by us as the unity of the freedom of His being if we approach it in this way. It will not confuse us by its manifoldness, but will comfort, warn and rejoice us if we see that it derives from Jesus Christ the Son of God, attesting Him, serving Him and leading to Him, as is in fact disclosed to our sight and hearing in God's revelation. There is no caprice about the freedom of God. . . . It cannot, therefore, be reduced to the level of the regularity of a cosmic process.[10]

Barth perceived that the distinction between God as Triune Creator and the Creator who becomes the creature with universal effects could not allow for some general or hybrid metaphysic. The fullness of the role of Christ constitutes an order of being in him; it is not an order that identifies nature with him or him with nature but one in which the fundamental distinction between Creator and creature finds its axis through the incarnation, Christ the Mediator of all uncreated and created reality, the image of God (Col. 1:15). The schema of metaphysical order emerges such that the eternally active God includes the multiplicities of creation in this singular activity of the divine being and does so without dissolving this distinction integral to the revelation of God in Jesus Christ. This is the reason the rejection of religion and natural theology also became necessary.

Romans and the "End" of Religion

Barth, then pastor in Safenwil, introduces the reader to his conviction that Paul speaks through Romans to every generation of all humanity. He does not discount the fruits of historical scholarship as part of understanding the text; neither can there be a discounting of the older doctrine of inspiration of the Bible, which is a "greater, deeper, more important" factor.[11] On the way to the substance of Paul's argument in Romans, Barth handles the key text of 1:16–17 (citing Albrecht Bengel on this *"Centrum Paulinum"*) as the truth that is the gospel against all other rival truths, whether religious, philosophi-

---

10. *CD* II/1:317–18.
11. Karl Barth, *Der Römerbrief* (Bern: Bäschlin, 1919), v.

cal, or psychological. The spiritual power of God that is the gospel of Jesus Christ now revealed is decisive in superseding the old alternatives, "churchly" or "worldly," with the new alternatives, faith or unbelief.[12] The power of God is his new righteousness, which is no longer his longsuffering of human unrighteousness; rather, he makes his righteousness effective again by justifying the ungodly. Barth denies the possibility of some tumultuous experience of the divine as human willfulness, morality, or religiousness; instead, Christian faith is being led by the knowledge of God in the strictest sense *(Erkenntnis Gottes im strengsten Sinn)* of "the light of the knowledge of the glory of God in the face of Jesus Christ" (2 Cor. 4:6). This knowledge is a powerful, liberating, newly creating word spoken uniquely by God that "breaks the tragically unfruitful earnestness of morality and religion." It is nothing other than a free union with God: Through God's faithfulness human beings find faith.[13]

The logic of this theological exposition is also rooted in the interpretation of what Paul goes on to say in Romans 1:18–21, what Barth calls "The Night." The great problem with human beings as sinners and above all as religious is that in every case we wish to have God/god on our own terms. Indeed, Barth identifies "πᾶσαν ἀσέβειαν καὶ ἀδικίαν ἀνθρώπων" (all irreverence and unrighteousness of human beings) (1:18)[14] as religion that leads to actual irreligiousness:

> Thus there is a false morality which eventuates in immorality in the promethean self-absorption which lifts itself to the righteousness of God. This is its "unrighteousness." Thus we see the contradiction of man under which his whole world suffers: which is always seeking God but always finds idols, always intends to serve God and always lives for itself and in both loses God himself. . . . False religion and irreligiousness, . . . products of a false morality. . . . [Humanity] knows the truth, but wills not to know it and therefore it cannot become a reality. . . . What God ought to be to him he is himself.[15]

One can detect the way in which the Reformation focus on personal faith, human depravity, and the error of human religion are interrelated forces. Barth's antipathy toward human religion because of human depravity even leads him to such expressions as *"Religionswahn"* (religion craze) in the most pejorative sense. This is because in the end all religion robs the true God of glory for the sake of self-glorification. Religion is actually unfruitful because it tends toward moralistic impositions or construes its own clever answers. Borrowing from Kant's interchangeable "concepts without perceptions are blind" and "perceptions without concepts are blind," Barth points to the indispensability of God's Word to overcome the unfruitfulness of religion. Although in 1919 Barth does not wage theological battle against natural theology, he is holding

12. Ibid., 9.
13. Ibid., 10.
14. Literally, although the NRSV translates the two terms "ungodliness" and "wickedness."
15. Barth, *Römerbrief,* 12–13.

high the Reformation priority of salvation in revelation. Revelation from God comes to human beings because they need a gracious God, not because they need a better concept of God.

The basis for Barth's rejection of religion as he reads Paul's great epistle is twofold: (1) the fall into sin and irreligion and (2) the kingdom of God. The first of these reckons with the profound judgment, "Claiming to be wise, they became fools" (φάσκοντες εἶναι σοφοὶ ἐμωράνθησαν) (1:22) such that, as Barth writes, *"Gott ist nicht als Gott erkannt"* (God is not known as God).[16] Focused on the noetic effects of sin with respect to the knowledge of God, Barth describes this other knowledge as rooted in "a subjective, naturalistic religiosity," which amounts to a willful absolutizing and deifying of fantasized notions. Barth couldn't be more emphatic: The natural religious impulse is nothing other than

die Verkapselung und der Misbrauch der Wahrheit zu gunsten des auf den Thron erhobenen Ich bricht, wie zuerst in der Verderbnis des inner Lebens (1, 21), so nun auch nach außen durch und erscheint in der Geschichte als die große Kultur- und Morallüge: Die Menschheit wird, was sie Kraft ihres Widerstandes gegen das göttliche "Es werde!" sein muß: ein *Tummelplatz* aller möglichen Nichtigkeiten, ein Weltkriegschauplatz, ein Narrenhaus.[17]

The encapsulation and misuses of the truth to benefit the enthroned "I" brings firstly the corruption of the inner life (1:21) and thus also outwardly through and appearing in history as the great cultural and moral lie: Humanity will be what the power of its opposition to the divine "it will be" must be: a *playground* of every possible nothingness, a grandstand for world war, a house of fools.

Nothing like this sentence appears in the second German edition—indeed, it is quite tempting to assume that Karl Adam got his inspiration for the famous comment on *Römerbrief* from this passage in the first edition—the book that "fell like a bomb that dropped on the playground [*Tummelplatz*] of the theologians."[18]

The *Romans* commentary was meant to inaugurate an end in a number of senses. In the first instance, it is an inquiry into the radicality of the apostle's first three chapters, which so prophetically assault human conscience and the ways of religious imagination. *Der Römerbrief* of 1919 inaugurates a way of thinking that is more than its own way. This publication becomes a paradigm for many outside theology because of its new apologetic and its apology against the cultural dictates of its day.

16. Ibid., 17.
17. Ibid., 18.
18. Karl Adam, "Theologie der Krisis," *Hochland* 23 (1926): 385.

Banishing "a Different Spirit": Natural Theology

I have consciously used Luther's parting words to Zwingli at the conclusion of the Marburg Colloquy of 1529, "You have a different spirit from us"—so personal and yet so concretely dividing—because the tragic conflict between Karl Barth and Emil Brunner bore so many similar marks of a theological parting of ways.[19] This allusion is not in the first instance about one or the other of the Reformers being theologically correct. Certainly, Barth has made natural theology (with its apologetics, polemics, and metaphysics) something for many theologians to eschew, although on the other hand it continues to enjoy a robust existence through Christian theism and philosophical theology. What was the problem with natural theology?

At one level, the problem of natural theology for Barth was rooted in his problem of the theology of cultural Protestantism. Since Enlightenment philosophy of religion had brought into question the possibility of revelation and the legitimacy of exclusive truth claims by any particular religion, natural theology became a way of suggesting if not proving the existence of the kind of God witnessed to in the Bible. In some respects, Christian theology had always offered this kind of apologetic for its truth claims by building a case that suggested that the truths of the Bible about God at least are not in conflict with what could be known about God. If this could be done satisfactorily, then one could move on and by means of a little jump proceed to the doctrines of revealed truth. To Barth's mind, this would be an immense jump, one that rendered the previous hopes of a rationalistic argument for God's truth a false hope and, even worse, a *sacrificium intellectus*.

A great deal separated the pre-Enlightenment theological world from the modern one. Barth defended Anselm's famous ontological argument of his book *Proslogion* as a way of showing "the impossibility of conceiving the non-existence of God."[20] What Anselm was not doing, Barth contended, was offering an argument to establish "the certainty with which faith conceives the existence of God." Because of this, Barth was making an important implied claim: Anselm's *Proslogion* was not a project in natural theology; above all, it was not a prolegomena to a dogmatics that built an intellectual link from the knowledge of human existence to the knowledge of God in the existence (in the fullest sense) of Jesus Christ. Toward the end of his book, Barth wants to distinguish Anselm's interest in demonstrating God's existence on account of the impossibility of conceiving of his nonexistence from the interests of the Enlightenment philosopher Descartes, who was intent on demonstrating the

19. For the precise delineation of the issues between Barth and Brunner, see McCormack, *Karl Barth's Critically Realistic Dialectical Theology,* 502.

20. Karl Barth, *Anselm: Fides quaerens intellectum: Anselm's Proof of the Existence of God in the Context of His Theological Scheme,* trans. Ian W. Robertson (London: SCM, 1960), 94; trans. of *Fides quaerens intellectum: Anselm's Beweis der Existenz Gottes im Zusammenhang seines theologischen Programms,* 2d ed. (Zollikon: Evangelischer Verlag, 1958).

impossibility of his own nonexistence, not God's. But it is this latter issue that is bound up in the fundamental religiocultural difference between the Enlightenment and Christianity, as introduced by the Enlightenment. With the shift of concern from the particular existence of God to the particular existence of self, truth in the most generalized and reductionist sense became a dogmatic demand of the Enlightenment program. With respect to religion, the Enlightenment program had distilled what was regarded as the essence of religion into a number of basic principles regarding existence, moral and religious obligations, and human destiny. These principles were developed extensively in Enlightenment theories of religious phenomena and were enjoined upon free thinkers of the seventeenth and nineteenth centuries as natural religion. In the first instance, natural theology was the expository expression of natural religion. Only in its Christianized forms did these principles become apologetic components of dogmatic prolegomena. Barth's exercise with Anselm did not win over many convinced historians of philosophy, but it did ground Barth's theology more clearly in two principles: the objectivity and reality of the God of revelation, and the revelatory particularity of this God—Father, Son, and Holy Spirit—known only in and through Jesus Christ. How could natural theology make any positive contribution to the knowledge of God?

Barth's rejection of natural theology is a subtheme running throughout the *CD*. He was a discerner of its many forms, reasons, contexts, and representatives. At the center of his critique was his alertness to the anthropological character of all natural theology.[21] In every case, intentionally or not, something self-justifying about the human subject is being claimed, something to be humanly achieved at the highest level of awareness and motivation, by which to credit the self before God. This problem with the natural theology was rooted, however, in the statements of Scripture attesting to what is called the *natural knowledge* of God and the exegetical and theological traditions that took up these statements in positive ways. That Genesis 1:26–27 had presented the human being as created according to the image of God suggested to many early theologians that a deposit of divine being was to be found in the former. Theologians had long contended that however corrupted human nature had become, this implanted deposit could be revived through the rebirth of faith and intellectual renovation by the Spirit of God. The natural knowledge of God could be taught to the world not only as part of the expositions of Christian truth but also as part of that which is essential to human nature. The fact of existence could be said to be true of creatures as well as God, when thought of in binary terms, in contrast to nonexistence; yet matter was a created continuity of divine existence between God and the human on account of the *imago Dei*. Human beings owed their nature to being created by God in his image, according to his likeness; hence, an absence of the image, so the classic theologians

---

21. Cf. *CD* I/1:126f.; and II/1:143ff.

reasoned, would be the cessation of human existence. This type of reflection stood behind the Catholic theology of *analogia entis* (analogy of being), which held the concept of a knowable correspondence between human beings and the divine Being that is part of the necessary movement toward faith in God, which God accepts and counts worthy of himself. Indeed, much of the appeal to that which persists in the goodness of God's human creature is part of the apologetic that derives itself from the *analogia entis,* reflection on the *imago Dei.* Indeed, one could assert that the best argument for the unique value of the human being flows from this very type of reflection. The problem with this reasoning with respect to Christian theology, in its dogmatic expression of what is to be taught, is that it misses two basic truths: the judgment and the grace of God.

Barth's lengthy discussion of religion in section 17 of the *CD,* "The Revelation of God as the Abolition of Religion," is both a theological exposé of "religion as unbelief" (i.e., under divine judgment) and "true religion" (i.e., that which comes to us by the gracious revelation of God in Jesus Christ).[22] The German original *Aufhebung* has a double meaning: Translated as "abolition," it could also carry the sense of "lifting up," referring to the other side of the discussion that presents religion in its true form in Christ. Barth could not be clearer: "Revelation does not link up with a human religion which is already present and practiced. It contradicts it, just as religion previously contradicted revelation. It displaces it, just as religion previously displaced revelation."[23] Barth's exposition of Romans 1:18–21 along with and in light of Acts 14:15–17 and 17:22–31 is particularly instructive here. In all of these texts, Barth takes the references to revelation not as a natural knowledge of God but as knowledge of Jesus Christ and thus God's gracious offer through him. Therefore, anything and everything else that human beings have regarded as divine is denied here. Although Paul refers to natural knowledge of God, one must not miss the judgment of God in every case: Instead of worshiping the true God, human beings turn to their idols, and this we do because of our unrighteousness. And so the idols of our own contrivance represent fully our own attempts at mediating the relation between God and ourselves by ourselves. In the case of the Romans text, the revelation of Christ is first of all the revelation of God's wrath against all suppression of the truth, which is quintessentially unrighteousness. Barth is intent on avoiding any kind of abstraction regarding pagan humanity. What the apostle writes about human actuality is that in every case human beings are in an inexcusable situation before God. Barth acknowledges

---

22. There is great sensitivity about this subject in Barth. Cf. J. A. Di Noia, O.P., "Religion and the Religions," in *The Cambridge Companion to Karl Barth,* ed. John Webster (Cambridge: Cambridge University Press, 2000), 243–57. Barth has in the background the influence of Ulrich Zwingli's important treatise on true and false religion (Ulrich Zwingli, *Commentary on True and False Religion,* ed. Samuel M. Jackson and Clarence N. Heller [Durham: Labyrinth Press, 1981]).

23. *CD* I/2:303.

the revelation of God in creation but reminds us how emphatic Paul is that no one, Jew or Gentile, has held fast to this knowledge. Thus, nothing in Paul's argumentation appeals to this natural knowledge of God. The problem of humanity is its defection precisely at the point of departure—the displacement of this knowledge from creation along with the attempt at replacement with human religion. In the face of this universal reality is Jesus Christ: "As the self-offering and self-manifestation of God He replaces and completely outbids those attempts of man to reconcile God to the world." Religion in effect tries to do what only Jesus Christ could and has done once and for all for us all: "Our justification and sanctification, our conversion and salvation" are such that our faith in him "consists in our recognising and admitting and affirming and accepting the fact that everything has actually been done for us once and for all in Jesus Christ." Barth adds, "There is an exchange of status between Him and us: His righteousness and holiness are ours, our sin is His; He is lost for us, and we for His sake are saved. By this exchange (καταλλαγή, 2 Cor. 5:19) revelation stands or falls."[24] The importance of this use of revelation cannot be overestimated for understanding Barth. Revelation is the saving action and saving knowledge of God. In view of Jesus Christ, nothing else can define revelation.

Thus, inherent in the denial of religion is the lifting up of true religion in Christ. And the entirety of the matter is acknowledging that God comes to us in Christ with every grace for salvation and that this demands of us, not any kind of bridge-building between ourselves and our religions but utter confidence in the God who saves us—which produces a profound self-confidence. Theology in every respect is an investigation into and elaboration on this gracious reality. In a most illuminating passage, Barth penetrates into the religious psychology of natural theology to expose it and to hold it up to the light of revelation in Christ:

> The Christian religion will always be vital and healthy and strong as long as it has this self-confidence. But it will have this self-confidence only as its adherents and proclaimers can look away from themselves to the fact of God which alone can justify them. In so far as they still rely on other facts, this self-confidence will inevitably receive one inward blow after another and in the long run completely disappear. It makes no odds whether these other facts consist in ecclesiastical institutions, theological systems, inner experiences, the moral transformations of

---

24. *CD* I/2:308. One fascinating example of where religion as secularized Christianity has arrived in Germany is described by Dietrich Korsch as the Christianity of "as if." Two approaches have emerged as a kind of theologizing replaces religion: (1) Words and meanings are used fundamentalistically in an attempt to bring one's world under the authoritative truth of faith, and (2) words and meanings from the surrounding culture are given a theological interpretation. Korsch is clearly searching for ways, in the face of massive ecclesial losses of outward health and vitality, to find a place on which to stand alone. Cf. Dietrich Korsch, *Dialektische Theologie nach Karl Barth* (Tübingen: Mohr, 1996), 296–305.

individual believers or the wider effects of Christianity upon the world at large. . . . Those who believe in their Church and theology, or in changed men and improved circumstances, are on exactly the same road, the road to uncertainty. This is betrayed by the fact that all of them, incidentally but quite openly, and with the unteachable ferocity of a secret despair of faith, have to take refuge in reason or culture or humanity or race, in order to find some support or other for the Christian religion. But the Christian religion cannot be supported from without, if it can no longer stand alone. If it does stand alone it does not allow itself to be supported from without. Standing alone, it stands upon the fact of God which justifies it, and upon that alone. There is therefore no place for attempts to support it in any other way. . . . In fact, they are a renewal of the unbelief which is not unnoticed or unassessed by God, but covered up and forgiven. But such attempts are bound to be made if once we glance aside at other facts side by side with the one justifying fact. In that case unbelief has already returned. It already has the decisive word. And it will see in such attempts, not a waste of time and energy, but an urgent necessity. The secularisation of Christianity is then in full train, and no subjective piety will avail to halt it. And the result will be a loss of all outward health and strength and vitality.[25]

Barth could not have been more poignant in his assessment. After all, the constructing of the supports does reflect the struggle of a faith that is slipping away from itself. In too many cases, even a feeble combination of the supports with the justifying fact of God seems to be lacking. Barth is acutely aware of the many ways that natural theology manifests itself in general religious thought: the eliciting of existential awareness of dependence on God, which enamored Brunner to such a degree; rationalistic demands; and questions of general truth. It is natural to construct a method of knowledge acquisition positing a point of initiation followed by a lifelong progression in further learning and understanding as the way of appropriating the saving knowledge of Christ. Nevertheless, this cannot justify a natural theology for the sake of supporting the Christian faith.

By way of bringing this discussion of dispensing with natural theology and indeed external religious supports of any kind to a close, we can cluster together three conceptual tools that reinforce this entire matter. The first of these three is *analogia fidei* (analogy of faith), whereby our speaking, through faith that receives and proclaims the Word of God, corresponds as a human word of testimony to the Word of God that has been received. The second is the disjunction between *theologia crucis* and *theologia gloriae*, both terms derived from Martin Luther's writings in connection with the Heidelberg Disputation. The former is the method of knowing and reflecting on the revelation of God through the cross-destined life of Jesus Christ; the latter is the method of abstract contemplation toward the attainment of immediate and transcendent knowledge of God. Finally, there is the dialectical polarity between *Deus*

25. *CD* I/2:357.

absconditus (hidden) and *Deus revelatus* (revealed),[26] whereby the way of the knowledge of faith as *theologia crucis* is ever an experience of the God who is at once revealed and concealed in the conditions of Jesus' life and death. In the case of the first two, leaving *theologia gloriae* behind to the natural theologians, we have the rule that qualifies the testimonial nature of all Christian theology: "not I but Christ." The massive possibility, advantage, and source of confidence in Christian theology is that our words can correspond with God's Word. But this happens only with reference to Christ, the One who as God became human together with us and who in terms of his cross and resurrection reveals the content of this Word to which our words may correspond by faith. In the third instance, the dialectical polarity between *Deus absconditus* and *Deus revelatus* reflects the combination of humility and confidence that must characterize all of our theological speaking and writing. We have this certain truth about God in Jesus Christ: It is available to us, sealed in our hearts, and always gives us hope. But at the same time, faith, hope, and love, the theological virtues, reflect realities much more hidden than revealed.

Grasping the *Pro-legomenon*

What then is the *pro-legomenon* that overcomes all the *prolegomena,* the false supports that have nervously and furtively been included in the history of theological first things and initiations? Regarding his emphasis on *analogia fidei,* Barth declares:

> With our statement about man's conformity to God in faith and therefore in his possibility of knowing God's Word we are saying . . . that when and where the word of God is really known, . . . this knowing corresponds to that of the Word of God itself. . . . We have thus described what acknowledgment of God's Word by man is, not in the form of an analysis of man's consciousness of faith, but in the form of a postulate directed to man's consciousness of faith by the nature of the Word of God. We have to think of man in the event of real faith as, so to speak, opened up from above. From above, not from below! . . . The true believer is the very man who will not hesitate to acknowledge that his consciousness of faith as such is human darkness. Hence we cannot omit to investigate the consciousness of our known ego with reference to the content of God's Word. The opening up from above that takes place in the event of real faith remains just as hidden for us as the event itself or God Himself. But we must also say that it is as manifest to us as this event is manifest or God is manifest; i.e., in the recollection of the promise and hope of its fulfillment. As we can and should believe the Word of God itself, as we are summoned to believe it, so we must believe our faith in the word, our possibility of knowing it or its knowability for us, the presence of the *forma Dei* in the midst of human

26. *CD* II/1:362–65; 541–50.

darkness, Christ's presence in the *tenebrae* of our heart. . . . Thus the possibility of man, inadequate in itself, can become the adequate divine possibility. . . . In affirming the knowability of God's Word as it is promised to us and as it takes place in the event of faith, we affirm the divine possibility. To the extent that we can affirm it only in its concealment, in the husk of the human possibility that meets us as darkness, we will not deny the dissimilarity between the divine possibility in itself and what it becomes in our hands. For all the dissimilarity, the possibility of grasping the promise in faith is not without similarity to the divine possibility of its actualization: not in itself, not as a human possibility, but, according to our first definition, in terms of its object, as the possibility of grasping the promise. In virtue of this similarity our possibility of knowing God's Word is the possibility of a clear and certain knowledge, not equal but at least similar to the clarity and certainty with which God knows Himself in His Word. In virtue of this similarity the confession of faith, corresponding to the knowledge of God's Word, acquires the definiteness which distinguishes it basically from all human convictions, however profound or serious; it acquires the final human seriousness which belongs only to confession, to the confession of faith. In virtue of this similarity the Church, Church proclamation and dogmatics are possible. The clarity and certainty of knowledge, the confession of faith and the Church rest on the fact that whenever and wherever the Word of God is really known it is known after the manner of the word of God itself, in this similarity of what is believed and known.[27]

A rich array of crucial factors comes together in this passage. With "conformity" to the Word of God by faith comes the possibility of correspondence with this same Word. The dissimilarity and similarity of our knowledge is brought out; it derives from the method of analogy, but in this case, not of being but of divine knowledge. Barth here is clearly speaking of the sacramentality of the Word of God to produce this fulfillment of relative similarity, the relativity being on account of both creaturely limitations and the human darkness. And yet because of this similarity of knowing as God knows, we are able to speak as God speaks and so to instantiate the gathering of the church and the instruction and reflection that is theology.

But what is the content of this Word of God? It is nothing other than Jesus Christ, the Word that is the person of God, the Word that is incarnate in Jesus of Nazareth, the Word of the gospel that the Holy Spirit ever illumines in the life of the church and in the believer. The purpose is that they might participate in the active recollection that is the appropriation of Scripture by faith and of the Word that comes to us in the presence of Jesus Christ, mediating here and now all the promises of God conveyed in Scripture to us and for the mission of Christ through us in the world. This is the Word of Jesus Christ that is, the Jesus Christ who mediates the truth of the trinitarian reality of God both at the beginning and in the coming end of all things, to the

27. *CD* I/1:242–43.

glory of God the Father and the fellowship of the redeemed in the kingdom of God. The christocentric positivity of theology is a testimony to the ever-freeing, gracious love of the Triune God. Jesus Christ is the first Word of the word of theology because he is the Word behind the words of Scripture. Jesus Christ is also the Word to which our words are to conform so that they might engender the confidence promised them as they become the testimony of the theologian. This Jesus Christ is the Word of God, the *pro-legomenon* of all our words in theology and proclamation. As such, theology is self-sustaining[28] as the product of the theologian's relationship with Jesus Christ, together with the testimony of the entire the church.

Two aspects are considered here. First, the christocentricity,[29] the *Christus solus* of the entire *CD,* is finally the surest way of locating its organizing principle and that of all future Christian theologies. Indeed, this point is the source of Barth's radicalism—in the sense of going to the root, the *radix* of the knowledge of God. In doing this, Barth aims at the concrete and actual form of the revelation of the Triune God. This does not mean that the three are somehow incarnate but that through the life of the man Jesus Christ, the life of the Son of God is known, and it is through him that the life of the Trinity is known and introduced to the world. It becomes clear, however, that all of what Barth has to say about the eternal nature of God; creation; the *imago Dei;* the freedom, revelation, and love of God; election; atonement; justification; faith; community; and the eschaton is mediated through his Christology. Part of Barth's approach to this is highlighted by his continual resistance to any moment in theology in which a concept, however scripturally based, takes precedence over the person of God, the person of Christ. Since the content of revelation is God, as is all divine action, God and supremely God in Christ is always the content of theology. While the arrangement of the *CD* can even be outlined according to the Trinity, the positive content always is a question of its means of conveyance, and this is always Jesus Christ, the Mediator of God to humanity, and vice versa. As Bruce McCormack writes regarding Barth's christocentrism, it was "a methodological rule—not an a priori principle, but a rule which is learned through encounter with the God who reveals Himself in Christ—in accordance with which one presupposes a particular understanding of God's Self-revelation in reflecting upon each and every other doctrinal topic, and seeks to interpret those topics in the light of what is already known in Jesus Christ."[30] Probably nothing concentrates our attention on Barth's christocentrism as much, however, as his contention that Jesus Christ is the only true sacrament. Indeed, the work of Christ has secured

---

28. Cf. Thies Gundlach, *Selbstbegrenzung Gottes und die Autonomie des Menschen: Karl Barths kirchliche Dogmatik als Modernisierungsschritt evangelischer Theologie* (Frankfurt a. M.: Peter Lang, 1992), 293ff.

29. *CD* IV/4:19.

30. McCormack, *Karl Barth's Critically Realistic Dialectical Theology,* 454.

once and for all the entire fulfillment of salvation for us and does so entirely in himself and as he is present exclusively by the work of the Holy Spirit and the witness of the Word of God. Hence, it is the humanity of Jesus Christ, itself the mediation and therefore not in need of other modes of mediation, that supremely conveys all the benefits of God and indeed God himself to us. This learning through encounter with God then leads to our second point: testimony or witness.

The testimonial form of the entire *CD* has to be taken into account as a fundamental characteristic of its rhetoric and stylistic forms. No one can read the pages of these volumes and not be struck by the unity of theological objectivity with the sources and contemporary debates and not, at the same time, be struck by the writer's intent to express himself as a witness of the things about which he writes. They are to him his meat and drink, work and leisure, worship and love. Everywhere Barth is testifying to the factual claim that he everywhere wishes to make clear: Instead of the possibility of the knowledge of God, there is the possibility that God has made himself known and will be known by sinful human beings. Since Barth is captive to the object of his study and teaching, he is clearly intent on captivating his audience in some way. Instead of doing so existentially, as Brunner's testimony led him to do, Barth wanted the *CD* to reflect a pedagogic that suggested something almost liturgical, certainly a kind of echo of the sermonic. Theology becomes testimony, and vice versa, as for Barth it must.

5

GOD'S "GOD OF GOD"

O Thou Beauty of ancient days, yet ever new!

Augustine, *Confessions* 10.27.38

The chapter title's reference to the chief clause of the Nicene-Constantinopolitan Creed points to an internal, eternal participation of God in his own life of living relations as Father, Son, and Holy Spirit. It also points to our participation in the self-knowledge and self-disclosing activity of God. The creed is an invitation to the Johannine Gospel, its prologue and especially its seventeenth chapter, as well as to the writings of Paul. God knows himself through the Son, who is "God of God," and through a relationship that is dialogical but not dialectic, since God is not self-reconciling but reconciling others. Our knowledge of God is expressed tautologically since in our inclusion in God's self-knowledge, God is incomparably God. At points there is nothing other to say than that God is who he is (Exod. 3:14).

But there is more to say also on account of the gospel. In this chapter, then, we explore with Barth his exposition of the doctrine of God in *CD* II/1. We should be mindful of the time in Barth's life when he is writing—at the height of his powers, with maturity and energy, and profoundly attune to the unity of God's communicative being. Barth discerns the terms of the knowledge of God, who is his own divine being in action, and determines to include the creation and, above all, creatures created in his image to share in his self-knowledge. By doing so, God who is God knows us in order that we might know him and in knowing him become caught up in a knowledge that is at once both true and redeeming. In *CD* II/1, Barth sums up what he has said about the divine

Word in *CD* I and what he will say about divine creation in *CD* III and divine reconciliation in *CD* IV.

God's Identity as Self-Communication

Theology includes the contemplation of God, both in terms of the objectivity of revelation through the canonical Scriptures and in terms of the subjectivity of theology's symbols and their function in the practices of prayer, worship, and mission. The contemplation of God always includes the self as the dialogical lesser member but exalted through justification to be a recipient of God's self-communication. We might call this a kind of "theositic"[1] inclusion of the sinner in God's self-knowledge as he communicates himself to the object of his gracious favor.

Barth attends to Augustine's mystical theology of ascent to the pure being of God, which he recounts from a particular day in Ostia. Barth refers to "one of the most beautiful but also most dangerous passages," in *Confessions* 9.10, and Augustine's account of himself and his mother, Monica, caught up in a spiritual rapture. In this account, Barth points out, we find the claim of *ascent* and *transcendence* by and of the self. He fixates on phrases from this passage: "We lifted ourselves with a more ardent love toward the Selfsame [*idipsum*]." "We came at last to our own minds and went beyond them." "Wisdom is not made, but is as she has been and forever shall be. . . . We just barely touched her with the whole effort of our hearts."[2] What Barth faults Augustine for is his abandonment of the creation as the context for divine revelation. Barth reflects on the Augustinian claim:

> If we really soar up into these heights, and really reduce all concepts, images, words and signs to silence, and really think we can enter into the *idipsum,* it simply means that we wilfully hurry past God, who descends in His revelation into this world of ours. Instead of finding Him where He Himself has sought us—namely in His objectivity—we seek Him where He is not to be found, since He on His side seeks us in His Word. It is really not the case, therefore, that if we have a knowledge of God in the form of that experience, we have reached a higher or the highest step on a way which began with an objective perceiving, viewing and conceiving of God, as though that were an early [*kindlich*] and sensuous mode of thought. It is not the case that in the non-objective we are dealing with the real and true knowledge of God but in the objective with a deceptive appearance. Just the reverse. If we regard ourselves as bound by God's Word we shall certainly find a deceptive appearance in that *ascendere* and *transcendere* so far as what happens there—whatever else it may be—claims to be knowledge

1. Pressing the Orthodox term for salvation, *theosis,* into adjectival service.
2. Albert Outler's translation of Augustine's *Confessions* 9.10.24–25, www.ccel.org/a/augustine/confessions/confessions.html.

of God. For how can it make this claim except where the fulfillment of the real knowledge of God in God's Word has either not yet begun or ceased again? Where it is being fulfilled, the hasty by-passing of God's revelation or the flight into non-objectivity cannot possibly occur. Where it is being fulfilled, knowledge is bound to the objectivity of God just as it is bound to this definite object who is the God who gives Himself to be known in His Word. And it is bound to the fact that His very revelation consists in His making Himself object to us, and so in His making a flight into non-objectivity not only superfluous but impossible. Thus the straight and proper way in this matter can never be from objectivity into non-objectivity, but only from non-objectivity back into objectivity.[3]

With the frame of reference that faithfully denigrates the opposite—eschewing the *theologia gloriae* for the revelation hidden in the cross, the *theologia crucis*—Barth exposes Augustine to fundamental critique as an early paragon of mystical theology. Barth reminds us that God comes to us in his revelation by means of a divine act of condescension or descent *(heruntersteigt)* into our world. God accommodates himself to us, to the contingencies of our existence, which he does supremely in the flesh of Christ, the man Jesus. This is the very structure of the incarnation of the Son of God. But in mystical apprehension beyond the creaturely form of the Word of God, we "wilfully hurry past" *(mutwillig vorbeieilen)* God in his revelation. The clearest way Barth expresses this is in God's "objectivity" *(Gegenständlichkeit)* in his act of self-giving to human knowledge. To hurry past it to some other knowledge of God is to attempt an impossible nonobjectivity because of what God's Word accomplishes in the way of positive knowledge of God.

When God becomes an object of human knowing, it means that he has offered himself for human

consideration and conception. On the strength of this it becomes possible and necessary to speak and hear about God. If it were not so, there would be no knowledge of God and no faith in Him. God would simply not be in the picture. We could not hold to Him. We could not pray to Him. To deny the objectivity of God is to deny the life of the church of Jesus Christ—which lives on the fact that God is spoken of and heard. It is to deny prayer to God, the knowledge of God, and with knowledge faith in God as well. But not every object is God; and so not all our human consideration and conception is knowledge of God. For although God has genuine objectivity just like all other objects, His objectivity is different from theirs, and therefore knowledge of him—and this is the chief thing to be said about its character as the knowledge of faith—is a particular and utterly unique occurrence in the range of all knowledge. Certainly the same thing happens in faith that happens always and everywhere when man enters into that uniting and distinguishing relationship to an object, when his subjectivity is opened up to an objectivity and he is grounded and determined anew. But in faith the same thing happens quite differently. This difference consists in

3. *CD* II/1:11–12.

the difference and uniqueness of God as its object. Knowledge of faith means fundamentally a recognition of the union of man with God who is distinct from him as well as from all his other objects. For this very reason knowledge becomes and is a special knowledge, distinct from the knowledge of all other objects, outstanding in the range of all knowledge. What our consideration and conception mean in this context cannot be determined from a general understanding of man . . . but only in particular from God as its particular object. On the strength of the fact that God in His particularity is its object, and as such is also known, it becomes possible and necessary to speak and hear about God. It must again be said that if God is not object in this particularity there will be no knowledge of God at all. God is not God if He is considered and conceived as one in a series of like objects. But then prayer and the life of the church will necessarily cease, i.e., dissolve into the relationship of man to what he knows or thinks he knows as one object in a series of other objects. As one in this series He will not be worshipped, nor will He have a Church.[4]

Here Barth is unpacking what he means by God's objectivity to human knowing, to "human consideration and conception" *(menschlicher Anschauung und menschlichen Begreifens).* I take these as the two functions in human knowing of critical observation and realistic ideation.

We are at the threshold of theological epistemology—but not in a way conceived of by epistemologists from Immanuel Kant to Karl Popper. What theology means by "critical observation" certainly overlaps with valid rules of human knowing or even scientific data collection and theory building. But theology does not object to the limits of philosophical and scientific epistemology just because there are exaggerated knowledge claims such as universality and uniformity. Much of the postmodern critique of modern epistemology has effectively rooted out the culture of scientism, which exalted scientific method to a level of instrumentality for the achievement and advancement of utopia. In Barth's day and throughout much of the twentieth century (barbaric as it was), philosophical and scientific epistemologists practiced one of several types of secular eschatologies—we must remember that the immensely popular fascism, Marxism, and scientific-capitalist perfectionisms achieved their potency through using eschatological terms. This is scientism, the culturally exclusivist outlook whereby the only claims to knowledge and truth are to be justified by scientific methods. To dismantle scientistic culture and its overbearing hubris, still expressed through various futurological approaches, is a laudable achievement. In the famous exchange between Barth and Heinrich Scholz,[5] resulting in a lifelong friend, scientism was not at issue but rather the status of theological knowledge claims. Heinrich Scholz, trained in theology and professor at Münster, had also become an expert in the philosophy of mathematics and was invited by Barth in 1930 to Bonn, where they discussed

4. Ibid., 14–15.
5. *CD* IV/2:737–41.

Anselm's *Proslogion* and its "ontological argument" for God's existence. This was a healthy debate and one in which an amicable difference of opinion could thrive. Barth's book on Anselm would arise principally from the stimulus of this conversation. Indeed, it would lead him to a whole new definition of theology in the modern context, as a science founded on the nature of its Object in the objectivity of revelation. Theology's knowledge of God is "scientific" to the extent that it a posteriori formulates its statements from disciplined attention to the content and media of the revelation. The possibility of theology based on divine self-revelation is the fact that this revelation takes place freely within the limitations and under the conditions of created reality, which are the same for all paths of knowledge. When the revelation as such is taken not only as a given for what it is, divine disclosure within a prophetic knowledge claim, but also for what it more fundamentally is, the self-giving of God for the sake of human knowing and relationship with God, then theology as science becomes an actuality: knowledge of God and therefore the science of God as an actual object of knowing.

Nonapplicability of Myth

The primary limitation to which the knowledge of God will not submit, however, is the logic of myth. Barth takes aim here against the detemporalizing and departicularizing of the reality and truth of God in Jesus Christ and Christian faith. Without denying the power of myth, he claims that the knowledge of God is simply not in the same species. In Barth's well-known discussion of the creation narratives, he first approvingly quotes Adolf Schlatter:

> As the concept of creation is given to us, we stand at the frontier of our power of vision. The apprehension of how things began and came into existence is every where denied us. We know only that which has come into being, only the results of the operation. Even in ourselves the processes of coming into being are completely veiled from us. . . . Because we are not the Creator we cannot see or understand any creative act.[6]

In connection with the creation stories of the Bible, Barth's distinction between history (according to modern canons of historiography) and saga (ancient history guided by conventions of cultural memory and therefore

---

6. *CD* III/1:78, quoting from Adolf Schlatter, *Das christliche Dogma*, 2d ed. (Stuttgart: Calwer, 1923), 60. Barth makes the distinction between historicist *"Historie"* (discrete history), which is a stringent telling of observed events without reference to unobserved causes, even if they were observable; and then the telling that includes judgments as to causes and effects and to truth, even the invisible working of God by revelation, which necessarily are *"Geschichte"* (interpreted history). Interpreted history uses the materials of historical record to answer larger historical questions of cause, of extended effects, and of meaning.

"prehistorical history") excludes the possibility of myth in connection with
the Bible and theology:

> The customary definition of myth as the story of the gods is only superficial. . . .
> The real object and content of myth are the essential principles of the general
> realities and relationships of the nature and spiritual cosmos which, in distinc-
> tion from concrete history, are not confined to definite times and places. The
> clothing of their dialectic and cyclical movement in stories of the gods is the
> form of myth. The fairy tale . . . which inclines not to concrete history but to all
> kinds of general phenomena, truths or even riddles of existence, is a degenerate
> form of myth as are legend and anecdote of saga.
>   The creation stories of the Bible are neither myths nor fairy tales.[7]

The issue of myth in religion and theology is complex. Beyond the logical
positivist banishment of myth out of the world inhabited by the likes of Scholz,
this category, both of literature and of creative and intentional narration, has
been vastly rehabilitated. The forces of this cultural shift are massive under
several rubrics, such as hermeneutical turn; postcritical, poststructural, post-
secular reenchantment of the world; remythologization; and quintessentially
the postmodern. In the last quarter of the twentieth century, there emerged a
continuum of interpretive moves that betray the thoroughgoing humanness of all
knowledge and truth claims. The questions of interest and purpose stand behind
every knowledge and truth claim, including those of natural science.[8] Who is
making a claim and why? Immediately, evidential and propositional forms of
knowledge must include accounts of the reasons for prioritizing or privileging
certain claims over others and provide an autobiographical/biographical account
of commitment. What had once been a careful boundary setting, between hard
and soft sciences, between humanities and physical sciences, now agglomerate
once again into a complex cultural system of all-too-human ways of communication. Knowledge and truth are not simply elemental resources like air and
water but complex systems inseparable from the structure and maintenance of

7. *CD* III/1:84.

8. In Philip Kitcher, *Science, Truth, and Democracy* (New York: Oxford University Press,
2001), 63–80, Kitcher lays out the role of narrative and persuasion essential to the public support for the advancement of science. But no one has demonstrated the problems of simplistic
objectivity along these lines like Nicholas Rescher in his *Priceless Knowledge? Natural Science in
Economic Perspective* (Lanham, Md.: Rowman & Littlefield, 1996); cf. esp. chap. 8, "Human
Science as Characteristically Human," and chap. 9, "Problems of Scientific Realism." As strong
a defense of scientific realism as Christopher Norris makes in his book *Truth Matters: Realism,
Anti-Realism, and Response-Dependence* (Edinburgh: Edinburgh University Press, 2002), 195ff.,
he cannot manage to cope fully with the issue of human interest and purpose. This is not to
say that some kind of scientific realism is unwarranted but that the cultural imbeddedness of
scientific knowledge cannot by its very nature provide the purely objectivist account on which
so much of scientific realism relies. Such accounts are themselves part of science's myth-making
so necessary to the human success of science.

culture and community. Without the narrative of commitment, all knowledge claims virtually beg to be subjected to a "hermeneutic of suspicion" to uncover the social, economic, and political ends a particular claim is serving. Thus comes the narratival demand, not merely because narrative has a persuasive power that rivals propositional statements but because there are constant social and personal demands to understand the wider context of interest and purpose now always at hand. It is the very construction of a narrative that mixes yet another level of decision-making as to the contents of that human story to embody reasons for commitment that make contemporary knowledge claims rhetorical and narrative events. For many, such processes of narration take on features regarded as forms of modern myth-making.[9]

At literary, philosophical, and finally theological levels of discourse, questions of narrative interest and purpose become acutely important when discerning the limits and functions of truth claims. What a novelist, poet, or literary interpreter means by belief in truth, and what a philosopher means by truth, is communicated by narratival means: Belief and myth become coterminus since the framework of the narrative suggests or exemplifies for the reader how belief in a truth claim can or ought to be embraced and embodied. Can theology be an exception to the mythic character of narrative truth claims? Since Barth recognized that theology as church dogmatics could not be other than narratival as testimonial while it strove to be objective about objective revelation, it certainly did not offer itself as mythic and does not intend to offer myth. One way of getting at this intention is evident in the careful hermeneutics of Hans Frei.[10] Frei was acutely aware that both the history of Christianity and most of all its Scriptures could be and were read by non-Christians as myth, or more modernly as fiction. Indeed, that he perceived this is as much a witness to the actuality of a secular mind-set as any. Of course, Frei also worked under the conditions of the American absence of a national religion, where conscious intellectual avoidance of religion was and is both a possibility and a reality. Theology at least had to deal with the consciousness that its truth claims could be read in an entirely secular way and thus regarded as fiction in the reductionistic sense, leaving these claims not to be believed or not believable. But this was before the postmodernist redefining of fiction as myth and as therefore ideally truth-conveying. Frei's hermeneutical strategy includes a regard for the multiple audiences of theology

---

9. Of course, in many respects the resort to myth is a default strategy in a time of extreme disaffection with metaphysics. This disaffection has many causes, not least of which was why Barth rejected especially its idealist forms as involving "harmful and dangerous deceptions" (*CD* II/1:73). But more fundamentally, Barth viewed metaphysics as always an exercise in anthropological speculation, no matter how much discoursing upon God might be found there; see *CD* II/1:269f.

10. Cf. the outstanding discussion in David E. Demson, *Hans Frei and Karl Barth: Different Ways of Reading Scripture* (Grand Rapids: Eerdmans, 1997), 25–40, which argues for the "indefiniteness of myth" as incompatible with the particularity of the gospel.

and their overlapping perspectives, both believing and secularist. But the problem with this approach is that it is too conscious of critical categories and interpretive strategies to ever enunciate a theology. As the testimony of Christian faith, Christian theology ultimately hazards to give full expression of its living commitments to what it has taken as the objective truth of God revealed in Christ, along with the full range of its obedience-based practices in proclamation, worship, and mission.

Barth answers the question of Christian theology as myth in the negative, on grounds inherent to his understanding of the nature of God and God's relation to the world. He does not believe that it is necessary for theology to account for readers who do not believe the Christian message. He also does not believe that a certain kind of descriptiveness or rhetorical strategy, even one following rules of "speech-act theory," according to an interest in remystification and/or a purpose in cultivating religious believing, compehends Christian faith and theology at all correctly. Some passages of Scripture display sensitivity to the distinguishing of the Scripture-faith nexus from a myth-belief one. First Timothy 1:4 sums up most acutely what is viewed to be at stake, that "μύθοις καὶ γενεαλογίαις ἀπεράντοις" (myths and endless genealogies) do nothing but "promote speculations" (ἐκζητήσεις) rather than the divine training that is known by faith. In addition, 2 Peter 1:16 contrasts the apostolic proclamation by an eyewitness of Christ to the "σεσοφισμένοις μύθοις" (cleverly devised myths) or sophistries of myth from other traditions. There is no case in the New Testament in which "myth" is a category corresponding to the truth of revelation in Christ.

For Barth, the mythic is to be rejected as an aspect of theological understanding and formulation on account of the eternity of God. This is not a nontemporal eternity but the eternal uninterruptible duration of God's being.

> What distinguishes eternity from time is the fact that there is in Him no opposition or competition or conflict, but peace between origin, movement and goal, between present, past and future, between "not yet," "now" and "no more," between rest and movement, potentiality and actuality, whither and when, here and there, this and that. In him all things are simul, held together by the omnipotence of His knowing and willing, a totality without gap or rift, free from the threat of death under which time, our time, stands. It is not the case, then, that in eternity all these distinctions do not exist.
>
> . . . Eternity is not the negation of time *simpliciter.* On the contrary, time is absolutely presupposed in it. Eternity is the negation of time only because and to the extent that it is first and foremost God's time and therefore real time, in the same way as God's omnipresence is not simply the negation of our space, but first and foremost is positively God's space and therefore real space.[11]

11. *CD* II/1:612–13.

Because of God's possession of all things already in himself, particularly time and space, he may graciously endow creation with its own created time and space. That our time and space have, as their condition, God's real and boundless time and space means that what we have we have by God's creative and gracious act. Creatureliness from the Creator establishes a kind of correspondence where we can know that we are known by God in terms that correspond to God's knowing of us and our world. Under the conditions of created, graced time, there is interruption, fleetingness, separations of past from present, present from future, future from past through forgetting, deaths, and destruction—stoppage of time for this and that. But not with God. God is beginning and end without end in himself, in the triunity of his being, in eternal living relation that is uninterrupted duration. This is his eternity out of which he grants us ours.

God's gracious creation of time for us is not at all the full extent of his relation with our time, temporality. Through the incarnation of the eternal Son, our temporality has been taken up into the life of God, without any diminution of God's Godness and greatness. God in Jesus Christ becomes time-ful in the reconciling work that his union with human nature achieves for himself. Indeed, on account of Jesus Christ, God is fully temporal in the creaturely sense so that his time is now truly our time. This is the capacity of eternity in itself, that it can absorb created, bounded, interruptible time into itself through the participation of God in our lives and through his assuming creaturely, human life and applying time to himself, for our sakes and for his. Barth describes the relation of divine eternity to creaturely time in terms of "the pre-temporality, supra-temporality and post-temporality of eternity. . . . God himself, who has the power to exist before, above and after time, before its beginning, above its duration and after its end."[12] Time flows within God's eternity such that, rather than a kind of dissolving droplet in an eternal, timeless sea, it is a striating wave within the immense, all-temporal, uninterrupted flow of God's duration.

Out of this discussion of God's eternity with human time, Barth presents his rejection of theology as myth:

> "He who was, and is, and is to come." . . . Not figuratively or metaphorically, but in a divine, unsurpassable reality which is not to be relativised. We have good reason to give clear emphasis to this truth and therefore to the concepts of the pre-temporality, supra-temporality and post-temporality of the eternal God. For a great deal depends on this truth and on the legitimacy of these concepts. It is only if they are true and legitimate that the whole content of the Christian message—creation as the basis of man's existence, established by God, reconciliation as the renewal of his existence accomplished by God, redemption as the revelation of his existence to be consummated by God (and therefore as the revelation of the meaning of

---

12. Ibid., 619.

His creation)—can be understood as God's Word of truth and not as the myth of a pious or impious self-consciousness, the comfortless content of some human monologue which lays no real claim upon us, the substance of a well-meant pastoral fiction, mere wishful thinking or a terrifying dream. The Christian message cannot be distinguished from a myth or dream of this kind unless God's eternity has temporality in the sense described, and God is really pre-temporal, supra-temporal and post-temporal. If God's eternity is not understood in this way the Christian message cannot be proclaimed in any credible way or received by faith. . . . Without God's complete temporality the content of the Christian message has no shape. Its proclamation is only an inarticulate mumbling. Therefore everything depends on whether God's temporality is the simple truth which cannot be attacked from any quarter because it has its basis in God Himself, which is not then a mere appearance, a bubble constructed by human feeling or thought.[13]

Barth could not be any clearer about the nature of myth: It is a construct with a possible claim to truth only at some psychological level. Instead, his plea is for an understanding of the Christian message as the "simple truth" that is unassailable on any other basis, including the hermeneutical narratology of myth. What is at stake is the actual, temporal, and spatial renewal and redemption of creation as much as cosmic event as original creation. The eternity of this God who has become temporally related to creation through Jesus Christ makes for a saving relationship based in eternity's "readiness for time." Nothing about created time incapacitates God from participating, indeed, from entering into it as a creaturely participant while remaining God, albeit in the humbled manner of the servant Lord, Jesus Christ.

But Barth is also intent on expounding the nonmythic character of the Christian message, which "binds and comforts" human beings—apparently only as the truth that engenders such faith in a reality nothing short of redemption. This message

attests itself as God's Word and therefore destroys, so to speak, from within the suspicion that we have to do only with the imaginative drama of a myth. But because this is the case, it is quite impossible to deny to God's eternity the possession of preparedness for time and therefore temporality. It is for this reason that this is true, and the concepts of pre-temporality, supra-temporality and post-temporality are legitimate because they simply spell out and analyse what the Christian message guarantees to be the Word of God and therefore the truth. This message can neither be proclaimed nor believed as the truth without the proclaiming and believing of these statements about God. They are not simply inferences from the Gospel. As certain as the Gospel tells us the truth about God, they are elements in the Gospel itself and as such. The Gospel itself and as such cannot be spoken and take shape without these statements being made and this understanding of the divine eternity forcing itself upon us.[14]

13. Ibid., 620.
14. Ibid., 621.

Now here we also detect a way of speaking about the truth of God that has become so familiar in the theology of Thomas Torrance—divine reality "forcing itself upon us" as our knowledge of this reality's truth is directly and simply communicated to us through the gospel. As expressed in the words of Revelation 1:4, 8; 4:8, this therefore is part of the gospel, as is the entire New Testament for Barth: "ὁ ὢν καὶ ὁ ἦν καὶ ὁ ἐρχόμενος" (who was and is and is to come). And of course, the priority here is the temporal ontology of the ὁ ὢν, the three Greek letters directly associated with every presentation and representation of the παντοκράτωρ, Pantocrator, ruler of all things, the One who is the Ἐγώ εἰμι of Sinai and the Johnanine Gospel (Exod. 3:14; John 4:26; 6:35; 8:12; 9:5; 10:7, 38; 11:25; 13:19; 14:6; 15:1; 18:5), "τὸ Ἄλφα καὶ τὸ Ὦ" (the Alpha and the Omega; Rev. 1:8; 2:16; 22:13) in orthodox thought and life.

One understands the meaning of cultural and literary experience, communal bonds of memory and ritual, but these cannot be the basis of Christian faith in the least. This is the great danger in local expressions of Christian culture and popular belief. In North America and Britain, this has particularly been found in the evangelical fascination with Christian fiction, whether C. S. Lewis's Chronicles of Narnia or more recently the immensely popular and influential Left Behind series of Tim LaHaye and Jerry Jenkins or the most widely distributed piece of myth-making, overlaying the spoken text of Scripture, the *Jesus Film* of global mission. Of course, these all have their counterparts in Romantic[15] and Victorian literatures of the nineteenth century and represent the ultimate domestication of the gospel in the mythic constructionism of religious imagination, regardless of its pious intentions. The most striking thing about the Left Behind series is that it is read as a form of theology, as a resource in Christian eschatology. The authors link the reading of their painfully poor narratives of the end times smoothly with discussions of eschatological passages of Scripture in the church. By the same token, numerous Christian college and seminary teachers rely on the mythopoeia of Lewis, J. R. R. Tolkien, George MacDonald, and others as a resource for knowing the Christian faith. Of course, once knowing the Christian faith becomes attached to the media or reenchantment and remythologization, use of almost any media to communicate the gospel seems to be justified.

In the case of the *Jesus Film,* celebrated for its having been shown to over one billion people, it is not so much a problem of dramatic portrayal of the life of Jesus as it is that because its auditory text is taken from the Gospel of Luke, it is presented as the proclamation of the gospel. The drastic mistake in this, however, is that the written text has been wedded to a visual text so that part of the claim of those who use this film for proclamation, inadvertently but surely, is that Jesus looks like this man in the film. The irony of the film

---

15. Frederick C. Beiser, *The Romantic Imperative: The Concept of Early German Romanticism* (Cambridge: Harvard University Press, 2004), surveys the powerful developments of poetic, mythopoeic intentionality in literature and interpretation.

is that for the iconoclastic evangelicals who made it, its iconographic power and therefore sacramental intention are far more imposing than any Eastern Orthodox or Roman Catholic icon. At one level, the *Jesus Film* is yet another manifestation of the belief that Christians have at their disposal sacramental media, which in this case convey the gospel for faith. The problem is that the gospel is not to be communicated with additives: "So faith comes from what is heard, and what is heard comes through the word of Christ" (Rom. 10:17). And part of the reason why the gospel is strictly an auditory medium[16] is so that something of the *simul* of God's pretemporal, supratemporal, and post-temporal relation to us cannot first and finally be detected until the fullness of the eschaton, God's posttemporal, comes upon us.

The Beauty Irreducible to Myth

Although it cannot be said that Barth constructs an argument that would render a mythic interpretation of theology unjustified, his point is clear: The reality of God and our relation in time to God, if true, make theology much more than myth. To the extent that those who might be interested in Christianity seek to find in it another classic example of human aspiration toward "the true, the good, and the beautiful," it is conspicuous that on his own terms Barth, after his lengthy discussion of God's perfection and temporality, moves to his glory. In the glory of God as expressed in the gospel is the sum of divine perfections and the divine self-sufficiency in revelation to us and for us; yet the true and the good in the flow of God's purpose in Christ reach their expression in his love, not in mystical visions and mythic descriptions of heavenly opulence.

> If we can and must say that God is beautiful, to say this is to say how He enlightens and convinces and persuades us. It is to describe not merely the naked fact of His revelation or its power, but the shape and form in which it is a fact and is power. It is to say that God has this superior force, this power of attraction, which speaks for itself, which wins and conquers, in the fact that He is beautiful, divinely beautiful, beautiful in His own way, in a way that is His alone, beautiful as the unattainable primal beauty, yet really beautiful. He does not have it, therefore, merely as a fact or a power. Or rather, He has it as a fact and a power in such a way that He acts as the one who gives pleasure, creates desire and rewards with enjoyment. And He does it because He is pleasant, desirable,

16. Of course, the gospel is based in a written text. But in the case of the Bible, we must remember its part in the history of books, which made certain speech transportable and certain arrangements of words precisely repeatable to an audience. Indeed, it is only after the fifth century A.D. that reading books silently became common for those who could read. The experience of silent reading, however, does not in any way negate what the book and its lettering represent: a relatively permanent form of a speech, whatever the genre, whatever the report.

full of enjoyment, because He is the One who is pleasant, desirable, full of enjoyment, because first and last He alone is that which is pleasant, desirable and full of enjoyment. God loves us as the One who is worthy of love as God. This is what we mean when we say that God is beautiful.[17]

Barth goes on to reflect on the great passage concerning the *"pulchritudo"* of God in Augustine's *Confessions* (10.27.38): "Late have I loved Thee, Beauty ever ancient and ever new! Late have I loved Thee!" And yet Barth also points out that Augustine did not attribute the idea of beauty to God, but that God is beautiful because he is God.[18] He considers the evident discomfort of generations of theologians over the category of beauty and therefore discomfort that desire and pleasure are so fundamental to its experience. Indeed, the connection with nineteenth-century Romanticism and theology make it one of the chief pathways to the domestication of theology, bringing God "into the sphere of man's oversight and control, into proximity to the ideal of all human striving." Barth certainly disallows any sense in which an "aestheticism" would put the knowledge of God "under the denominator of the idea of the beautiful," particularly because "it is not a leading concept," since it is always one of the descriptors for divine glory. And yet, as in the quote above, the pleasantness, desirableness, and fullness of enjoyment that is God is the divine beauty. Beauty is not an autonomous reality, just as truth and goodness are not. All three are dimensions of the life and attributes of God, above all, which is love and the inevitable joy that this produces. Indeed, this experience of the beauty of God in the joy of knowing God is what Barth calls "the evangelical element in the evangel."[19]

Beyond the above, it is perhaps the realism of Barth's theology that guards against a strategy of remythologization and reenchantment as the overarching task of theology. No one has explored the theological realism of Barth more than Bruce McCormack in his study of Barth's "critically realistic dialectical theology."[20] Although this intellectual biography is not the full critical biography, which is yet to be undertaken, it is certainly the most thorough treatment of Barth's background and development as a theologian up through his mid-career.

17. *CD* II/1:650–51.

18. Augustine, *On True Religion* 32, 59.

19. Ibid., 651–55. At the same time, Barth emphatically denies that obsessive concern with sin should be allowed to blot out the biblical emphasis on the beauty of God. Acknowledging that desire is deformed and wicked in the human being, the supreme desirability of God and pleasure in God must always be affirmed. "This is a fact, and the radically evangelical character of the biblical message has to be denied if this is rejected" (654). The evangelical, however, must also be reminded by Barth of the beauty that is the joyousness of the theological task: "A theological proof is in itself a *delectation*." One can best perceive this beyond being able to converse about it, and yet not to perceive it is a "good cause for repentance" on the part of any theologian (657).

20. Bruce L. McCormack, *Karl Barth's Critically Realistic Dialectical Theology: Its Genesis and Development, 1909–1936* (Oxford: Clarendon, 1995).

McCormack has made his mark in Barth studies particularly at the point of showing the great continuity of Barth's thought, overturning an assumed paradigm of a radical break between an earlier orientation to dialectical method and a later orientation to analogical method. In his most in-depth discussion of the topic, McCormack points out that Barth's realism must not be confused with the realism of the Catholic theological tradition, stemming from Aquinas's *analogia entis*. The mythical being is nowhere in sight; anyhow, the reason for the rejection of Aquinas—on down even to Przywara—is that the Catholic knowledge claim regarding God is fundamentally based on the created similitude between God and the human being. Regardless of considerations given to the "greater dissimilitude," the natural connection is still the basis of the appeal for theological understanding. Such an appeal, however, makes revelation superfluous, and it also contradicts the very content of revelation as the necessary act on God's part, affording to humanity what it could not know on account of sin and making humanity the redemptive vehicle for human salvation.

God's Attributes and Person as Triune Self-Opening

The doctrine of the Trinity flows out of the life of Jesus Christ as the personal presence of the Son of God incarnate and his historically revealed relationship with God the Father and God the Holy Spirit. This is the grounding of the *Church Dogmatics'* christocentrism, not christomonism (which would make it non-trinitarian). The knowledge of the Trinity is not something pieced together through an isolation of theological concepts that are amalgamated into a triadic complex concept of being suggestive of physical, mathematical, and psychological analogies. Rather, it is the life of Christ, the gospel narratives together with their theologies of the embodied, humanized *Logos,* that engenders an unfolding of the knowledge of God into a living multiplicity and complexity of relations that is the eternal and perfect life of the one true God. Certainly, Barth can use classic formulations for this doctrine:

> We are speaking about the God who is eternally the Father, who without origin or begetting is Himself the origin and begetter, and therefore undividedly the beginning, succession and end, all at once in His own essence. We are speaking about the God who is also eternally the Son, who is begotten of the Father and yet of the same essence with Him, who as begotten of the Father is also undividedly beginning, succession and end, all at once in His own essence. We are speaking about God who is also eternally the Spirit, who proceeds from the Father and the Son but is of the same essence as both, who as the Spirit of the Father and the Son is also undividedly beginning, succession and end, all at once in His own essence. It is this "all," this God, who is the eternal God, really the eternal God.[21]

21. *CD* II/1:615.

In such a statement, the essential truth of the one God eternally subsisting in three divine Persons gives rise to such a formulation. Distinctions and identity are carefully balanced, and their dynamic relations are maintained, as in all classic, orthodox definitions. Barth has certainly come in for critique by the social trinitarian Jürgen Moltmann as insufficiently scriptural and relational in his articulations, as too Augustinian, and therefore as fundamentally monotheistic. Because Barth sees the person of God as no more than an expansive, repetitive, solitary subject, he is, if fully trinitarian, a "trinitarian monarchist."[22] Granted, early in the *CD* Barth is reticent to use the terminology of "person" because it has been so determined in its meaning by the German philosophical psychology of the nineteenth century. In this modern tradition, stemming from Johann Gottlieb Fichte and others, person is defined apart from relations, and this seemed to Barth to put any relational understanding of person in jeopardy. This move was strange on Barth's part for someone who not only commandeered language through exhaustive redefinition but even rehabilitated theological language that had been lost from the memory of many of his contemporaries. Barth instead used "three modes of being" *(Seinsweisen)* eternally within the one Being of God, "the Revealer, the Revelation, and the Revealedness."[23]

The backdrop for Barth's thinking in terms of eternal "modes" of divine being reflects his uncovering of the historic theological struggle to match divine simplicity of substance with multiplicity, diversity, and complexity in God. Classically understood, the perfections of God would preclude any definitions that indicate anything other than pure undifferentiated being. Indeed, even a multiplicity of perfections or attributes eternally qualifying the divine being could be regarded as in tension with his eternally and utterly simple substance. The fact that theology acknowledges divine attributes was seen as stemming economically from the divine anthropopathic condescension to create and govern the universe. In this regard, Barth alludes to statements by numerous theologians, from John of Damascus to Aquinas to Calvin, where God's "*nuda*

---

22. Jürgen Moltmann, *The Trinity and the Kingdom of God: The Doctrine of God,* trans. Margaret Kohl (Minneapolis: Fortress, 1993), 139–44.

23. *CD* I/1:295–347. No one uncovers Barth's reasoning for the use of *Seinsweise* better than Alan Torrance. With great erudition, although concentrating his attention only on *CD* I/1, Torrance points out that Barth puts forth reasoning for using this term when it is difficult to explain the otherwise exclusive use of *hypostasis* in the doctrine of the Trinity. Further, Barth uses *Seinsweise* in relational ways, including perichoretic *koinōnia* and dynamic mutuality in divine love. Some confusion arises in connection with "absolutisation" of terminology, and here it seems that Torrance is on shaky ground. Not only *hypostasis* but also *homoousion* could be left out of absolutely necessary terms. The example of Alisdair Heron, pitting "Word made flesh" as necessary against *homousion* as nonnecessary, at least confuses primarily christological terminology with trinitarian terms. Thus, Torrance's suggestion of balancing a "doxological model" with "equally important New Testament notions" without exploring Barth's further expositions of Scripture and formulations finally turns out to be unsatisfactory. Cf. Alan J. Torrance, *Persons in Communion: An Essay on Trinitarian Description and Human Participation, with Special Reference to Volume One of Karl Barth's Church Dogmatics* (Edinburgh: T & T Clark, 1996), 251–62.

essentia" (pure being) is the fundamental truth of God's nature. Indeed, the normativity of denying that the divine attributes are essential to the being of God is overwhelming in the history of theology, so much that the attributes identifiable in Scripture are entirely a matter of divine initiative in created relations. Only in the nineteenth century among the theologians F. H. R. Frank, G. Thomasius, and I. A. Dorner do full affirmations appear to the effect that "the attributes of God are nothing other than His being."[24] Taking his cue from them, Barth goes on to explicate the attributes of God according to their multiplicity, individuality, and diversity. The being of the one God alone possesses these eternal attributes and exists nevertheless in utter simplicity since there is no division in God; therefore, they are rooted in God's being and not in his relationship to other beings. Barth moves to the Scriptures, to Gospel narratives, which Moltmann seems to have overlooked, and asserts, "If we do not wish to deviate from Scripture, the unity of God must be understood as this unity of His love and freedom which is dynamic and, to that extent, diverse."[25] To probe the depths of this entire matter of the diversity of God in his attributes and therefore in the multiplicity of his personhood, Barth advances a number of questions reflecting upon the classic distinctions between what is "incommunicable" and what is "communicable" in relation to creatures:

> For which of the attributes of God, in which as Creator, Reconciler and Redeemer He allows His creatures to share, is not, as His own, utterly incommunicable from the creaturely point of view, i.e., communicable only by the miracle of grace? And again, which of these incommunicable attributes has not God nevertheless communicated to the creature in that His Word was made flesh? Is not God's mercy completely unfathomable and inaccessible to us? And has He not implanted His eternity utterly in our hearts? In His Son God has opened up to us and given us all, His own inmost self. How then can His sovereign freedom be understood as a limitation of His love? How can it be sought elsewhere than in this love itself? . . . God must be recognised as eternal love. . . . He must be understood as the freedom personally entering our world of time. What He is there in the height for us and for our sakes, here in the depths He is also in Himself. And we are speaking of God only when we know that He is both—and both in this reciprocal relation, and differentiated unity.[26]

Far from reasoning from either monotheistic or Christian idealist perspectives, Barth keeps in mind the entirety of the gospel events as well as the biblical concepts of divine identity. Of the biblical concepts, Barth is particularly interested in holding divine love and holiness together.[27] But even more

24. *CD* II/1:330.
25. Ibid., 343.
26. Ibid., 345.
27. In a striking section, Barth writes, "Our concern is that at this point the truth emerges that God's righteousness does not really stand alongside His mercy, but that as revealed in its

pointedly, the death of Christ reveals the attributes of God, God's participation in the condition of the creation and human creatures, and, above all, the trinitarian life:

> The meaning of the death of Jesus Christ is that there God's condemning and punishing righteousness broke out, really smiting and piercing human sin, man as sinner, and sinful Israel. It did really fall on the sin of Israel, our sin and us sinners. It did so in such a way that in what happened there (not to Israel, or to us, but to Jesus Christ) the righteousness of God which we have offended was really revealed and satisfied. Yet it did so in such a way that it did not happen to Israel or to us, but for Israel and for us. What was suffered there on Israel's account and ours, was suffered for Israel and for us. The wrath of God which we had merited, by which we must have been annihilated and would long since have been annihilated, was not in our place borne and suffered as though it had smitten us and yet in such a way that it did not smite us and can no more smite us. The reason why the No spoken on Good Friday is so terrible, but why there is already concealed in it the Eastertide Yes of God's righteousness, is that He who on the cross took upon Himself and suffered the wrath of God was no other than God's own Son, and therefore the eternal God Himself in the unity with human nature which He freely accepted in His transcendent mercy.[28]

At this point, the Scripture texts Barth marshals all correlate with God's self-revelation on the cross as man for us and for himself, the expiation and propitiation on our behalf (John 3:16; Rom. 8:3, 32; 2 Cor. 8:9; Gal. 2:20; 4:4–5; Phil. 2:6–8; Titus 2:14). But also the act that fulfills the inner trinitarian counsel of God's will, that God should take the sinful condition and the righteous punishment of humanity on himself to reverse this condition and finalize this judgment for the sake of saving rather than annihilating human beings, both Jewish and non-Jewish. Barth's embrace of the scriptural theology and theological traditions of substitutionary and propitiatory atonement is arresting given his modern context. It is not surprising that his contemporaries and ours so often find him hopelessly beyond the pale of rational limits in religious and philosophical thought. He is simply following the trajectory

---

necessary connexion, according to Scripture, with the plight of the poor and wretched, it is itself God's mercy. Just because He is righteous God has mercy, condescending sympathetically to succour those who are utterly in need of His help, who without it would in fact be lost. God is righteous in Himself, doing what befits Him and is worthy of Him, defending and glorying His divine being, in the fact that He is our righteousness, that He procures right for those who in themselves have no righteousness, whose own righteousness is rather disclosed by Him to be unrighteousness, yet whom He does not leave to themselves, to whom rather He gives Himself in His own divine righteousness and therefore becomes the ground on which, against their own merit and worth and solely by His merit and worth, called away from themselves and summoned to surrender themselves to His will, they can truly stand and live. This standing and living of man is not, therefore, threatened but in the true sense established by the righteousness of God when in his confrontation by God man must necessarily confess that . . . he is a sinner" (ibid., 387).

28. Ibid., 396–97.

from the prophets, the apostles, the confessions, and the central dogmas of the Christian faith.

What Barth is doing here also speaks comprehensively to the matter of God's relationship with the creation and his action in the world. In the same way scriptural narratives and concepts become foundational to the knowledge of God, quite against the metaphysical ways of thinking about God, *via positiva* or *via negativa,* kataphatically or apophatically, particularly with reference to the being of God as speculatively approached, beyond attribution. As we have already noted, God is who he is internally and externally as portrayed in Scripture. The narratives and concepts of God in Scripture generate their own foundation in contrast with others that are philosophically determined, whether monist, pantheist, panentheist, process, or Openness.

Jesus Christ, crucified yet rising the third day, is his own paradigm for the God-human-world relation and for the way of God's action in the world. By focusing on the person and work of Christ, distinctions such as Creator/creature, omnipotence, freedom, and love find their definitive context, their truest explanation and portrayal of what these concepts mean to us and to God. In a most arresting passage, Barth sums things up through his category of "double proof of omnipotence" in Jesus Christ:

> Because He was God Himself, He could subject Himself to the severity of God. And because He was God Himself He did not have to succumb to the severity of God. God has to be severe to be true to Himself in His encounter with man, and thus to be true also to man. God's wrath had to be revealed against the ungodliness and unrighteousness of men. But only God could carry through this necessary revelation of His righteousness without involving an end of all things. Only God Himself could bear the wrath of God. Only God's mercy was capable of bearing the pain to which the creature existing in opposition to Him is subject. Only God's mercy could so feel this pain as to take it into the very heart of His being. And only God's mercy was strong enough not to be annihilated by this pain. And this that could happen only by the divine mercy is just what did happen on the cross of Golgotha: that double proof of omnipotence in which God did not abate the demands of His righteousness but showed Himself equal to His own wrath; on the one hand by submitting to it and on the other by not being consumed by it. In virtue of this omnipotence God's mercy could be at one and the same time the deepest and sincerest pity and inflexible and impassible divine strength. He could yield to His own inexorable righteousness and by this very surrender maintain Himself as God. He could reveal Himself at once as the One who as the servant of all bore the punishment of death which we had deserved, and the One who as the Lord of all took from death its power and for ever vanquished and destroyed it. In this twofold sense God's righteousness triumphed in the death of Jesus Christ.[29]

29. Ibid., 400.

The entire range of doctrinal issues is summarized here: the vicarious representation of God in his own humanity for the sake of our humanity. God is at once "passible" *(des Leidens fähig)* and has deepest "compassion" *(Mitleid)* and yet in the exercise of his power is "unalterable and unmovable" (a better translation than "impassible," as found above).[30] Of course, theology based on the narratives of the life of Jesus and the doctrines about this life from Scripture simply will not comport with Neoplatonic, Aristotelian, Kantian, Hegelian, or process philosophies. The Kantian and neo-Kantian, the Schleiermacherian, Ritschlian, Troeltschian, Herrmannian trajectories looking to reduce the narratives to ethical norms, signs, and symbols of human aspiration for the "kingdom of God" in history or in the intensely religious heart of the human being are wholly inadequate to the matter. But also inadequate are those classic metaphysical trajectories of the divine absolute, existing in transcendent distance and utter simplicity of being, or those in which the divine initiator is radically immanent, so attached to the natural world that some compatibilist, Openness,[31] or process scenario is employed to model the God-world relation.

30. Ibid., 450.

31. The curious theological phenomenon of Openness theism in American evangelical contexts is built on various tendencies in late-twentieth-century theistic philosophy of religion, which emphasize models of divine relationality and bounded interactions with nature and the cosmos. The starting point for this perspective is a determinism and freedom dichotomy that must be decided for the latter pole. Connected to the issue of God's influence in a world in which human beings are bounded but truly free agents is the question of the degree of divine knowledge of future events. In this modeling of the God-world relation, what can be said about God's involvement, either at the point of knowledge or action, is determined entirely by the logically possible conditions in the world as discerned by a particular philosopher. This is the approach found in, e.g., Richard Swinburne, *Providence and the Problem of Evil* (Oxford: Clarendon, 1998), 130–34. The Canadian theologian Clark Pinnock has explored concepts of a relational God who is highly passible and mutable, given the random and free-agency conditions of nature and human beings. "God rules the world in such a way as to allow for creaturely input" means that "the counsel of God is not timeless and fixed." Pinnock appeals to the narratives of God in Scripture that present God as repenting and acting unexpectedly and himself surprised by events as they take place. God's involvement in the world, therefore, entails fundamental risks that he is willing to bear and, although Pinnock does not emphasize this much, that he is willing for human beings to bear as well. His most outstanding work on the subject is Clark Pinnock, *Most Moved Mover: A Theology of God's Openness* (Grand Rapids: Baker, 2001), 55, 59. Pinnock's younger colleague, John Sanders, explores the model of divine risk-taking in a more systematic way and by doing so extends the metaphor of God as risk-taker into an overall theological hermeneutic. The limitations of the logically possible give shape to his entire project and, like Pinnock, he must carve his way through the preponderance of classic theological positions from Irenaeus to Aquinas to Luther to modern theology—the "no-risk model"—since the "risk model," while always a known possibility, was rarely adopted. Sanders does seem to indicate that the future is uncertain for God and for human beings, even God's own victory, but God's victory is something for which God and humans can hope. What is at stake for us is not substituting "belief in an immutable principle for trust in a personal God, so we must not exchange a demand for rational certitude for hope in the living God." The curious point here is that Sanders equates the theological understanding of the certainty of faith in the promises of God and the rational certainty in observable phenomena or logical argument. Cf.

It is quintessentially at this point that Barth as exegete of Scripture and biblical theologian of the doctrinal conceptuality of Scripture is decisive for the whole of the *Church Dogmatics.*

The question of divine immutability and creaturely mutability is discussed by Barth, not in terms of an underlying dualism or monism but in terms of trinitarian life and the constancy of God's love:

> The fact of resistance to God in the sphere of creation does not involve any conflict in God Himself. It is a mark of the divine nature as distinct from that of the creature that in it a conflict with Himself is not merely ruled out, but is inherently impossible. If this were not so, if there did not exist perfect, original and ultimate peace between the Father and the Son by the Holy Spirit, God would not be God. Any God in conflict with Himself is bound to be a false God. On the other hand, it is a mark of created being as distinct from divine that in it conflict with God and therefore mortal conflict with itself is not ruled out, but is a definite possibility even if it is only the impossible possibility, the possibility of self-annulment and therefore its own destruction. Without this possibility of defection or of evil, creation would not be distinct from God and therefore not really His creation. . . . A creature freed from the possibility of falling away would not really be living as a creature. It could only be a second God—and as no second God exists, it could only be God Himself. . . . It follows inevitably only from the incomprehensible fact that the creature rejects the preserving grace of God. What belongs to the nature of the creature is that it is not physically hindered from doing this. If it were hindered in this way, it could not exist at all as a creature. In that case, grace would not be grace and the creature would inevitably be God Himself.
>
> Further, no conflict in God is involved in the fact that He for His part opposes the opposition of the creature to Himself. . . . He is not diverted from His purpose. He is not mocked. He does not allow limitations to be set [beset] Him by the opposition of the creature. And He certainly does not allow Himself to

John Sanders, *The God Who Risks: A Theology of Providence* (Downers Grove, Ill.: InterVarsity, 1998), 235; and Gregory A. Boyd, *God of the Possible: A Biblical Introduction to the Open View of God* (Grand Rapids: Baker, 2000). Curiously, neither Pinnock nor Sanders engages Barth in these matters. The problem with extending the metaphor of risk, so that risk-taking actually becomes one of the names for God, is its vagary as a term. Risk and associations of probabilistic logic evoke further associations with, for example, military strategy in terms of minimizing casualties, of medics on the battlefield necessarily practicing triage, of an insurance actuary calculating and minimizing losses, ironically, even of the crapshoot approach to life that leads to the tragic "eat and drink, for tomorrow we die" (Isa. 22:13; 1 Cor. 15:32). Risk, in a world of loss, is primarily a conservative's game and is driven entirely by self-interest, however virtuous the intent. The problem with the model of Open theism is that it suffers both from philosophical bias and terminological weakness. Such works in philosophical theology will continue, in this case stimulated largely by offensive models of God from opposing views read into the traditions of Christian theology. In responding to revelation in Christ and in finding one's way through the great tradition of Christian theology, there is little that has not been treated in great depth, and there are few points where new questions cannot uncover unforeseen inferences that deliver new insight together with coherency in the tradition.

be drawn into the conflict. . . . The salvation revealed and given by Him to the world in this new work does not in any sense consist in making concessions of any kind or withdrawing in the face of it, as if He had to take its defection seriously in the sense that, faced with a *fait accompli,* He could only be different, retracting or qualifying the law of His will, or letting mercy take the place of justice and the like. . . . It is not by His abandoning His opposition, but by His maintaining and exercising it that the world is saved from the evil of its own opposition.[32]

The constancy of God in his vital freedom and love toward humanity is not rooted in either a law of being or a cosmic law of any kind. Even a kind of abstracted triadic logic of interpersonal, person-constituting relations or of sociality cannot be said to be at work here. As illuminating as social normativity and relational values may be even within the context of ecclesial traditions,[33] they can never take priority in theological reasoning. At base the contours, features, communications, nominatives, and subjunctives of the life of Jesus engender everything that we know of the trinitarian life of God, but as importantly, they constitute a structure of knowledge and systematic reasoning that of themselves are generative of trinitarian theology in all its richness and without remainder. However, we have been following Barth's reasoning on the constancy and omnipotence of God at the point of his gracious opposition to all sinful opposition of humanity and the certainty of his victory in retaining humanity as his and unto his glory. But Barth has also been writing of the free omnipotence that engenders free humanity, so free that it can opt for self-destruction and divine wrath. Obviously there is the potential for tremendous stress in Barth's conceptuality between his account of the God who is determined to overcome human opposition and the God who is determined to let human beings decide against his decision to redeem and restore them. Surely this free choice and option of the human being is sinful when acted upon, just as any sin, and yet, Barth contends, sin—and one would assume this sin as well—"is already outstripped and overcome. . . . If He is the Creator and Lord of the world, this settles the fact that even in creation sin can only be the impossible

---

32. *CD* II/1:503–4.

33. Alan Torrance's basic approach acknowledges the power of language but under the pressure of divine reality as it is taken up in the life of the church: "In sum, the use of a theological term presupposes a community which provides the context of its use, that is, the rules of use of the term. Terms are used in the context of social participation with respect to which certain rules of use apply. . . . There is simply the language-game which is constituted, which 'takes place' within the Body of Christ by the Spirit and which we are brought to indwell as the means for the communion which stems from the triune life. The very articulation of the Trinity takes place, therefore, within this context. What has traditionally been conceived . . . as theological *pre-dication* might be more properly . . . interpreted as . . . theologically 'ex-pressive' (in that the meaning of our terms submits to the 'pressure' of the God-humanward dynamic) *post-dication*." He admits some clumsiness here, but the a posteriori nature of theological language, i.e., their derivation from faithful reading of Scripture, is clearly in view. Torrance, *Persons in Communion,* 336.

possibility, the possibility rejected by His sustaining grace."[34] Since we must understand the Trinity through the life and work of Christ, and through Christ the attributes of God through the revealing and reconciling work of God, we find ourselves at the heart of the matter in the heart of God. With God the Lord of all things at the beginning, he in the same way is determined to be Lord of all things, while being in a new way, through his Son, at the end of them as well. This is his immutability, "the Creator's saving opposition."[35]

The christocentricity of our knowledge of God through the narratives of Jesus indicate that

> God's work in Jesus Christ, as the centre and content, the presupposition and ground of creation and reconciliation makes clear to us that in Jesus Christ God Himself has become a creature. That is to say, He has become one with the creature, with man. He has not simply entered into fellowship as He did in creation, causing the creature to become and be as His creature, or as He does in reconciliation, befriending His fallen creature, or as He does in redemption, granting life in His perfect kingdom to His creature. Among all the events in which God in His free love has granted His fellowship to what He has created, this event is distinguished by the fact that in it, in Jesus Christ, He becomes one with the creature.
>
> He does this as the One He is because the incarnation is as such the confirmation of the triunity of God. Without abrogation of the divine unity, there is revealed in it the distinction of the Father and the Son, and also their fellowship in the Holy Spirit. He does it as the Creator because the incarnation is as such the confirmation of the distinctive reality of creation. . . . He does it finally as Reconciler and Redeemer, because the incarnation as such confirms and explains the fact that God has befriended and continually befriends fallen creation, and will lead it on to a full redemption. . . . To this extent it is the constancy of God which is revealed and which is recognisable in Jesus Christ.[36]

We are now seeing the great integrative power of Barth's systematic thinking, given already the intensity of his attention to the distinctiveness, depth, and richness of God's revelation in Christ. The christocentricity of the action of God is the basis of our trinitarian knowledge of God. The person of Christ is the locus of God's activity and as such the sign of his claim upon all of creation, since Christ is the Lord of all through whom all things were made and will be reconciled. The great question for Barth is the nature of human freedom under the reconciled relation, where the peace of Christ will reign but where peace can be both the fellowship of love and the pacification of opposition. Since God in his omnipotence and constancy is able to bring creation through its opposition to a place in Jesus Christ beyond any question of the perpetuation

34. *CD* II/1:505–6.
35. Ibid., 509.
36. Ibid., 514–15.

of that opposition, pacification is not the same as willing, repentant, exultant embrace of God in the fellowship of Father, Son, and Holy Spirit.

The crucial question arises as to God's exercise of his omnipotence and the destiny of free creatures. But here again, Barth is emphatic about following the self-revelation of God as it is found in Scripture. The attributes of God's holiness, righteousness, and wisdom coalesce around and imbue his omnipotence so that it is never naked power, never power without principle: His power is entirely determined by what is possible for him and by the fact that, primarily, morally, and justly, "there is nothing He can do *de jure* that He would not also do *de facto*."[37] Barth is also emphatic that the attributes of God, exemplified in omnipotence, hold for inner-trinitarian relations as well as for extra-trinitarian relations with creation. Along with this emphasis is the insight that post-Reformation theology, right down to Schleiermacher, had left out of its formulations the distinctions between the potentiality of God's action and the actuality of his action. Instead, theology had always stated the latter so that what God has done is the full exercise of his omnipotence, indeed, his omnicausality. But Barth counters:

> God and God alone has real power, all the real power. This is the statement of the Christian knowledge of God. The alternative that all the real power that we encounter (what we think real) is God's power is the statement of a blind deification of nature or history or fate, and finally of man himself. The identification of God's omnipotence with His actual omnicausality drives us to this deification, which is more or less concealed in it. That is why it is to be rejected. Certainly all true reality is based on God's omnipotence as the only true possibility. But what this true reality is cannot in any way be known a priori. It is God's revelation which decides what true reality is, and therefore what may and must be the occasion and object for our glorification of the divine omnipotence.[38]

The history of theological contemplation of divine omnipotence is fraught with as much abstraction as at any other point.

What can be and not be fathomed about the omnipotence of God finds speculative expression in overabundance. The wildly speculative nature of it can begin in something as apparently safe as the most basic law of noncontradiction in logic: $A \neq B$. But this is not a statement about God from God. Only God's Word can provide direction in this:

37. Ibid., 526.

38. Ibid., 531. In the discussion of God's omnipotence, Barth takes Aquinas's approach to task for its speculations regarding potentialities and contradictions. Barth concludes, "We cannot accept the idea of an absolutely possible or impossible by which even God's omnipotence is to be measured. On the contrary, we have to recognize that God's omnipotence is the substance of what is possible. Necessarily, then, we dispute the reasons offered by Thomas and his followers for rejecting the statement that even what is to be described as absurd in creation is the object of God omnipotence" (534).

We are not summoned by God's Word to assert that through God's omnipotence two and two could also be five. We will not be restrained from doing this out of respect for the law of contradiction. . . . It is well known that respect for the law of contradiction is not able in fact to protect us from this kind of absurdity and all kinds of much more serious absurdities. What can protect us is the fear of God, and the knowledge of the grace and patience and wisdom in which He has called the world into existence and causes it to consist in its nature and existence for His own sake and by Himself. It is this knowledge alone in the realm of creaturely reality and reason which can definitely and finally protect us from holding the impossible to be possible. . . . They are shown us by God's Word. It is there that we are told who and what God is and therefore what is possible and impossible for Him. Every meaningful statement about God's omnipotence must be able to base itself on God's Word. If it cannot do this, it is directed against God and is a denial of His omnipotence, even if, as far as its content goes, it seeks to say the most tremendous and wonderful things about the infinity of His power. If it is not based on God's Word, it denies His omnipotence just as definitely as a statement which denies or limits the capacity which according to His Word is His will and is therefore a real capacity. . . . The limit of what is possible, if it is to hold good and therefore if there is to be any certainty or security in the created realm, must be guaranteed by God's Word as the order of the divine grace, patience and wisdom which is set up and maintained by God because freely chosen by Him, and is therefore to be accepted and respected by us and not therefore doubted through any discoveries of our imagination.[39]

Scripture is not the rule for the knowledge of God because of a religious rule but because it alone is the place where God has made known what he has actually done in the completely free exercise of his will. Only in Scripture do we know the trinitarian form of divine omnipotence in the free love of God exercised through Christ and in the unity of the Holy Spirit to make, to sustain, and to redeem the creation. Indeed, omnipotence is the key to all of the divine attributes as the source of the activities by which God identifies himself for who he is with the particular qualities of being and personality that he possesses for himself and constantly expresses in creating and to the creation.

But appreciation of this requires the miracle of God's work in us, by which we say, "Thy will be done." God must create fellowship within us, the reality of a faith that is established by God's sovereignty over our wills. Anything else produces knowledge of a different god. What Barth is conveying is "a recognition that can be brought about only by the grace of His Holy Spirit."[40] This recognition comes about through a fellowship that God establishes with us by his Spirit. This fellowship is established by grace where

the Reconciler Himself is the reconciliation, and the reconciliation the Reconciler. The result of this insight is, then, that we may and must revere God's being

39. Ibid., 537.
40. Ibid., 548.

wholly under the form of His will, and in His will His being. This means that we cannot think of God at all without being summoned in the same instant to faith, obedience, gratitude, humility and joy.[41]

God is both his knowledge and his will. To truly know the will of God is to know God, for God gives himself in order that we may know his will. The gift and the Giver are one and the same (cf. the abundance of Barth's preferred texts here: Gen. 3:8–9; 1 Sam. 2:3; Pss. 1:6; 56:8; 90:8; 94:5–7; 121:4; 139:1–18; Isa. 40:27; Jer. 16:16–17; Hosea 5:3; Matt. 6:4, 6, 18; 10:29–31; 1 Cor. 2:10; 2 Tim. 2:19; Heb. 4:13; 1 John 3:2). In light of these, we discover that there is only one sphere of created being in relation to uncreated being and that it is all exhaustively subject to the will of God. We are free to decide against him, but God wills to be who he is toward us just as much as he wills to be who he is toward those who love and obey him. Even death and nothingness remain under his will. In terms of God's decision to be who he is and to have creation in his life, there is nothing but agreement or objection; neutrality is not possible:

> It is, therefore, impossible—really impossible—to fall out of or escape from the lordship of the divine will. His will is done in heaven and on earth both when we are obedient and when we are disobedient. But God's will is God Himself, and God is gracious and holy, merciful and righteous. Therefore . . . to say that God is the One to whose will all things are subject is a word which is full of warning and yet at the same time full of comfort.[42]

The real moment of joining the knowledge of God's lordship with that of his omnipotence is in gaining the knowledge of his omniscience. The personality of God as God comes into full exposure only to the extent that we can receive it, by Scripture's declarations concerning the all-knowing-ness of God, all in terms of time and space, the conditions of everything that would be from all eternity stemming directly and entirely from God's absolute freedom to be who he is and to create according to his omnipotence. Since God is eternal in his knowing, his omniscience is as a single event such that

> if we ask . . . why we must believe the Word of God spoken in this event, and obey it, again and above all the only answer we can give is that this is God's free will, and therefore His holy and righteous and good will, and as such His omnipotent will. This is all absolutely above us, and we are absolutely account-able to it all, because it is all in some way God Himself, and God is free to be God in this way both in Himself and therefore also for us.[43]

41. Ibid., 550.
42. Ibid., 557–58.
43. Ibid., 561.

Interestingly, the first Scripture quoted by Barth immediately in support of the foregoing is "The wind [spirit] blows where it chooses" (John 3:8; followed by Eph. 1:11; Rom. 9:18–26; 11:33–36, all emphasizing God's utterly independent prerogatives and impenetrable depth). Yet it is Scripture that leads us in this fundamental understanding of God and his relation to all that is not God. In focusing on the texts that identify God in himself and then in his relation to all that is not God, one discovers that independent metaphysical conditions dominate a whole raft of systems whose knowledge foundations are an amalgam of Christian faith and independent metaphysics:

> The right understanding of the freedom of God's will excludes all those views which seek to represent the relation between God and the reality distinct from Himself as a relation of mutual limitation and necessity. In the first instance this includes all pantheistic and panentheistic systems, according to which the existence of this other reality belongs in some way to the essence and existence of God Himself. With whatever necessity God acts in Himself, He is always free in relation to these. As God He wills the world, but He does not will a second God.
>
> The right understanding of the freedom of God's will also excludes all non-deterministic and deterministic standpoints—the two really belong together. According to these the creature constitutes a factor which in some way conditions and limits the will of God. It does so either by its relative contingency on the basis of its *liberum arbitrium* [free choice] or by its relative necessity in the continuity and limitation of its existence as it obeys the law of its being. Pelagianism and fatalism are alike heathen atavisms in a Christian doctrine of God. They both ascribe to the will of the creature an autonomy in relation to God's will which it cannot possess either in its relative freedom or its relative subjection.[44]

Probably the most significant point is not the valid expulsion of so many rival systems but the necessity of maintaining God's continuing freedom and not a special limitation with respect to the already-created world and relations with humanity. The nature of the relations with creatures is ever unilateral and irreversible. The mutuality that indeed exists by grace between the divine and the human exists on account of the incarnate humanity of the Word and the gracious self-giving of God to humanity through Jesus Christ. Further, this mutuality has its own order also modeled in Scripture, and that is prayer, the permission and the commission to reply to God with the yes of adoration and obedience, as well as to address the plea for God to act. We otherwise know nothing of God, and yet in knowing so much that is definite in him through Jesus Christ, we have a pattern of mutual relations that we must learn in order to freely embrace them.[45]

44. Ibid., 561–63
45. In a fascinating discussion of Molinism as the Counter-Reformation Jesuit alternative to the Augustinian-Thomistic tradition of the Dominicans, and therefore perceived as too close to

In all of Barth's discussion, then, it really is the being of God as the One who is from eternity, the Creator and Redeemer, known through Jesus Christ, that is the content of Christian knowledge:

> We have simply to think of God Himself, recognising and adoring and loving the Father, the Son and the Holy Spirit. It is only in this way that we know eternity. For eternity is His essence. He, the living God, is eternity. And it is as well at this point, relation to the threefold form of eternity [pretemporal, supratemporal, and posttemporal], to emphasise the fact that He is the living God.
>
> At God's end, His beginning is operative in all its power, and His present is still present. At this point, as in the doctrine of the Trinity itself, we can and must speak of a *perichoresis,* a mutual indwelling and interworking of the three forms of eternity. *God* lives eternally. It is for this reason that there are no separations or distances or privations. It is for this reason that that which is distinct must be seen in its genuine relationship. . . . In this distinction and unity . . . God is eternal, and therefore the Creator and Lord of time, the free and sovereign God.[46]

Thus, we come to God as Trinity, where God in himself is distinguishable from himself in three irreversible, noninterchangeable relationships. Although Barth maintains his use of *Seinsweise,* these three in the one God are not merely in relation but in relationship, bearing personal pronouns and communicating in intimacy

> to the extent that these three are distinct in God but no less one in God, without pre-eminence or subordination but not without succession and order, yet without jeopardising or annulment of the real life of the Godhead. We can now state more explicitly the decisive truth that it is the content of the divine being which creates the particular form of the divine being. . . . As the triunity . . . God Himself—is the basis of the power and dignity of the divine being, and therefore also of His self-declaration, His glory, so this triune being and life . . . is the basis of what makes this power and dignity enlightening, persuasive and convincing. For this is the particular function of this form. It is radiant, and what it radiates is joy. It attracts and therefore it conquers. It is, therefore, beautiful. . . . It does not do this materially. . . . It does it formally. . . . It does this to the extent that in it there is repeated and revealed the unity and distinction of the divine being particular to it as the being of the triune God. To this extent the triunity of God is the secret of His beauty. If we deny this, we at once have a

---

the Reformation theological view, Barth recounts the struggle over the former's *scientia media,* the doctrine of "middle knowledge"—God's knowledge of the future based on his knowledge of all contingencies in the future and his impartation of resistible prevenient grace. "Yet we have to recognise that the continued existence of the Thomistic counter-theory means that the door to the Reformation doctrine [of grace and divine foreknowledge] has not been altogether slammed. It remains an inch open" (ibid., 568–69ff.). This is part of one of Barth's most extended excurses in the *CD.*

46. Ibid., 639–40.

God without radiance and without joy (and without humour!); a God without beauty. Losing the dignity and power of real divinity, He also loses His beauty. But if we keep to this, fulfilling the whole Christian knowledge of God and all Christian theology with a knowledge of this basic presupposition that the one God is Father, Son and Holy Spirit, we cannot escape the fact either in general or in detail that apart from anything else God is also beautiful.[47]

And so we return to the theological aesthetic that is none other than the Triune God himself, whose very form makes our knowledge of him qualitatively, against any other, beautiful. It is then, also finally, that Barth comes again to Jesus Christ, the incarnate Son, by whom alone in his name and person we have knowledge of the Trinity. The glory of Christ is the glory of the Father is the glory of the Spirit, beheld by John and the apostles (John 1:16), and is quintessentially the beauty of God and the miracle of God as we creatures could ever possibly know it.[48] This is because God has taken our humanity into himself and has caused himself to be taken into our humanity. The glory that is his, a knowable beauty that is his alone, without a medium of disclosure, is the man Jesus Christ, that medium, the sole Mediator, the new form of the beauty of God that discloses the Trinity and its beauty in a way we can see:

> For the beautiful in God's being, that which stirs up joy, is the fact that so inexhaustibly and necessarily . . . He is One and yet another, but One again even as this other, without confusion or alteration, yet also without separation or division. What is reflected in this determination of the relationship between the divine and the human nature in Jesus Christ is the form, the beautiful form of the divine being. In this way, in this rest and movement, God is the triune, and He has and is the divine being in the unity and fulness of all its determinations. Because He is this in this way, He is not only the source of all truth and all goodness, but also the source of all beauty. And because we know that He is this in this way in Jesus Christ, we must therefore recognise the beauty of God in Jesus Christ.
>
> The beauty of Jesus Christ is not just any beauty. It is the beauty of God. Or, more concretely, it is the beauty of what God is and does in Him. . . . If we do not see this, if we do not believe it, if it has not happened to us, how can we see the form of this event, the likeness of the essence of God in Jesus Christ, and how can we see that this likeness is beautiful? In this respect, too, God cannot be known except by God.[49]

47. Ibid., 661.

48. In quoting from Friedrich Schiller's poem "Auch das Schöne muß sterben!" also set to music by Johannes Brahms in *Nänie*, Barth means that the beautiful who must die is Christ, and therefore God himself is embracing perishability, and yet this is not the end of beauty but the inclusion of death in the aesthetic of its triumph. See Eberhard Jüngel, "'Even the Beautiful Must Die'—Beauty in the Light of Truth: Theological Observations on the Aesthetic Relation," in *Theological Essays,* ed. John Webster, trans. U. Lohmann (Edinburgh: T & T Clark, 2000), 59–81.

49. *CD* II/1:664–65. Barth continues, "He can and will not only exist but co-exist. This is the δόξα τοῦ θεοῦ, the *gloria Dei,* and all God's works from the greatest down to the least,

The glory of God can be known to us only through a form, an image, a likeness given to us by God, and it must be revealed to each one in order to see it for what it really is and is meant to be for us, the joy-instilling beauty of God. To see this beauty in Jesus Christ (in this vein, Barth directly cites Isaiah 53) is to behold the form of the Trinity as it can be known, which is only through God as man. But there is a profound question here that makes all the difference for theology, and that is whether the capacity for glimpsing this beauty has happened to us. Without it, something other than a theology grounded in the faith that we are knowing God by God is the substance of our work and reflection in the church and in the world. This is nothing other than our worship, ever increasing the effulgence of glory that creatures can render to God through Christ in the Holy Spirit.

This third member of the Trinity is sometimes incorrectly deemed to be in need of defense from Barth's supposed neglect, and yet this is entirely not the case.

> It is as well to realise at this point that the glory of God is not only the glory of the Father and the Son but the glory of the whole divine Trinity, and therefore the glory of the Holy Spirit as well. But the Holy Spirit is not only the unity of the Father and the Son in the eternal life of the Godhead. He is also, in God's activity in the world, the divine reality by which the creature has its heart opened to God and is made able and willing to receive Him. He is, then, the unity between the creature and God, the bond between eternity and time. If God is glorified through the creature, this is only because by the Holy Sprit the creature is baptised, and born again and called and gathered and enlightened and sanctified and kept close to Jesus Christ in true and genuine faith. There is no glorification of God by the creature that does not come about through this work of the Holy Spirit by which the Church is founded and maintained, or that is not itself, even in its creatureliness, this work of the Holy Spirit. It is the Holy Spirit who begets the new man in Jesus Christ whose existence is thanksgiving. It is in virtue of His glory, which is the glory of the one God, that what this new man does is the glorification of God, and therefore the creature may serve this glorification.[50]

Thus, there is nothing in Christian theology that can be done without the inner working of the Holy Spirit in the life of the theologian. The Holy Spirit is the revealer of the Trinity, whose knowledge is manifest in Jesus Christ, who introduces the Father to us for a life of grace-inspired gratitude, of which

---

each in its own way, are works of this divine glory, witnesses of the overflowing perfection of His Godhead. But the beginning, centre and goal of these works of the divine glory is God's Son Jesus Christ. He is their beginning because [he is] prior to all God's action *ad extra*, . . . because the Son in His relation to the Father is the eternal archetype and prototype of God's co-existence with another. . . . It belongs to the essence of the glory of God not to be *Gloria* alone but to become *glorificatio*" (ibid., 667).

50. Ibid., 669–70.

theology is simply the verbal manifestation. Theology is obediential, and this means thanking and praising God. Obedience as the act that comes from being vivified by the Holy Spirit is the content of the divine intention that the creature participate in God's self-glorification and thus in beholding the beauty of the Lord.

6

GOD WITH US
AND WE WITH GOD

The previous chapter investigated a couple of things that are vital to understanding Barth: The trinitarian knowledge of God is christologically mediated and discerned, and all theological method proceeds from the reality of knowing Jesus Christ through his contemporaneous presence. The title of this chapter reflects the christological center of the *CD,* that in Christ the Triune God and humanity are both fully represented and fully reconciled. Here, after the totality of divine initiative apart from us and yet to us, after the almighty and unrivaled privilege of God and yet his gracious address to us and coming to us in Jesus Christ, after our response to God by the faith that hears and receives and by grace is a qualified yes to the eternal and unalterable yes of God in electing us to himself comes what is accomplished in Christ, is ontologically settled in him, and partakes of a divine activity of life that consummates the movements of creation and redemption in reconciliation and the reconciled existence: God with us and we with God in the person of Jesus Christ.

This second aspect, particularly running right through Barth's lengthy discussion of the knowledge of God in *CD* II/1, shows how one must hold together both volumes I and II in order to gain a full appreciation of his method. In *CD* I, Barth's great concentration on the Word of God in its three modes—incarnational, scriptural, and proclamatory—has the scriptural as the church's form of recollecting the history of God's revelation and of the Holy Spirit mediating the objective and contemporaneous knowledge of God in and through "biblical concepts" *(biblische Begriffe)* of God. But in *CD* II/1, the contemporaneous knowledge of God comes to us in the personal presence of

Jesus Christ to the believer and to the church in the form of the christological formula "God with us and we with God," a relation mediated by Christ.

In this christological "God with us and we with God," we have the only reversible theological formula that is possible solely because of the unique mediatorial and sacramental divine-human reality that is Jesus Christ. Nothing about human life and faith determines the being of God, which is already self-determined to be for humanity, its past, present, and future. Barth continues to elaborate on his theological method in *CD* IV, with *CD* III on creation being largely the act of recollection, which he elaborated and in no way disavowed in *CD* I. But because the historical Christ must also be *Christus praesens* (present) to the church, the objective and contemporaneous content of the knowledge of God is not only the vital understanding of biblical concepts of the true God but also the vital presence of God himself as human for our sakes. After the lengthy discussions of *CD* III on creation and the order of life established by Jesus Christ, we return again to themes of the presence of Jesus Christ through the divine act of reconciliation that binds God and the human together, which is reconciliation: God with us and we with God. This will be the basis for Barth's claim that Jesus Christ is the only sacrament, since his full incarnational presence is a reality to the believer and to the church, by which the sacramental, mediatorial function and the fullness of grace are conveyed to sinful but elect creatures and are entirely fulfilled.

The exposition in this chapter develops the thesis that the entire *CD* can be read according to Barth's simple triadic structure: "*Deus extra nos, Deus pro nobis, Deus in nobis*" (God outside us, God for us, God in us). Understanding this structure takes its cue from Eberhard Jüngel (as outlined in chapter 2, above). As Jüngel notes, for most of the *CD* and not until IV/2 does the third node of the triad, *Deus in nobis,* find expression.[1] Until then, the "God outside us" and the "God for us" secures for Barth the objectivism, the critical and eschatological realism, and the irreversibility of theological knowledge based on the nature of God's initiatory relation to creation in gracious revelation. All theological reasoning has its basic structure as proceeding from the side of God. Out of God's unbounded freedom in granting freedom to the creature, he provides for human life in infinite anticipation of all that human beings require and are to become because he himself is already and ever will be their life. Far too little is made of the third node of the triad, "God in us," on account of the at-times overwhelming objectivism of the *CD*. Perhaps also the profound emphasis on the presence of Jesus Christ to us in *CD* II remains objectivist because it is still "to us." We recall that in Christ the Gift and the

1. Nevertheless, Barth's formulation for the early section of *CD* IV/4 (1967) appeared already in 1962 in the Wolf *Festschrift* under this very title: "Extra nos—pro nobis—in nobis," in *Hören und handeln: Festschrift für Ernst Wolf zum 60. Geburtstag,* ed. H. Gollwitzer and H. Traub (München: C. Kaiser, 1962), 15–27. This fact should also guard against reading IV/4 as all too fragmentary or as a part of the *CD* to be discounted in relation to the previous volumes.

Giver are one: When God gives his gracious life to us, he gives us himself. And yet the work of the Holy Spirit in *CD* IV/2, whereby God's relation to us and with us is most fully "God in us," is required to illumine fully where Barth was going already by II/1. Even in reading the "God with us" structure of reconciled relationship in IV/1, one could miss this dimension, which we need to investigate here. If the biblical conceptual focus of *CD* I is not acknowledged to have been enriched by the *Christus praesens* focus of *CD* II, then one can miss the fact that the knowledge of God in his being "with us" has as its content "God in us," which of course is Barth's full development of pneumatology. And as we will see in the last chapter, the knowledge of God according to this triadic node is always and ever new, a progressive knowledge of the richness and vital fullness of the Triune God. Hence, we are ever pilgrim theologians to whom and in whom God is ever unfolding himself through the One who is our goal in life, in death, and in resurrection: the Lord Jesus Christ. In this, the testimony of one lifetime is added to the testimony of many others to whom Christ is present and active.

In coming to the *CD* through Barth's development of his christocentric theology, several things must be kept in mind: (1) In his theology, there is no question of a Christ-monism (i.e., that the only knowledge of God available is Christ or that the only subject of Scripture is Christ). (2) Christocentric theology is the consistent outworking of the affirmation that Christ is the only mediator and therefore the prime vehicle of the rich and varied knowledge of the Triune God. (3) In Christ, the paradoxical union of natures, divine and human, are related in the utterly unique incarnational union of hypostases that are one and the same time an- and enhypostatic (i.e., without particular human individuality and also with a particular human individuality in the person of Jesus of Nazareth). (4) Incarnation does not function analogously after the doctrine of election (*CD* II/2) in the *CD,* and thus (5) one cannot speak of an incarnational ecclesiology in view of the sole sacramental reality that subsists in the person of Jesus Christ. Finally, (6) the bond of relation between Jesus Christ, the church, and its individual members is one of *Entsprechung* (correspondence), where through the internal work of the Holy Spirit in faith, the believer is enabled to obey the gracious command of God in Scripture and so to act in ways analogous to divine action.

Deus: Extra Nos, pro Nobis, in Nobis

If the reader focuses on Barth's statements about the relation between the Triune God's being and act *extra nos,* and his being and act *pro nobis* both in and through Jesus Christ, we can see emerging a kind of overarching development of the covenantal relation between God and humanity. This covenantal relation manifests itself in a correspondence form of the human knowledge of God, which is progressively clarified as to its nature according to faithful correspondence with God in knowing and acting through receptive and obediential response to God's Word. Although CD I as a kind of *prolegomena* sets out the science of theology as the "self-examination of the Christian church with respect to its speech about God,"[2] theology takes its content from the nature of that which is examined, namely, God himself. Drawing on the Second Helvetic Confession, the threefold Word of God bears an analogy to the Triune God[3] and is known through the gracious activity of the Holy Spirit. Knowing the God revealed in Scripture is not a matter of mere literacy and critical attentiveness to the content of Scripture, a result of an inherent capacity to know God on God's terms, which is revelation. Instead, it is the result of an enabled acknowledgment by the vivifying action of God's Spirit. The human need to understand is preceded by the gift of faith, which is entirely the result of the gift of God who is the Spirit of God, a faithful knowledge that fundamentally is *acknowledgment,* the grace-induced receptivity that in fact receives what is delivered by this objective revelation in the Word of God by the faithful knower.[4] From this graced and Spirit-filled vantage point, one can embark on the task of understanding and making understood what has been acknowledged, the doctrinal or dogmatic task of witness, the preaching and teaching of this Word in the continuous process of the church's and the believer's "*fides quaerens intellectum*" (faith seeking understanding).

The knowledge of God through the revelation of God's Word manifests God's eternal Trinity in unity as the One who in omnipotent freedom is, to all that is not God, the following: Creator, Reconciler, and Redeemer; Father, Son, and Holy Spirit, interpenetrating (perichoretically) one another in the divine being and act of eternal *(ad intra)* and temporal *(ad extra)* relations.[5] The knowledge of the Trinity is rooted in the divine and human historical life of Jesus Christ, especially in the Johannine Gospel of Jesus' testimony, and particularly in the ontological reality and relationality exhibited in his prayers. Thus, through the incarnation God's self-revelation becomes particularly objective, as it is with Israel, only now as intensified fulfillment in time and absolutely as the *extra nos* activity of God, which is at one and the same time absolutely *pro nobis* in its purpose and character.[6] The unity of these two fundamental terms is actually displayed in the person of Jesus Christ, "the Word [who] became flesh" (John 1:14). God's Word (*extra nos*) was united to creaturely flesh (*pro nobis*) and yet irreversibly so. Nothing about humanity imagines, decides, or in any way lends to the engendering of this reality but instead receives—as in the faithfulness of Mary—and benefits entirely from this sovereign, free, and yet "for us" action on God's part. Through his humanity, God the Son participates in human

2. *CD* I/1:3.
3. Ibid., 162–86.
4. Ibid., 198–240.
5. Ibid., 368–490.
6. *CD* I/2:25–44.

life, in full exposure to human sinfulness and yet without sin. Through the incarnation of the Word by means of God's direct action—"conceived by the Holy Spirit"—Jesus Christ is both objective knowledge of God as revealed and yet entirely unique because unlike any other fact or class of objective knowledge, our knowing is entirely dependent on God's intention that we know it on God's terms as revelation, as prime mystery, that "Jesus Christ is very God and very Man."[7] In this his being, we have not only the objective revelation of the Triune God in the life of a historical human being but also the condition by which communion between God and humanity is reestablished in God's covenantal love.

For this communion between God and human beings to effectively take place in Jesus Christ through the knowledge of the Word of God, God the Holy Spirit must cause this knowledge to become as subjective reality within the human knower. Through the outpouring of the Holy Spirit into the lives of human beings, an entirely new freedom to know and to be for God is created within the human subject, a freedom that now corresponds to the original divine freedom to be for human beings.[8] Objective knowledge of God—as we have it given to us in "the doctrine of the Trinity, and ultimately and decisively by Holy Scripture as the source and norm"[9]—must be given to us, to be subjectively known by us in a creative action of God the Holy Spirit on us and in us. In doing so, God the Spirit creates the church, where the objective knowledge of God is operative in its fullness. God is God's own witness to the truth of Scripture and to the truth of his own triune being, both through the person of Jesus Christ and through the Holy Spirit given to us. By giving us the Holy Spirit,

> God also adopts us, in such a way that He Himself makes us ready to listen to the Word, that He himself intercedes with us for Himself, that He Himself makes the speaking and hearing of His Word possible among us. Therefore the decisive answer to the question of the existence of the Church must certainly be to indicate the mystery of Pentecost, the gift which men who themselves are not Christ now receive in their entire humanity for Christ's sake, the gift of existing from Christ's standpoint for Christ and unto Christ, "the power to become the sons of God" (John 1:12).[10]

At this early stage in the *CD,* Barth is working along traditional Reformation lines and with this subjective reality inseparably connected to the objective reality of God in Christ and through the Holy Spirit. This means that since the subjective appropriation of the Word of God by the Holy Spirit is God's use of created signs for us—mediated by the life of Jesus Christ, the Scripture, and

7. Ibid., 172ff.
8. Ibid., 203–79.
9. Ibid., 204.
10. Ibid., 221f.

the preaching of Jesus Christ and the Scriptures in the life of the church—all of this has a particular "sacramental" nature. Indeed, the

> sphere of subjective reality in revelation is the sphere of sacrament. This has nothing to do with the Roman *opus operatum* or with heathen "magic." The sphere of sacrament means the sphere in which man has to think of himself as on the way from the baptism already poured out upon him to the Lord's Supper yet to be dispensed to him, the sphere in which he beings with faith in order to reach faith, ἐκ πίστεως εἰς πίστιν (Rom. 1:17). On this way our perception will certainly be a true one if we think of ourselves as the recipients of revelation. And it is in this sphere that theology has to seek both its beginning and its goal, and by the law of this sphere that it must direct its methods.[11]

Significantly, Barth brings sacrament into the sphere of the work of the Holy Spirit to make us hearers of the Word of God and therefore believers in this Word. What constitutes the church is not an ecclesial *actio sacra* (sacred act) but the activity of the Holy Spirit creating and nurturing "recipients of revelation." In the course of the *CD,* Barth will reserve sacrament and the sacramental exclusively for the life of Jesus Christ for us, and yet from the beginning Barth had been concerned with the priority of Word and faith, *solo verbo* as the content of God's gracious communication in revelation and *sola fide* as faithful reception of it. For Barth there will no longer be a "sphere of sacrament"; instead, there is the One who is God's one and only sacrament, who by the Holy Spirit's free and freeing sacramental action makes us hearers and doers of the Word—sacramental action that is always and exclusively God's, but God for us, with us, and in us. On account of this, what we do can become ours and, in gratitude, ensue in spiritually liberated human action that corresponds to God's action and thus bears faithful witness to the world.

In one of the great pneumatological passages of the *CD,* Barth's penetration and comprehensiveness is striking:

> As God, the Holy Spirit is a unique person. But He is not an independent divinity side by side with the unique Word of God. He is simply the Teacher of the Word: of that Word which is never without its Teacher. . . . The Word is never apart from the Holy Spirit. And it is by this very work of the Holy Spirit, and because in the Holy Spirit we recognise that God's Word is the truth. . . . It is God Himself who opens our eyes and ears for Himself. And in so doing He tells us that we could not do it of ourselves, that of ourselves we are blind and deaf. To receive the Holy Spirit means an exposure of our spiritual blindness, a recognition that we do not possess the Holy Spirit. For that reason the subjective reality of revelation has the distinctive character of a miracle, i.e., it is a reality to be grounded only in itself. In the actual subjective reality of

11. Ibid., 232.

revelation it is finally decided that apart from it there is no other possibility of being free for God.[12]

What is important about this text is that although Barth's overarching concern is with the objective knowledge of God, a great deal regarding his future interest in the work of the Holy Spirit in the life of the believer is already here. Barth is not ready to include a fundamental principle of *in nobis* with *extra nos* and *pro nobis,* but the content is already present.

With Barth's full discussion of Scripture as the Word of God for the church, as the church's authority, and as defining Christian freedom within the church, Barth clarifies his distinction between revelation, God's direct and objective self-giving to the knowing subject and Scripture, and the indirect witness to this act of the revealed Word. Secondarily, Scripture is revelation but yet through human witnesses, the authors of Scripture, and those whose witness of the Word of God is recorded in Scripture.[13] Scripture is the Word of God formally and in its content, which being human is fallible in God's infallible will to have it as his Word. In any case, the constant, miraculous work of the Holy Spirit, creating hearers and learners of this Word, takes place to effect the objective knowledge of God.[14] Barth expounds his doctrine of Scripture this way chiefly because he is at odds with strategies of reading that bring Scripture itself under various kinds of human sovereignty, failing to receive it for what it is and on its own terms. When received under the direction of the Holy Spirit, the Scripture becomes the format of the bounded freedom that is the basis for Christian ethics. The profoundest direction of the Holy Spirit in the matter of Scripture is actually the further extension of the Word of God through proclamation. Although proclamation is the embodiment of the church's responsibility, it is executed as a human act entirely as the impossible is made possible through the action of the Holy Spirit and prepared for through deep and regular acts of prayer. Indeed, proclamation is a duty and is itself the test of theology and ministry of the church. Here is where dogmatics is essential as the extension of the proclaiming function of the church and therefore is a function of the Word of God.[15]

As Barth moves on to his account of the knowledge of God, he moves beyond the *prolegomena* volume of the *CD* and in a sense begins over again. This beginning anew, however, is essential to the distinctions between the divine and human that will lead to Barth's distancing of his later definitions from certain of those embodied in I/1 and I/2, particularly at the point of sacrament and proclamation as virtually sacramental. While Barth is attentive to created signs and their effective signification as vehicles for knowing what

12. Ibid., 244.
13. Ibid., 457–537.
14. Ibid., 502–37.
15. Ibid., 743–884.

God is communicating to human beings about himself, he does not carry over as forcefully the sacramental sense of a sign. In the revelation of the knowledge of God, human words and human dependency on the conditions of creaturely existence to know anything make obvious the "secondary objectivity" of all knowledge of God by faith. But even this divine secondary objectivity is not natural to any sign and is only the result of grace. Any sense of human ability is a question of gracious enablement to respond to and obey this Word.

> God stands before man as the One who awakens, creates and upholds his faith, and where God offers Himself to man as the object and content of the knowledge of his faith, He does it in this being and action—as the One who remains mystery to us because He Himself has made Himself so clear and certain to us. . . . Within obedience the knowledge of God cannot be destroyed, because its object cannot cease to be this object and God cannot cease to be the One who is and acts in this way. If our obedience springs from God, necessarily we are always in the same obedience towards God. In this obedience we are set on the circular course in which we can go only from faith to faith and similarly from knowledge to knowledge. Because we do not in any sense begin with our selves, with our own capacity for faith and knowledge, we are secured against having to end with ourselves, i.e., with our own incapacity.[16]

God is the mystery of the world in that he is claimed to be known and obeyed yet is not known simply as the result of his will to be known and yet is not at all something naturally accessible to us. But what natural religion and natural theology cannot do, no matter how supposedly authorized, through the Holy Spirit and the grace of God we have a genuine knowledge of God because it is knowledge on terms set by this One who is known. This knowledge is alone genuine: "We possess no analogy on the basis of which the nature and being of God as the Lord can be accessible to us. . . . The decisive distinguishing mark of the lordship of God is this fact that He is really the Lord over all things and therefore supremely over ourselves, the Lord over our bodies and souls, the Lord over life and death."[17] This knowledge of God can be received only as a gift. Since this gift is entirely christological, the Gift and the Giver are actually one and the same. But there is something extraordinary about this extraordinary claim, namely, that in Jesus Christ we have not only the God who reveals himself to be known but also our humanity, which knows him and makes him known as God in Christ. Once the knowledge of God by the gift of faith becomes operative, a degree of understanding results regarding the hiddenness of God and therefore recognizes that God is naturally inapprehensible. This apophatic knowledge is also part of the positive knowledge of God that is by faith through grace since it is part of the greater truth that God wills to make himself apprehensible. But this knowledge is always obediential; always

16. *CD* II/1:43.
17. Ibid., 75.

a function of joyous, grateful, awestruck response; and therefore always the work of the Spirit of God. Because God gives himself in our knowing of him, what we know is always a share in God's own self-knowing.

God is, and therefore our knowing of him is already the knowledge of his existence. There is no movement from a prior demand and capacity on the part of confident believers in God to establish his existence. Instead, God's reality in making himself known immediately confronts us with his attributes. God's being is in his act, and his act is in his being and as such is self-grounded and not acted upon or acting because of anything other than himself. Here is God in his actual and entirely *extra nos* existence. As personal God he is, however, utterly distinct in his attributes, and yet he is who he is entirely in his unbounded freedom and love, which are essential to him.[18] In God's absolute freedom vis-à-vis all that is not God, he is spatial, temporal, and omnipotent. By laying these dimensions out we come to that point where the *CD*'s distinctive *extra nos* structure comes to expression in the doctrine of election. Barth embraces the classic Reformed view that election is the sum of the gospel, where God's free decision establishes the freedom of human beings to become free for God through justification and the assurance of the Holy Spirit. In election God establishes his covenant and his covenant partner because he has, in the most basic way and according to his freedom and love, willed not to exist apart from his creation.

> In light of an evangelical understanding of the election of grace, what is the meaning of the mystery of the freedom of this divine work? . . . If we tried to call God to account for His decision we should be questioning and indeed denying God Himself. But if this is the case, then it means that the creature must bow before the gracious God and submit itself to Him. Confronted with the mystery of God, the creature must be silent: not merely for the sake of being silent, but for the sake of hearing. Only to the extent that it attains to silence, can it attain to hearing. But again, it must be silent not merely for the sake of hearing but for that of obeying. For obedience is the purpose and goal of hearing. Our return to obedience is indeed the aim of free grace. It is for this that it makes us free.[19]

This is the gospel not only *in nuce* but also ultimately *in nobis*. Here in Barth's interpretation, he precisely lays out the linkage guiding us and maintains a dynamic model of distinction and relation.

But one aspect of the *extra nos* and *pro nobis* formula looms largest here, and that is the election of God the Son in the election of Jesus Christ, through whom and in whom humanity is elect. Barth's account here is not so much about the fall of humanity as about the condemnation of humanity for its sin and sinfulness. Christ is elect for humanity, the sign of God's willingness to

18. Ibid., 322–50.
19. *CD* II/2:30.

include humanity in his life. In the divine life of the Trinity, the Son elected himself to serve the divine purpose for humanity. Indeed, God's decision is matched and inseparable from the decision of Jesus Christ, who thus is the self-electing God and the self-elected human being:

> In the beginning with God, i.e., in the resolve of God which precedes the existence, the possibility and the reality of all His creatures, the very first thing is the decree whose realization means and is Jesus Christ. This decree is perfect both in subject and object. It is the electing God and also the elected man Jesus Christ, and both together in the unity the one with the other. . . . And this decree is really the first of all things. It is the decision between God and the reality distinct from Himself.[20]

Barth emphasizes the distinction between God and humanity, which is fundamental to the covenantal relation. Everything becomes caught up in this divine decision, which includes both rejection and acceptance in Christ, and ultimately the community of those accepted in him and who in turn will accept him. There are also those who are rejected, are reprobate, and spurn the free, loving offer of God. As above, election secures human beings for salvation and also for obedience. And yet election originates and is operative entirely outside us, in Christ.

The election of God in Christ is the root and foundation of everything else that is to follow in the *CD;* by this election the divine act and human act, while united covenantally, are ontologically distinct on account of the former as *extra nos,* eternally grounded in the being and action of God. The covenantal union is never a union in which divine being and human beings perichoretically interpenetrate, where the human being has some kind of claim or forceful influence on the divine life. Instead, on account of the representation of human life in the life of Jesus Christ and of the penetration of the divine life of the Holy Spirit in the life of the human being, we are enabled and thus able to act in ways that correspond to divine action upon the analogy of divine revelation, in terms of the Word of God and our words, spoken and performative, and in acts that bear witness to the gracious reality of God in us. That election takes place according to supralapsarian doctrine (that God is the universe's and humanity's origin, purpose, and meaning):

> [God's] purpose is the beginning of all things, the eternal reality in which everything future is already determined and comprehended. And in this purpose . . . God does not will at random. He wills man: not the idea of man, not humanity, not human individuals in the mass or in particular, but *in concreto* and not *in abstracto.* He wills man, His man [Jesus Christ], elected man, man predestined as the witness to His glory and the object of His love. In this man, but only in him, He wills humanity and every individual man and what we may describe

20. Ibid., 157.

as the idea of humanity. . . . His intention is that this man should testify to His glory and thus reveal and confirm and verify both positively what He is and wills and negatively what He is not and does not will. The latter part of the intention is not positive but negative; a marking off, a separating, a setting aside. It is not a second Yes on God's part, but a No which is of God only to the extent that it corresponds and is opposed to the Yes, a No which forms the necessary boundary of the Yes: so assuredly is God God and not not God; so assuredly does He live in eternal self-differentiation from all that is not God and is not willed by God. In this sense God is and is not; He wills and does not will. . . . In this way the witness can truly exist and live in covenant with God. . . . It is not God's will that elected man should fall into sin. But it is His will that sin, that which God does not will, should be repudiated and rejected and excluded by him. It is God's will that elected man should repudiate what He repudiates, and that thereby the Yes of God should be revealed and proclaimed.[21]

God's action in his self-differentiation from all that is not God and yet as the God who is for us eternally in establishing who we will be on account of and through the unique elect man Jesus Christ sums up Barth's view at this point. In all that God is in himself and for us, yet the ultimate purpose of God in us is that we should do as God does in repudiating sin, in faithful analogy to God's thinking and acting, and according to his yes and his no. This is all because

"primarily God elected or predestinated Himself." God is determined to give and to send forth His Son. God determined to speak His Word. The beginning in which the Son became obedient to the Father was with Himself. The form and concretion of His will, the determination of his whole being, was reached in Himself. All God's freedom and love were identical with this decree, with the election of Jesus Christ. This is the one side of the matter. And the other is that God elected man, this man.[22]

The *extra nos* character of God's being and act then could not be clearer, and it is essential for grasping how Barth understands what is grounded in God for God. But by concentrating all attention on divine election in the person of Jesus Christ, what election is is entirely visible in him. There is no decision behind the election of Christ and of God behind him in static depths of hiddenness or arbitrariness. This is not the place to offer a full discussion of this crucial doctrine for Barth, only to make explicit the *extra nos* basis of our relation with God.

When there is discussion of the elect community in Israel and the church, both of which belong to God on account of election, the latter included in the former, the former included in the latter, we see that human beings become

21. Ibid., 140–41.
22. Ibid., 162.

witnesses of the mercy and grace of God. And in discussing the election of individuals as well, we can understand nothing about it in abstraction. Barth does not shy away from the significance of the election of individuals within the elect community on account of the work of the Holy Spirit through Christ.

> It is exactly because of the original election of Jesus Christ that the *particula veri* of "individualism," so far from being eliminated, is given a lasting validity. This same is true of the election of the community. This too, has a relativising, but at the same time a confirmatory, significance in relation to the election of the individual man, both inside and outside its confines. . . . It is in their election alone that election can really be visible and effective for the community. The fellowship does not lead any independent life in relation to its members. It lives in them. It does not rob those to whom it mediates the election of Jesus Christ. . . . The *particula veri* of "individualism" is not curtailed but genuinely assured and honoured when we understand the election of the "individual" as the *telos* of the election of the community.[23]

Authentic individuality is neither an absorption of individuals in community nor an affirmation of their sinful tendencies in isolation from God. Indeed, God himself acts as individual being in absolute purity of moral action.[24] And yet because of the individual election of Jesus Christ, the end of election is individuals in him. This is the "particular truth" that secures the individual in the grace of God and by the Spirit will transform them into new life and new freedom.[25] Through God's election, as we can see, gracious preparation for the human being as a true actor in a particular historical life is already appearing. There is no question of election merely to vocation; election is first of all the eternal realization of the gracious saving will of God. But what this saving will of God accomplishes is reflected in its *telos* (outcome): the redeemed and faithful individual subject within the community of Christ and in the world.

23. Ibid., 310–11.

24. Cf., John Webster, *Barth's Ethics of Reconciliation* (Cambridge: Cambridge University Press, 1995), 43. God in his being as *ens concretissimum* and in his action as *"purissimus et singularis"* (*CD* II/2:260–62).

25. In no way, however, can Barth's emphasis here be saddled with the accusation of fostering individualistic autonomy. By highlighting the particularity of the individual and the reality of human agency in thought, will, and action, Barth points to the scriptural balance of community and individual, against collectives and communes and nationalism that would reduce the human person solely to communal significance. At so many points, the analysis in John Macken, S.J., *The Autonomy Theme in the Church Dogmatics: Karl Barth and His Critics* (Cambridge: Cambridge University Press, 1990), is based on a close reading of Barth mixed with overdrawn characterizations, e.g., that IV/4 on ethics represents "an axiomatic disjunction between God's act and man's" (80), which skews all that Barth has been expounding in terms of covenant and correspondence in volume IV as well as teaching the impossibility of water baptism without its grounding in Spirit baptism. While Macken has no appreciation for Barth's—as with all evangelical—rejection of synergism, he actually ends up faulting Barth for asserting full human dependency in the realization of autonomy through the grace of Jesus Christ, as one freely embarks on a life of *imitatio Christi* in the power and presence of the Holy Spirit.

On the basis of the election of God, Barth highlights the connection between divine decision and divine command. Rooted in the doctrine of God,
the election of Jesus Christ is the election of a freely obedient human being,
partnering with God for the purpose of also bringing sanctification to humanity and to individual human beings. Indeed, the theological inseparability of
divine decision and divine command provide an important methodological
signal that Christian ethics may not and cannot be grounded independently
of the gospel itself, nor does it borrow anything from a basis foreign to itself.
Along with the unity of decision and command in God is the more explicit
grounding of ethics in the human life of Christ; indeed, his life is the demonstration of this unity in Christ living. This Barth explores in profound depth in
his discussion of the Reformed employment of a "practical syllogism," ranging
from Calvin to the context of the Heidelberg Catechism and beyond, whereby
the individual believer can know his or her own elected status through action
that graciously corresponds with divine action:

> As Christ is certainly the source and object of faith, so Christ Himself assuredly
> ([Calvin] *Instit.* III, I, 1; 2, 24, etc.) lives and works in the believer through
> faith, and is one with him. But this being the case, it is inevitable that we should
> understand faith itself (as a human deed and attitude) and the believer as such
> and his human life . . . as an incidental, but certainly not on that account su-
> perfluous, confirmation of the one, decisive witness. A man is sure that this is
> established in itself, and is true, by its own weight, and therefore in the power
> of the witness of Jesus Christ and the Holy Spirit. But he is so only in the
> form of his own decision, his own faith and confession, his own corresponding
> being. Christ cannot be to him a witness of his election without his receiving
> His witness, and therefore himself—even in opposition to himself—becoming
> a bearer of this witness.
>
> I do not think it possible to deny . . . that . . . what was later called the
> *syllogismus practicus* did constitute one element in the theology of Calvin
> himself. . . . The problem which he here sought to answer was and is a genu-
> ine problem. The final witness of Jesus Christ to each individual, the least
> independent and least worthy of a hearing, yet the most indispensable in this
> situation and function, is the individual himself (in and with that which he is
> by faith in Jesus Christ). While his witness in and by itself does not give him
> the slightest assurance, he cannot receive the witness of Jesus Christ and the
> Holy Spirit—which gives the real and complete assurance—unless he receives
> it from himself, unless he himself gives it in his faith and life and "works." It
> is as I live as an elect man that I am and shall be assured of my election. This
> is perhaps the meaning of the well-known section in the *Heidelberg Catechism*,
> Qu. 86, when the question why we should perform good works is answered
> in the third paragraph as follows: "that we may ourselves be assured of our
> faith by its fruits."[26]

26. *CD* II/2:334–35. Calvin's view expressed in *"Christus mihi pro mille testimonies sufficit"*
(*De aet. Dei praed., Corpus Reformatorum* 8:321) and his careful qualification *"bonorum operum*

The Christian life confirms the primary witness of Jesus Christ, that what Christ has done for us is not only accomplished but also visible to an imperfect degree in faithful obedience. Here Barth is emphatic about the believing subject and the ethical action enjoined by the command of God, made entirely possible in the eternal election of God, which creates the individual to be a "corresponding being": "only in the form of his own [the believer's] decision, his own faith and confession, his own corresponding being."

According to Barth, the command of God makes ethics not a question of conforming to natural law or indeed of intuiting how natural law becomes encased in moral laws or rule but rather a question of correspondence in action, where the divine command serves this purpose of prescribing and proscribing as it does. This is how Barth can declare that "the Christian doctrine of God . . . is ethics." And more specifically:

> For the answer [to the ethical question] is not theology, or the doctrine of God, but their object—the revelation and work of the electing grace of God. But this, the grace of God, *is* the answer to the ethical problem. For it sanctifies man. It claims him for God. It puts him under God's command. It makes God's command for him the judgment on what he has done and the order for his future action. . . . The command of God is therefore the truth from which—whether he knows and wants to know it or not—man derives and which he will not evade. By the decree of the divine covenant with man, the ethical question as the question of human existence is put from all eternity as the question to which, on the basis of revelation and the work of grace, man will himself in some way be the answer.[27]

This then is the grounding of what will be said over and over in the *CD* about Christian ethics and moral action. Based on God's eternal covenantal decree and a command that arises eternally out of it, human beings are not only constituted and reconstituted in Christ but also have their spring of action in Christ. What human beings are to do and will do before God in Christ are acts of faithful obedience even when these are always, in the first instance, acts of prayers for mercy or of thanksgiving for having received it. But what

---

gratia . . . commonstrat," Barth says, created a problem for those like Beza, who based election not on Christ but on an absolute decree of God and only then on Christ. This resulted in a theological "bad choice" between treating assurance either as having nothing to do with works of obedience (with only the inner testimony of the Spirit), or as having very much to do with works that encroached on God's exclusive prerogatives in justification, making it virtually a crude self-justification. Calvin apparently did not fully detect this problem, and Barth writes, "The historical and psychological enigma which will always confront us at this point is that it could escape the perspicacity of the master that a choice had to be made here, and that it was a bad choice." Barth goes on to point out, on the basis of election in Christ and not merely a bald divine decree, that what Calvin did with the problem of self-assurance is the correct one: locating it in obedient works but defining them with extreme caution as in no way independent of election" (*CD* II/2:338–40).

27. *CD* II/2:515–16.

is crucial here is that God graciously creates the conditions for us and in us in order that the human action, faithful working, might have its own answer to the ethical question in itself. And what Barth means by this are human actions in which full responsibility is consciously taken before the judgment of God, whether rejected or accepted by God, and therefore accepted as truly just or truly unjust. But like any aspect of revelation, Christian ethics cannot work with possibilities other than those given to it, those things given that constitute Christian ethics in the command of God. God is the good to which one "clings," and in doing so the command of God is the good that the Christian strives to do. God's command engenders human action that in turn corresponds to divine action and thus achieves the relationality that is created beyond the distinctions between God and the human.

There is little space here to deal with what we are after in this chapter, namely, Barth's doctrine of creation. It must suffice that the creation, according to Barth, is that context of goodness fashioned by the good God, the context that Scripture enables us to regard as the place of God's good action toward human beings. While the creation is not immediately recognizable as such, as nature for its own sake, revelation imparts understanding of it as the "external basis of the covenant"—along with the covenant being the "internal basis of creation." What is crucial about this volume III of the *CD* is that creation becomes the context in which the actuality of God's presence comes to expression. From the radical *extra nos* of eternal election, however concretely purposeful in its *pro nobis* content and structure, it is only when we begin to consider the temporality of God's action instantiating the *novum* of created reality and therefore of God's temporality and history that we can speak of "God with us." Only with God's creating can the *opus Dei ad extra* actually become an event, whereby God is Lord of time as he is also of eternity.[28] In the context of creation with all its vastness and variation, the human created in the image of God comes to the fore, which is the created basis for divine-human correspondence: "the analogy of free differentiation and relation. In this way He wills and creates man as a partner who is capable of entering into covenant-relationship with Himself."[29] Barth begins to fill out further the nature of the Creator-creation relationality as he discusses God's Sabbath:

> [God] seriously accepted the world and man when He had created them, associating Himself with them in the fullest possible sense. To the reality of the creature there belongs constitutively not only the fact that it is created by God's grace and power, but also the fact that God willed to co-exist with it, and that when He had made it He constituted Himself its co-existing God in the historical event of the seventh day. In light of this event—with all that follows right up to the incarnation of the Word and then the resurrection of the body and

28. *CD* III/1:130. Some of the richest discussion of *imago Dei* in all theological literature is to be found in this volume of the *CD*.
29. Ibid., 185.

the new heaven and earth—it is meaningful to speak of God's immanence in the world. For in this work which completes creation . . . God, when He had created the world and man, made Himself temporal and human, i.e., He linked Himself in a temporal act with the being and purpose and course of the world, with the history of man.[30]

God's being with us, God's movement to become immanent in the world, signifies to human beings not only what he became for us but also what he became for himself in the incarnation and therefore within the being of God: temporal and human. This is the nature of God in the now of history, the temporal existence that constitutes us by that which "He constituted Himself." And in doing so he became the creation's "coexisting God." Thus, the condition by which God becomes human uniquely in Jesus Christ for us and for himself is there from the beginning in God and in God's determination to be with the creation, both in its present creatureliness and in its future new-creatureliness.

Jüngel *Absconditus*

Chapter 2 of the present work noted a few of the problematic readings of Barth. One that looms large in some ways disregards Barth's intention, or even, on account of the lateness of the work in Barth's lifetime, his full theological competency on the topic of baptism in *CD* IV/4. Against this trend stands none other than one of Barth's most penetrating interpreters, Eberhard Jüngel, who embraces Barth's teaching on baptism, traces its genetic support throughout most of the *CD,* shows how Barth has abandoned early notions of volume I, and further extends the discourse of IV/4. The argument, based on the entire theological development of volume IV on reconciliation being accomplished through the sole sacramental agency of Jesus Christ, is for a fundamental distinction between Spirit baptism and water baptism. In Spirit baptism, God initiates what he is accomplishing *in nobis,* effecting internally what he has been bringing to us all along through Jesus Christ as "God with us."

What is most unfortunate is the unavailability of Jüngel's work on baptism to English-language audiences that do not have a capacity for reading highly technical theological German. But there is a peculiarity about this unavailability that must also be raised. Virtually all of Jüngel's work has been translated; indeed, it is often singled out for quick translation. Perhaps because of his avid readership among English-language theologians, he is the only German theologian of recent memory whose work, when it was discovered that an earlier translation had some infelicities and mistranslations, was given an entirely new and bet-

---

30. Ibid., 216.

ter translation and introduction.[31] But too conspicuously Jüngel's material on sacrament and baptism, rooted in a profound embrace of Barth's doctrines, is absent from the translated material. The inattention to, or perhaps even the refusal to advocate for, the translation of these texts has had an abnormally severe effect of obscuring them to the English-language audience. The lack of attention to the essays by Jüngel on sacrament and baptism is readily apparent in the English-language literature. This is strange since Jüngel himself has been concerned with this topic since the beginning of his career, fresh from his contacts with the later Barth, who had posited the closest possible connection between baptism and Christian ethics.[32] For whatever reason, not mentioned in the translator's preface[33] to the essays on Barth,[34] only those parts of the edition that had nothing to do with Jüngel's views on sacrament and baptism were included in the English-language volume. Indeed, though Garrett Paul wants to point to a bit of a tiff between Jüngel and Friedrich Wilhelm Marquardt over Christianity and socialism, there is the much more fundamental matter of sacrament and baptism and the relationship to ethics and analogy, which in the German volume extends from pages 180 to 331 (the better part of a 347-page book). Although the English translation includes Jüngel's chapter on gospel and law, where he embraces Barth's ethics against some of the leading figures of the Lutheran tradition, we cannot know from this English edition that this chapter is only a prelude to Jüngel's radical embrace and elaboration of Barth's view of baptism. Paul's translation, and also John Webster's of other Jüngel essays, simply bypasses these. Indeed, the bypassing gives the impression of a kind of obscurantism by the time we get to Webster's extensive discussions of Barth and Jüngel. Consistently, when Webster critiques and rejects Barth's view of baptism, he never comments on the substance of Jüngel's work at this point. Webster is absolutely attentive to all of Jüngel's work except these essays and their cohesive relation to much of Jüngel's overall theological project. The

31. I refer here to Eberhard Jüngel, *Gottes Sein ist im Werden: Verantwortliche Rede vom Sein Gottes bei Karl Barth: Eine Paraphrase* (Tübingen: Mohr [Siebeck], 1967); in its first translation, *The Doctrine of the Trinity: God's Being Is in Becoming,* trans. Horton Harris (Grand Rapids: Eerdmans, 1976); and then, *God's Being Is in Becoming: The Trinitarian Being of God in the Theology of Karl Barth: A Paraphrase,* trans. John Webster (Grand Rapids: Eerdmans, 2001).

32. Cf. Eberhard Jüngel, *"Zur Kritik des sakramentalen Verstandnisses der Taufe,"* in *Zu Karl Barths Lehre von der Taufe,* ed. F. Viering (Gütersloh: Mohn, 1971); Eberhard Jüngel and Karl Rahner, *Was ist ein Sakrament? Vorstösse zur Verständigung* (Freiburg: Herder, 1971), 25–43; E. Jüngel, *Karl Barths Lehre von der Taufe: Ein Hinweis auf ihre Probleme* (Zürich: EVZ-Verlag, 1968); idem, "Das Sakrament—was ist das?" *Evangelische Theologie* 26, no. 6 (1966): 320–36 (republished in *Was ist ein Sakrament?*); cf. also idem, "Erwagungen zur Grundlegung evangelischer Ethik im Anschluss an die Theologie des Paulus: Eine biblische Meditation," *Zeitschrift für Theologie und Kirche* 63, no. 3 (1966): 379–90; idem, "Das Gesetz zwischen Adam und Christus," *Zeitschrift für Theologie und Kirche* 60, no. 1 (1963): 42–74.

33. Eberhard Jüngel, *Karl Barth: A Theological Legacy,* trans. Garrett E. Paul (Philadelphia: Westminster, 1986), 7–10.

34. Eberhard Jüngel, *Barth-Studien* (Zürich: Benziger, 1982).

most we get from Webster in footnotes, ever, is that Jüngel has published these essays and that they provide "an analysis . . . which relies heavily on Barth,"[35] or he simply quotes isolated statements by Jüngel that never convey the main argumentation put forward.[36] This is perturbing to say the least. Although Webster acknowledges that Jüngel has adopted Barth's radical christological view of sacrament as exclusively located in the person of Jesus Christ, none of the wider connections are made with respect to Jüngel's work on baptism.[37] What emerges is a consistent isolation of Barth's *CD* IV/4 on baptism from his supporters, most importantly, the support of Jüngel. What follows below is a paraphrase of Jüngel's contributions in *Barth-Studien:* a combination of free translation of Jüngel's work and comment on it. What is essential is to begin to grasp the gist of Jüngel's extensive work on baptism in Barth.

Part of Jüngel's embrace of Barth's argument for baptism in IV/4 is a series of contrasting themes showing how Barth has "corrected" himself from volume I to volume IV of the *KD* (the German original: *Die kirchliche Dogmatik*). In the first instance, Jüngel does this with respect to the Word of God and God's Word proclaimed: human speech about God (i.e., the form of the Word of God in which and through which God himself speaks).[38] Here Barth had drawn on a formula in the Second Helvetic Confession I.2: "*Praedicatio verbi Dei est verbum Dei*" (the predicate of the Word of God is the Word of God). This is an origin of Barth's assertion of the three foldform of God's Word as incarnate, in Scripture, and proclaimed. Drawing on an analogy from the unity of Christ's two natures, enhypostasis and anhypostasis,[39] Barth says that Jesus Christ's humanity is witness to his divinity, as are the three forms of the Word of God: Preaching refers back to the God who has spoken and becomes a true Word of God, not merely setting aside human speech about God but destroying it.[40] Barth "corrects" this position in IV/3, where he declares that Jesus Christ is the only true witness in the prophetic office, which he perfects and possesses.[41]

Jesus Christ calls the Christian community to be entrusted with and to serve his prophetic Word as his own earthly form of existence:[42] Each member is called to a task in Christ's name, and "being called means existence in the carrying out of this task"[43] because Christians have been made witnesses of the Witness

---

35. Jüngel, *God's Being Is in Becoming,* 127 n. 51.

36. E.g., ibid., 129, 136, 168.

37. Cf. John Webster, *Barth's Moral Theology: Human Action in Barth's Thought* (Grand Rapids: Eerdmans, 1998), 196–201.

38. *KD* I/1:97. *KD*=Karl Barth, *Die kirchliche Dogmatik,* 4 Bde. (Zollikon-Zürich: Evangelischer Verlag, 1932–67, 1970).

39. Ibid., 53.

40. Ibid., 97.

41. Jüngel, *Barth-Studien,* 276.

42. *KD* IV/3:780, 783.

43. Ibid., 658.

with a given message to preach.[44] Preaching as human action now has been distanced from the reality of the Word of God and is not in itself revelation but the highest fulfillment of the task of the Christian life, belonging under ethics of the doctrine of reconciliation. Preaching as testimony signifies and has its function as witness,[45] but there it is connected with the sacrament as means of grace, the self-objectification of God.[46] The church, however, is not itself reconciliation and does not take the position of Jesus Christ.[47] Thus, preaching is not itself the Word of God. Instead, preaching proclaims the Word of God, such that the use of the term "form of the Word of God" for preaching in *KD* I/1 has now been dispensed with; the term that has entirely replaced it throughout the *CD* is "correspondence." Thus, preaching has also been "de-sacramentalized," a shifting away from volume I's *prolegomena* together with its references to baptism, prayer, and the Lord's Supper.[48] This is the result, Jüngel asserts, of Barth's christological concentration, which although present in *CD* I comes to fruition only in the doctrine of election.

There is a radical differentiation between preaching and baptism and God's work and Word. At the same time, there is a much closer relation between preaching and baptism, which represents *solo verbo* and *sola fide*—a concentration on the Reformation formula. In contrast to the earlier formulations in which God causes himself to be presented and communicated objectively in preaching and sacrament as means of grace,[49] now Jesus Christ is the only sacrament, the only means of grace. Where Barth problematizes "sacrament," the baptism of the Spirit is a "sacramental occurrence," but now always in christological terms rather than in terms of preaching or water baptism—which is already well developed earlier in volume IV.[50] Thus, in full coherence with all of volume IV, Barth writes, "Baptism is the answer to that which is a 'mystery,' a 'sacrament' in the history of Jesus Christ, his resurrection, the outpouring of the Holy Spirit: it is itself not a mystery, not a sacrament."[51] Spirit baptism is called a "sacramental event," where the concept of sacrament rests entirely with the true witness Jesus Christ.[52]

This entire development, Jüngel contends, is a result of Barth's embrace of the phrase *in nobis* with respect to God's gracious action. The question of an original reticence about formulations with reference to God's action "in us" so that we may act has been fully achieved by 1959.[53] Human action "in which

44. Ibid., 660.
45. *KD* I/1:94.
46. Ibid., 53, 65.
47. *KD* IV/3:957.
48. Jüngel, *Barth-Studien,* 277.
49. *KD* I/1:53, 61, 65, 93–94.
50. *KD* IV/4:118–20. This is already rooted in IV/1:744; esp. IV/2:42, 59.
51. *KD* IV/4:112.
52. *KD* IV/3:1.
53. Jüngel, *Barth-Studien,* 270.

and through which"[54] is not only possible but commanded. Barth's emphasis moves from passive to active on grace and the possibility of beginning again; Barth is especially interested in the function of Paul's testimony of God's action "ἀποκαλύψαι τὸν υἱὸν αὐτοῦ ἐν ἐμοί" (to reveal his Son to me; Gal. 1:16). Barth explains the practical effect of the sole sacramentality of Jesus Christ in terms of Spirit baptism:

> Baptism with the Spirit is effective, causative, even creative action on man and in man. It is, indeed, divinely effective, divinely causative, divinely creative. Here, if anywhere, one might speak of a sacramental happening [*Geschehen*] in the current sense of the term. It cleanses, renews and changes man truly and totally. . . . It is (we recall the New Testament descriptions) his being clothed upon with a new garment which is Jesus Christ Himself, his endowment with a new heart controlled by Jesus Christ, his new generation and birth in brotherhood with Jesus Christ, his saving death in the presence of the death which Jesus Christ suffered for him. All this is to be taken realistically, not just significantly and figuratively. . . . This is the foundation of the Christian life on this side, . . . it's primary foundation. . . . The divine change, man's baptism with the Holy Spirit, is not half-grace, or half-adequate grace; it is whole grace and wholly adequate grace. . . . It is not just his enlightenment from without [*Beleuchtung*], but a lighting up from within [*feurige Erleuchtung von innen*]. It deserves and demands full, unreserved and unconditional gratitude.[55]

Jüngel points out that Barth's earlier reflection on the Augustinian concept of sacrament of sign/reality or thing structure has been in fact exploded, since the "sign" (water baptism) does not effect the "thing signified" (Spirit baptism). The sign is "exclusively" the function of the divine "thing" of human correspondence through obedience. Water baptism is then a "necessary principle" *(necessitate praecepti),* not a "necessary medium" *(necessitate medii).* But Barth is also not advocating some kind of gnostic or spiritualist understanding of baptism in which water baptism is devalued and inner conversion experiences are exalted, leading to "*Eigenmächtigkeit*" (arbitrariness). If one thinks about divine presence in terms of sacrament, as in the Lutheran tradition, then water baptism is a matter of corresponding to that reality/thing that is already present. And immediately, as human correspondence, it has an ethical, existential meaning.

No longer is the sacramental understanding of water baptism an "effective sign of grace" *(signum efficax gratiae)* in the believer but the other way around: The human being actively participates in the grace of God since water baptism is expressive of the human decision in conversion corresponding to the divine act of baptism with the Holy Spirit. Jüngel brings Barth's arguments to bear

---

54. *KD* I/1:97.

55. *CD* IV/4:33–35. The translation of *"feurige Erleuchtung von innen"* (*KD* IV/4:38) is really quite inadequate here and should be more like "fiery illumination from within."

directly on his own Lutheran tradition and its need for reform. Thus, rather than the definition of the Augsburg Confession, article 5,[56] the decision of community and believer in water baptism is grounded in the coming of the Holy Spirit, where the Christian life is established. It is then the fundamental act of obedience and hope, the objective activity of baptism with water. To the extent that human decision in conversion is identical with the "act of faith,"[57] faith of the baptizand, the baptismal candidate, is the condition for receiving water baptism[58]—certainly not as a work of the law; the baptizand together with the baptizing community confesses the deepest solidarity with unbelievers. The irrevocability of faith's beginning objectifies itself in water baptism as the irreversibility of human beings' decisions before God. And particularly in this irreversibility of human decision there is found its existential meaning that human beings obey and hope in their God.[59]

Thus, the connection between sacrament and proclamation remains, but no longer "proclamation through sermon and sacrament"[60] or baptism as sacrament where "reality also becomes truth"[61] or where reality is sealed with truth. Even preaching is no longer an act that is both truth and reality (*KD* I/1:60ff.) or "God's Word as God's Work." Jüngel points out that Barth no longer accepts what he had once meant by sacrament: It no longer means "means of grace." Thus, one can no longer say that human preaching is the Word of God or that baptism and the Lord's Supper are activities that confirm and make visible God's work (*KD* I/1:71). Instead, baptism and the Lord's Supper and preaching *correspond* to the Word of God.[62] Baptism and the Lord's Supper so correspond based on an analogy with prayer itself, the answer of the church to the Word of God: baptism as petition, Lord's Supper as thanksgiving.

Jüngel is intent to show that *solo verbo* and *sola fide* are maintained, with the human act of water baptism as an "answering act." According to Jüngel, Barth interprets baptism consistently as a phenomenon of the Word of God.[63] One can speak of it as an "act of the Word." In view of the foundational acts of obedience and hope, both make concrete the human word, where obedience is twofold: as human refusal (confession of sin) and agreement (confession of faith) and hope as prayer. By faith, human beings

---

56. "That we may obtain this faith, the Ministry of Teaching the Gospel and administering the Sacraments was instituted. For through the Word and Sacraments, as through instruments, the Holy Ghost is given" (Augsburg Confession, art. 5). Note the instrumentality of teaching and sacraments for the work of the Holy Spirit. Jüngel is not becoming Anabaptist, but he is distinguishing the particular work of the Spirit from human action.

57. *KD* IV/1:2.

58. *KD* IV/4:189f.

59. Jüngel, *Barth-Studien*, 280.

60. *KD* I/1:57.

61. Karl Barth, *Die kirchliche Lehre von der Taufe* (München: C. Kaiser, 1947), 19.

62. Jüngel, *Barth-Studien*, 281.

63. This is something of a speech act, as an "act word"; therefore Jüngel's term *"Tatwort."*

act in ways that correspond with the divinely given command on the ground of baptism and with the goal of baptism in divinely given hope. The *solo verbo* is brought forward so consistently by Barth that Christian existence is determined through the Word of God as being acts of the Word. The *fides*, which alone corresponds to the *verbum divinum*, corresponds to it in human acts of the Word.[64]

As to Barth's use of Scripture in grounding his view of water baptism, Jüngel notes that the New Testament speaks of baptism largely ad hoc. An isolated theology of baptism is not possible; nevertheless, the phenomenon of baptism appearing in the text requires that baptism be theologically and correctly understood. Taking Barth's exegesis seriously as sound and persuasive, Jüngel points out that Barth can identify God himself as the baptizer; baptism is effected only in the sending of God's Son.[65] Mostly, however, Barth sees Jesus Christ as the one who baptizes with the Holy Spirit.[66] Barth sees Spirit baptism and water baptism as two different acts of two different subjects in the same event. As to the question of how water baptism as such serves Spirit baptism as such, Barth gives an effective answer: It witnesses to it. This is the function of the uniqueness of water baptism.

Jüngel draws together themes of prayer for the Holy Spirit, ethics, and the uniqueness of water baptism. He shows how Barth deals with the problem of understanding the prayer "Come, Creator Spirit" as fulfilled in Spirit baptism[67] according to *sub specie aeternitatis* with the perichoresis of the three modes of time in the life and history of God, which allows for the one coming of the Holy Spirit to be understood as iterative. Jüngel then asks whether there should be a *sub specie hominis* to distinguish between a renewed coming with Spirit baptism and the already-come Spirit.[68] The ethical connection with Paul's statements on baptism is unmistakable. However, these statements do not refer back to a human act but to a specific being of the human based on the acts of the baptized. Baptism's uniqueness brings about an irrevocable addressability of the baptized and thereby a validation of "life in the Spirit." Water baptism is the church's and the believer's way together of "unsacramentally" establishing the validity of the Christian life, beginning with an "adult" act of obedience. Jüngel finally wishes to put forward an evangelical theology of baptism that is worth the conflict such reform will cause. To do that, the reforming work would have to be fully justified exegetically (something that Barth himself

---

64. Jüngel, *Barth-Studien*, 282.

65. *KD* IV/4:33; Jüngel, *Barth-Studien*, 283. Christologically, Jüngel wonders if baptism with the Holy Spirit demonstrates the human being of Jesus Christ (cf. *KD* IV/2:122–56, 327–89 his *status exaltationis* [state of exaltation]) as opposed to Jesus' being baptized with water in the Jordan as a specific demonstration of his deity (cf. IV/1:145–81, connecting the divine being of Jesus Christ with the *status exinanitionis* [state of self-emptying]).

66. *KD* IV/4:76f.

67. *KD* IV/4:40.

68. Jüngel, *Barth-Studien*, 284.

had not done) and based on dogmatic interpretation, all the while paying full attention to the phenomena of Scripture.[69]

Barth's doctrine of baptism, observes Jüngel, becomes more controversial than its dogmatic premises—this is readily seen in all of the extensive treatments by Webster. Its practical consequences would be attacked more than the doctrine itself. This is the point where Barth's rejection of infant baptism as integral to this doctrine of baptism confronts church practice.[70] Jüngel contends that one cannot proceed to other parts of the *CD* unless one passes through this one. Even at this negative point, the doctrine of baptism is not an appendix to the *CD*[71] but instead the test of any full embrace of it by means of an example. One cannot "sneak past" it. Thus, whoever wishes to baptize infants, declares Jüngel, should not proclaim their closeness to Barth's doctrine of predestination. The churches will have to decide on this. Implying a decision in agreement with Barth, Jüngel further asserts that it will be good for them to do so.[72]

At this point Jüngel wishes to test the reception of Barth. Is Barth understood as neoorthodox, as a "revelational positivist," or as a church father—even as a defender of the churchly status quo accredited by ecclesial authority?[73] Jüngel points out that Barth is for neither a "theology of human beings" nor a "theology about human beings" but wants a theology of God himself, and yet a theology of God himself for human beings. Therefore, in the *CD*, there can be no mixed image of divine *and* human being or act. As God demonstrates himself in his own acts, so also the human being should demonstrate himself in his own acts. God himself demands that one do this. When one does this, one corresponds to God himself. Thus, the human being is himself or herself. Barth's theology is of God speaking with human beings and therefore at the same time of humans speaking with God.

Jüngel concludes with his own outlining of the argument of *KD* IV/4. In Spirit baptism, Barth is focused on the prior divine turning to human beings in Jesus Christ, which is the origin of human conversion. Barth is rejecting both anthropomonism and christomonism. The resurrection of Jesus Christ is the divine disclosure of his history for all human beings, whereas the work of the Holy Spirit is the divine disclosure to particular human beings for the disclosure of the history of Jesus Christ. Barth then interprets Spirit baptism as the epitome of the entire Christian life, founded on the divine turning toward human beings. The beginning of the Christian life occurs in an immediate (not requiring ecclesial mediation) self-witnessing and self-mediation of Jesus Christ through his powerful and active Word, taking place with particular human

69. Ibid., 285.
70. Ibid., 286.
71. Ibid., 287.
72. Ibid., 287. Cf. H. Gollwitzer, "Theologisches Gutachten über die Freigabe der Erwachsentaufe," in *Ecclesia semper reformanda: Theologische Aufsätze,* ed. Ernst Wolf, W. Schneemelcher, and K. G. Steck, *Evangelische Theologie,* Sonderheft (München: C. Kaiser, 1952), 65–82, 76 n. 16.
73. Jüngel, *Barth-Studien,* 288.

beings in the work of the Holy Spirit. Spirit baptism is a newly founded form of effective and reality-creating grace—which water baptism is not. Spirit baptism engenders thankfulness in obedience and inseparably so. Spirit baptism is the hope-filled beginning of a life in special solidarity with the Christian church. It is the hope-filled and permanent beginning of the new life, with an ever-new beginning in daily repentance, as believers wait for the absolute goal on the other side of the entire Christian life.

In water baptism, as Jüngel further clarifies, Barth is focused on human correspondence, which points to Spirit baptism as the first form of the divine turning to which human conversion corresponds as the foundation of Christian life. After exegetically substantiating this claim,[74] Barth calls Jesus' baptism the basis for baptism with water. The command to be baptized is the explication of the knowable ground of Christian baptism in the baptism of Jesus. In interpreting this ground of Christian baptism, Barth notes the unreserved subjection of Jesus to God, the unreserved solidarity of Jesus with human beings, and Jesus' appearance as servant as the first and foundational act of his self-proclamation. The baptism of Jesus is the "necessary ground" *(necessitas praecepti)* for understanding that obedience that is carried out in water baptism.[75] The goal of baptism with water formally lies beyond itself as a completed act. Materially, the promised goal of water baptism is Spirit baptism.[76]

The meaning of water baptism is the establishing of the Christian life in human action. Negatively, the praise of baptism is its not being a sacrament by the necessary differentiation of Spirit baptism and water baptism. This requires the exegetical and systematic theological deconstruction of the churchly theological tradition of understanding baptism sacramentally. Positively, the praise of baptism is its being a human act, but not in Zwingli's sense. The formal characteristics of baptism are imitative action (technical completion), communal work between the baptizing and the baptizand, and a free human act (obedience as risk). The technical definition is an existential interpretation of water baptism: conversion as the unity of obedience (over against the basis of baptism) and hope (in the goal of baptism). Finally, Barth further explicates his existential interpretation formally as an act of a given freedom by which obedience is carried out, and materially as human rejection (based on divine justification) and human agreement (based on sanctification). Infant baptism must be rejected formally as a hopeful act of risky hope and materially as merely a hope-filled act of prayer.

In a final chapter on Barth's doctrine, Jüngel formulates a set of theological theses. First among them is that Barth's doctrine of baptism is a part of his *Church Dogmatics* and thus is to be understood, appreciated, and critiqued in relation to these dogmatics. Particularly difficult, of course, is the unfinished

---

74. *KD* IV/4:49–55.
75. Ibid., 73–75.
76. Ibid., 73–110.

nature of the *Dogmatics* and that the doctrine of reconciliation is missing the part on the Lord's Supper. Barth's doctrine of baptism is an immediate consequence of his Christology grounded in his doctrine of reconciliation. Barth's doctrine of baptism is the foundational part of his ethic within his doctrine of reconciliation.[77] As such, his ethic cannot be drawn from some general concept but rather must be a theological decision decided above the essence of ethics. Barth's doctrine of baptism is a conscious and decisive correction of his earlier formulation of the doctrine of the Word of God and the connected doctrine of sacrament. This correction is already prepared for in the doctrine of election.

The christological grounding of Barth's doctrine of reconciliation determines the concept of baptism and the structure of the doctrine of baptism in the doctrine of reconciliation. Barth's doctrine of reconciliation is the basis for understanding the being of Jesus Christ as a history that has revealed the reconciliation of all human beings and their world with God, destroying the traditional theological concept of baptism as a sacrament. This understanding of the being of Jesus Christ is basic to Barth's doctrine of the being of the elect man in Jesus from the beginning with God. This understanding knows only the human being of Jesus Christ as the mediating sacrament between God and humanity. Barth's struggle with the sacramental character of baptism would not be a minimizing of its worth but a proper honoring of baptism. Barth seeks to solve the contradiction of the double mediation of the present salvation in the being of Jesus Christ through Word and sacrament in the Reformation doctrine of baptism. He does this through differentiating between the exclusive divine action toward human beings understood as "baptism with the Holy Spirit" and what is exclusively human action understood as "baptism with water." The differentiation between Spirit baptism and water baptism is to be understood as a strict correspondence (analogy) of faith grounded in divine action and is foundational for the Christian life of human action. The differentiation between Spirit baptism and water baptism parallels fully Barth's differentiation in *KD* IV/1–3 between Jesus Christ as Word of God *(analogans)* and Christian proclamation *(analogatum)* (i.e., self-presentation of Jesus Christ [*analogans*]) and the corresponding formation of Christian existence of this self-presentation *(analogatum)*. The differentiation between Spirit baptism and water baptism presupposes an understanding of God whereby we are to think of God's omni-agency and sole agency. The christological point of the differentiation between Spirit baptism and water baptism is Barth's thesis from the ontological connection between Jesus Christ and Christians (between the *extra nos* [*in Christo*] and the *in nobis* of salvation). The anthropological point of the differentiation between Spirit baptism and water baptism is Barth's speech about baptism as a redemptive human activity.

---

77. Jüngel, *Barth-Studien,* 291.

Barth's doctrine of baptism is of fundamental ecumenical significance as far as it brings Reformation principles to more consistent validity. It conveys the possibility of understanding with Roman Catholic soteriology, and it also conveys the possibility of an understanding with evangelical Christianity (Baptists and others). Barth's doctrine of baptism brings consistent validity to the faith that alone corresponds to the being of Jesus Christ. Based on this, baptism (with water) does not establish faith, but the believer lets himself or herself be baptized. The necessity of baptism is not as a means of salvation but is perceived according to faith as *necessitas praecepti,* which as such is based on the baptism of Jesus. Barth's doctrine of baptism implies a positive interpretation of human action in view of human salvation, insofar as water baptism is a petition for the Holy Spirit, and this petition is understood as redemptive human action. Based on the strict differentiation of divine action and human action with the *particulae exclusivae solus Christus, sola gratia, solo verbo, sola fide,* there is the first correct validation of appreciation of the human being as subject of his own act, justifying the demand of Roman Catholic theology in an evangelical way. Barth's rejection of infant baptism based on a consistent application of his doctrine of baptism could contribute to an ecumenical understanding of the concept of the church in evangelical Christianity. Barth's doctrine of baptism does not confront the Eastern Orthodox understanding.

In evaluating Barth's doctrine of baptism, particular arguments are appropriate only as they make themselves understood according to baptism that is validated according to *solus Christus, sola gratia, solo verbo,* and *sola fide;* as they account for the necessity of a baptismal theology and doctrine of baptism interconnected with the entirety of Christian doctrine; as they account for the difficulties of New Testament statements on baptism; and as they presuppose that valid church practice is not the absolute criterion for the truth of the church doctrine of baptism.

Barth's doctrine of baptism has sought support in general critical exegesis of the New Testament baptismal statements, but the full range of critical aspects has not been explicated. This fact gave Barth's critics cause for justifiable criticism. A general critical exegesis would have been necessary (1) to clarify how such different and thoroughly contradictory understandings of baptism were possible; (2) to make the relation between baptismal theology and liturgical characteristics of primitive Christian baptismal practice critically thematic; (3) to make the relation between baptism and sin thematically clear, and with this criterion to work out a theology of baptism; (4) to lay out and overcome the terminological difficulties of the differentiation between Spirit baptism and water baptism; (5) to critically express the natural approach of baptism with water conferred on it or to deprive it of meaning in the framework of a hermeneutic of the symbol; and (6) to critically express the varying relevance of symbolic action in every respect for a religiously administered world and in a technically administered world. The baptismal theology of Barth should have done everything that a general critical exegesis would have to do.

Jüngel rounds out his approach with his "critique of the sacramental understanding of baptism." Essential to the task of theology is to reflect the church's constant inquiry of true kerygma and confession and therefore of baptism essential to these. In contrast to traditions that posit ecclesial infallibility, the church that exists in its earthly sojourn as *simil iustus et peccator* must be continually attentive to what comes to it clearly in the gospel, what it has formulated for itself in terms of what it proclaims, and what it confesses before God and other human beings. Penetrating reflection on the nature of baptism is in order. Jüngel writes this particularly in light of what the Roman church regards as the *"fratres seiuncti"* (disjoined brethren) of Protestantism, particularly those of the Lutheran communion.

The first task that stands before the church with respect to baptism is that the question of baptism must be aporetically worked on to dialectically expose the contradictions between New Testament and ecclesial statements. "Ways of escape are to be cut off"—Jüngel is saying something to himself as much as anyone else.[78] Ways that would hinder an aporetic of baptism are the following: (1) reducing the question of the nature of baptism systematically to the question of the legitimacy or illegitimacy of infant baptism; (2) answering the question of the nature of baptism primarily in terms of infant baptism, based on confessions and church canons as definitive on account of recurring instances; (3) based on the variety and contradictoriness of the exegetical contributions to the question of baptism, coming to the conclusion—in view of the present responsibility in dealing with the matter of baptism, the scriptural baptismal texts, and the church theological baptismal tradition—of avoiding a reworked doctrine of baptism, and thereby rather in practical terms theoretically leaving everything the way it was. Jüngel then lays out four principles by which reworking a doctrine of baptism must proceed: (1) Show responsibility to the matter of baptism in every respect, since it is to baptism that we are responsible. (2) Since responsibility to baptism is already expressed in the New Testament texts, present responsibility to baptism must lead to conformity to these texts of the New Testament in clear distinction from the history of the tradition, which bears very marked differences in response. It will be proper to bring forward the differences in the drive toward general critical decision. (3) Responsibility to baptism cannot take place as responsibility to the matter of baptism today without conflict with the tradition, where respect and criticism cannot be two-sided but must be one-sided. Uncritical respect for the tradition should be rejected just as much as disrespectful criticism of the tradition. (4) Present responsibility to baptism regards effective church canons as fundamentally revisable, and after revision the canons would demand to be respected. Jüngel then offers a set of theses as answers to fundamental questions about baptism, theses directly applicable to his own Lutheran tradition, down to the point

---

78. Ibid., 299.

of requiring revision of the *Confessio Augustana* (Augsburg Confession). After fully absorbing Barth's doctrine of baptism and then going back to the texts of Scripture, Jüngel begins reworking the Lutheran doctrine of baptism. He has cut himself off from every escape route.

The first principle: What does baptism have to do with sin? Jüngel answers this question by centering on justification alone, thus dissociating baptism, in the first instance, from the forgiveness of sins. Indeed, the doctrine of justification is the only basis for a connection between baptism and sin in a correct doctrine of baptism. Ultimately, baptism is an event that functions as "interpretation of the event of the justification of the sinner."[79] By "event of justification" Jüngel means sanctification, where to be "washed" in 1 Corinthians 6:11 is parallel to "being justified."

The second principle: Jesus Christ as ground of faith and therefore of baptism. Here is where Jüngel has most crucially recognized Barth's contribution, that the orientation toward the doctrine of justification in the evangelical doctrine of baptism requires the sacramental options of Lutheran and Reformed tradition to be overcome. This is based on the necessity of baptism not as a necessary medium *(necessitas medii)* but solely as the necessity of a gracious command *(necessitas praecepti)*. Thus, it follows that baptism is possible and meaningful only for believers. The theses that follow from this point are most crucial: (1) Baptism gives and works nothing other than what Jesus through the Holy Spirit in the Word of proclamation gives and works with faith, but it gives and works the same in a different way. (2) The special aspect of baptism exists in that the baptizand in baptism is established in his or her faith and thereby on Jesus Christ as the object and ground of faith and together with the baptizing community is irrevocably united to the body of Christ. (3) Through baptism and faith alone the believer is irrevocably separated from sin. (4) In baptism there takes place the irrevocability of Christian being (character) itself as the imperative for Christian action. (5) Finally, faith in a judgment that will judge Christian works is an eschatological reservation against a sacramental understanding of baptism.[80]

Barth's influence and overall continual reflection on the founding texts of Scripture for doctrine and practice are reflected in the work of another leading Lutheran theologian, Friedrich Mildenberger. In his theology of Lutheran confessions, he writes:

> This is an unusually critical matter for the Reformation's focus on the gospel as it is distributed in Word and Sacrament and received in faith. The problem is that the church's practice of infant baptism makes it impossible for us to see God working in the unified process of giving and receiving. . . . In discussing faith under . . . presuppositions about baptism, we cannot avoid the appear-

79. Ibid., 304.
80. Ibid., 310–13.

ance that this faith is really the work of the person who has been baptized. The question as to how the church's practice can be conformed to this theological insight remains an open question. . . .

The practice of infant baptism . . . isolates the objective side of the sacrament that is related to the person and work of Christ. Thereby it places the salvation gained by Christ into the hands of the church so that it now has to be distributed by the church. If the church fails in its task and a child dies without being baptized, then this child misses out on salvation. The church's function then becomes a work that is necessary to salvation and God's freedom to work in and through the gospel is set aside. . . . Such an understanding of baptism is inconsistent with the gospel.[81]

Mildenberger goes on to point out that both Lutheran and Baptist positions on baptism require a positive unification of objective and subjective poles of this one reality.

Jüngel actually has another chapter that profoundly complements what he has been expositing with regard to the fundamental implications of Barth's view of baptism.[82] Basic to this ethic would be an exposition of the Lord's Prayer and its particular petitions. In doing so, Barth would bring together the analogy between divine action and human action. The distinction is not nonrelational but achieves its concrete relation in and through invocation.[83] The "grounding act of the Christian ethos" is the invocation of God: "Our Father!" This invocation has the human being asking of God what only God may give, what only God can do: "Hallowed be Thy name! Thy kingdom come!" A "synergism" actually appears in Barth where, based on faith, a cooperative labor in the Christian life arrives, a *"Senkrecht von unten"* (perpendicular from below),[84] where believers' "being in action"[85] emerges as a genuine Protestant concept. Jüngel points out that Barth's ethic becomes even more radical than that of his teacher, Wilhelm Herrmann, who declared, "Real ethics . . . is the true obedience of the free."[86] What Herrmann grounded in general humanness,

---

81. Friedrich Mildenberger, *Theology of the Lutheran Confessions,* ed. Erwin L. Lueker (Philadelphia: Fortress, 1986), 108–11.

82. The chapter is "Invocation of God as Fundamental Ethos of Christian Action: Introductory Remarks to the Posthumously Published Fragments of the Ethic of the Doctrine of Reconciliation of Karl Barth" (Jüngel, *Barth: Legacy,* 315–31). By this Jüngel means not only *CD* IV/4 but also "Lectures from 1959–1961," in Karl Barth, *Gesamtausgabe,* vol. 2: *Akademische Werke 1959–1961: Das christliche Leben,* ed. H.-A. Drewes and Eberhard Jüngel, 2d ed. (Zürich: Theologischer Verlag, 1979).

83. Jüngel, *Barth-Studien,* 321.

84. Ibid., 254.

85. *KD* II/1:1.

86. Cf. W. Herrmann, "Religion und Sittlichkeit," in W. Herrmann, *Schriften zur Grundlegung der Theologie,* ed. P. Fischer-Appelt, Theologische Bücherei 36, Teil 1 (München: C. Kaiser, 1966), 264–81, quoting 265. This has interesting implications for the conclusion of Gary Dorrien, *The Barthian Revolt in Modern Theology: Theology without Weapons* (Louisville: Westminster John Knox, 2000), 187–96.

Barth brought out in christological uniqueness as the condition of being and the condition of understanding the "ethical question." Through christological uniqueness, Barth was pointing to a revealed goodness that is univocal whose corresponding truth is concrete faith in God, the One who is gracious toward human beings through Jesus Christ.[87]

Barthian Problems with Barth

Unfortunately, some of the leading readers of Barth working in the English-language context have not responded to the Barth of IV/4 in an affirming way. In a well-written article, George Hunsinger challenges what he calls the "bifurcation" in Barth's view between Spirit baptism and water baptism, whereby water baptism not only attests to but also conveys forgiveness. Certainly, the first thing to contest with respect to Hunsinger's article is the very judgment of "bifurcation": This is certainly not what Barth intends, but has he rendered the doctrine thus anyway? Or is there a more fundamental problem of consistency with respect to the relation between understanding God's saving work in Christ and a proper understanding of sacrament? By beginning his article with a presentation of baptism and forgiveness, Hunsinger hits on an important soteriological connection. Indeed, this was the crucial point for Jüngel in dismantling the traditional theological category of sacrament. Hunsinger does not interact with Jüngel on this point. He does wish to lay out a framework for the whole of soteriology and to allow its particular truths to speak within that whole. This is not an easy thing to do in any case, as Hunsinger acknowledges, and in proceeding with Hunsinger, one must resist quibbling over each particular term or definition that he introduces, as in the three tenses of salvation. Indeed, there is much to admire here; one sees Hunsinger's profound grasp of the matter of theology. His perceptiveness and articulation of the varied dangers of a soteriological model that neglects past, present, or future aspects is masterful.

From the outset, Hunsinger does not write his article as a close critical reading of Barth. Instead, as a theologian in his own right, Hunsinger lays out the contours of his theological approach, and central to this is what he calls "a *koinonia*-relations," "a relation of mutual indwelling between two terms (e.g., between Christ and the church)."[88] Employing an incarnational model[89] or, as he calls it, a "Chalcedonian pattern," Hunsinger explicates the dwelling "in" of two members who comprise a particular kind of unity. He does not lay out

---

87. Jüngel, *Barth-Studien,* 328.

88. George Hunsinger, "Baptism and the Soteriology of Forgiveness," *International Journal of Systematic Theology* 2 (2000): 247–69, quoting 248.

89. Thus, he defines unity as relation "without separation or division . . . and without confusion or change" (ibid., 248).

in critical relation the notion of a differently conceived unity by elaborating the other preposition accompanying *koinōnia*—"with"—or explaining how a nonincarnationally conceived "in" might operate as well. Hunsinger is laying out his model of relations based on his reading of theological tradition, and so one must bear with his explication according to examples stemming from an *a* related to a *b,* or a soteriological model according to tenses appended to *Christus—adventus, praesens, futuris*—and the priority of the first, the historical life of Christ, with respect to the other two, Christ's presence and future. The problem of generalizing what cannot be generalized, however, is the first chief problem with the logic of the model. The incarnation of the second person of the Godhead is not a shared condition of existence with any other than God and therefore is without analogy. This logic preserves the orthodox understanding of the incarnation from the other direction as well, rejecting what is viewed as a model of proper relation of unity between different members, according to a general logic of ethical relations based on "with" or "with-ness." In terms of Hunsinger's exposition, its rich christocentricity maintains the proper elements of soteriology in a lively fashion, but by turning the incarnational into a single model that comprehends the entirety of these elements, it fails at two points: (1) missing other kinds of appropriate relational models and (2) maintaining his own model through a defensive strategy of christological polemics (e.g., to deny "indwelling" would be a Nestorian error).

After laying out some basic notions regarding the nature of sin and of forgiveness, the sheer and infinite grace behind the latter, and the inadequacy of polarizing models of sin, Hunsinger asserts a generous orthodoxy that encompasses both sin and victimization realities in our account of a salvation-needy world. His article has two subsections titled "The Forgiveness of Sin" and "Generous Orthodoxy: Some Consequences for Forgiven Sinners," which are comprised exclusively of excerpts from the Heidelberg Catechism (questions and answers 81–83, 131, 119, 115, 52). Then Hunsinger includes "Baptism as the Liturgical Mediation of Forgiveness," where "baptism is integral to soteriology" since it not only attests to but also mediates the sheer grace of divine forgiveness by liturgical act of the church.

As Hunsinger moves into his discussion of Barth's view of baptism, in his short opening paragraph he asserts what he regards Barth as not doing. He cites a parallel section in *CD* I/1 on the "sacrament of God" with his exposition of the threefold Word of God. Hunsinger observes that finally Barth gets around to baptism "decades later," at the end of his life, and simply fails to maintain self-consistency, instead rejecting baptism as sacramental in favor of the sole sacramentality of Christ. Hunsinger calls "this latter argument peculiar" not only with respect to the Catholic tradition—the remnants of which in Protestant theology Barth and other significant theologians of the late-twentieth century were hoping to reform more fully out of thought and practice—but also with respect to the implied suggestion that Barth's view is an aberration, something entirely unprepared for, even though published within the *CD*. Granted, if one has adopted a rather fixed paradigm for reading the *CD* through the lens of I/1 and, on this very point of sacrament, sensing the sacramental language used by Barth early but soon to be rejected with respect to the proclamation of the Word of God, it would be nothing less than a most unwelcome jolt or unpleasant development to pick up IV/4. One might regard it as wholly anomalous to what had been proceeding so well up through IV/3 along traditional sacramental lines. But Hunsinger knows that he must tackle Barth's earlier assertion that Jesus Christ is God's only sacrament for the salvation of humankind. By quickly appealing to a following of "the earlier rather than the later Barth," and yet wanting to retain what only the later Barth had fully clarified, namely, the sole sacramentality of Jesus Christ, Hunsinger calls for a "thought experiment" by which he would simply reconfigure the *CD* to suit a call for a traditional model—that one could question was ever in the early Barth at all.

Hunsinger makes it clear that his interests in going against Barth are ecumenical and that if his theses are acceptable, no position would remain unchanged. Of course, from Barth's and Jüngel's perspective, what counts is not only the likelihood of incremental, ecumenical change where everyone exhibits some progress but also why any change might be advisable, in this case with respect to the Catholic tradition, which apparently has the most to lose. Hunsinger is not thinking with Barth already from the doctrine of election in *CD* II/2 in terms of Christ as only sacrament, the sole medium/Mediator of grace from eternity, giving rise to a unity based on the enablement of the believer and the church to actively correspond to God, maintaining the integrities of divine freedom in being and action and creaturely human freedom in redeemed being and action. Hence, he directs all of his attention to what he calls Barth's loss of a "proper sense of unity."[90] This is most unfortunate since it is merely the case that Barth does not conform to Hunsinger's model of unity. As above, since nothing about the corporate relation between Christ and the church is incarnational, since the incarnation is without analogy just as the activity of Jesus Christ's soteriological mediation is without distribution and completely *extra nos* and *pro nobis,* Hunsinger is the one who loses the proper sense of *koinonia* between Christ as head of the church and believers as never more than his members. This is unfortunate, since so much of Hunsinger's thinking on Barth is as penetratingly correct as any writing in the English language. In a footnote, Hunsinger declares that Barth saw Spirit baptism and water baptism as two separate events, and yet it is more correct to say that for Barth they represent two successive, irreversible, and irrevocable moments of one event, where Spirit baptism has priority and human obedience is necessary as the prayerful form of action that is water baptism for the community and those being baptized. Here Barth's extensive analogy between prayer and water

90. Ibid., 256.

baptism is essential for understanding him. Again, what Hunsinger is missing is that although Barth's understanding comes to full expression only in *CD* II/2 and the later parts of the *CD*, Barth no longer regards any human action as anything closely analogous to divine action. Like proclamation, preaching corresponds to the Word of God, but in Barth's formulations, it no longer becomes the Word of God. This is also the final deepening and systematic extension of *analogia fidei*.

But Hunsinger also becomes difficult to follow as he lays out what he means about the priority of Spirit baptism:

> Barth is again correct, however, that the efficacy of Spirit baptism is definitive. Spirit baptism stands on its own and does not require water baptism for its efficacy. Water baptism is best understood as the fulfillment of Spirit baptism. Dominically appointed it is the normal consequence of Spirit baptism. Spirit baptism can be and is (in principle) efficacious without water baptism, but water baptism is not efficacious without Spirit baptism. . . . Add water baptism to Spirit baptism, and the former becomes a means of grace . . . in a secondary and . . . non-synergistic way. The relationship between the *water* of water baptism and the *Spirit* of Spirit baptism is one of mutual coinherence. The Spirit is *in and with* the water and the water is *in and with* the Spirit in a distinctive form of mutual indwelling and accompaniment. Yet it is the Spirit who makes the water efficacious in a way that is not in any sense reversible.[91]

How can Hunsinger combine the assertion that "Spirit baptism stands on its own" with the assertion that "water baptism . . . becomes a means of grace"? It is important to note, as Hunsinger does, that Barth ascribes to Spirit baptism a sacramental quality, but this is precisely because the Spirit is the Spirit of Christ, whose sole gracious agency is consistently affirmed by Barth. As with many traditionalists, Hunsinger finds Barth's move to separate sacramentality from baptism—not to speak of the Lord's Supper, as Barth would have done with more time to write the *CD*—simply unthinkable or, better, truly counterintuitive.

The essay moves on to include what Hunsinger calls the "abnormality" of infant baptism, which must nevertheless be made intelligible in the church because of entrenched practice—the cause of the counterintuitiveness. The standard arguments are brought out along with a theologumenon of "proleptic faith," all to attempt a substantiation that the faith of one may be exercised on behalf of another *coram Deo* (before God)—which of course is the very point of fundamental contradiction with the Reformation doctrine of *sola fide*. Vicarious faith on the part of the community increases creaturely sacramentality, as Hunsinger anticipates, beyond the signs of water, bread, and wine to the institution of the church itself. But the real problem takes place at the point of

---

91. Ibid., 257.

Spirit baptism. The Reformed tradition, which has always affirmed the necessary connection between the work of the Holy Spirit and the sinner's hearing and confessing by faith, understood that the regeneration anticipated by water baptism was not present at the water baptism of an infant. But since Hunsinger is trying to hold on to Barth's prioritization of Spirit baptism, followed then and only then by water baptism, the reality of saving faith must be reserved for a later time in the life of the infant being baptized. The infant cannot hear the Word of God as the Word of God nor confess agreement with and trust in that Word from the heart. Hunsinger then claims that it is the "temporal sequence" of water baptism preceding Spirit baptism that makes infant baptism seem "abnormal," but that temporal sequence is a matter of "indifference."[92] In terms of Barth's view, this spells a total loss, but it is one of the possible "escape routes" that Jüngel had tried to close off in view of the need for the church to be ever reforming. The irony is that the ancient understanding of baptism as an act of confession on the part of the baptizand, which Barth is attempting to restore and to extend, can never be a part of actual experience on the part of those baptized in infancy. It must be remembered for them so that the vicarious element never gives way to actual experience in terms of the lived and communal experience of water baptism. The curious matter is that Hunsinger never suggests that what has been historically "abnormal" in Christian practice should not finally be rectified. Key to Hunsinger's proposal is that Spirit and water baptism not be separated from each other, that at the same time synergism be avoided, and that better attempts to become ecumenically unstuck by not condemning infant baptism be made. Long gone are the ecumenical theologians who argue for believer's baptism, but Barth, Jüngel, Jürgen Moltmann,[93] and others wish for reform to continue in this direction. How could theologians of the Reformation traditions think otherwise about ecumenical progress?[94]

92. Ibid., 262. Curiously, he regards the multiple texts of the New Testament that present temporal sequence as no challenge to his position.

93. Cf. Jürgen Moltmann, *The Church in the Power of the Spirit,* trans. Margaret Kohl (San Francisco: HarperSanFrancisco, 1991), 226ff.

94. In his latest book of essays on Barth, Hunsinger explores in a couple of chapters matters immediately relevant to the present discussion. In a chapter on the Holy Spirit, he is alert to Barth's stringency in distinguishing the divine and the human on this point but also his emphasis on the *in nobis* working of the Spirit, mediating a faith, although not a being, which is our *participatio Christi.* Most important, Hunsinger is sensitive to the work of the Spirit, which mediates the *Christus preasens* so crucial not only to Barth's theological deepening but also to his theological method—discussed at length in connection with *CD* II/1 in chapter 5, above. Much more than in the article, Hunsinger here clarifies the problem, as Barth saw it, of synergism in the relation between the Holy Spirit and the human being: Only the miraculous working of God can bring the divine and human into proper relation, never in a natural coexistence because of humanity's radical fallenness. Drawing on his translation of Barth's chapter "Extra nos—pro nobis—in nobis" in the Wolf *Festschrift* (ed. H. Gollwitzer and H. Traub), which becomes early pages of *CD* IV/4, Hunsinger makes the inseparable connection between divine and human

John Webster, however, is perhaps the theologian who has spent the most time with Barth's and Jüngel's view. Webster has certainly become the most sophisticated reader of both theologians in the English-speaking world and has done immense service in rendering translations of the two and carefully expounding and defending their views—except on this point. And the exception is complicated and fraught with torturous avoidance and even obfuscation,

---

action, accentuating "outside us, for us, and in us." Hunsinger identifies the uniting work of the Holy Spirit between Christ and his community, but he is careful to follow Barth in not identifying this work as incarnational (cf. *CD* IV/3:760–61; IV/2:652–53). Christ is the head of the community, his body where "two freedoms are mysteriously conjoined," one eternal from God's side and one temporal from the human side. Together, they are *totus Christus,* but in this other special sense of union that is real but not hypostatic. Indeed, Barth considered talk of the church as incarnational to be *"blasphemische Rede"* (*KD* IV/3:834). As Barth writes, "The coordination and unity is the work of the active grace of God. . . . It all takes place in the gracious act of the gracious power *(Gnadentat der Gnadenmacht)* of the Holy Spirit which co-ordinates the different elements and constitutes and guarantees their unity. In virtue of this gracious act it is always true and actual that the Head does not live without His body nor the body without its Head, but that the Head, Jesus Christ, lives with and in His community, and the body, His community, with and in Him. In virtue of the gracious act of the Holy Spirit, who is Himself God, *Dominus, vivificans, cum Patre et Filio simul adorandus et glorificandus,* there exists and persists . . . the people of His witnesses in world-occurrence" (*CD* IV/3:761–62). Everything is constituted and guaranteed by the gracious power of the Holy Spirit. In discussing participation in the life of God, Hunsinger notes Barth's point of the actual sharing in the love of God, Father, Son, and Holy Spirit. The ontological divide is in no way dissolved, but unity of "indirect participation" (*CD* II/1:59) is nevertheless established in the freedom of God to be with us, uniting us with Christ and on account of our *koinōnia* in the humanity of Jesus. This chapter becomes, then, a most helpful exposition of the pneumatology of volume IV, particularly at the point where Hunsinger holds together Barth's emphases on the universal scope of God's relations and the special relation to the individual, the *pro me* of his grace. He sums up: "The Holy Spirit's mediation of communion, as Barth saw it, is trinitarian in ground (not anthropological), christocentric in focus (not pneumatocentric), miraculous in operation (not "natural"), communal in content (not individualistic or collectivist), eschatological in form (neither epiphanist nor triumphalist), diversified in application (not unvarying or undifferentiated), and universal in scope (not simply ecclesial). Within these contours of Barth's theology of the Holy Spirit is a theology of *koinonia,* and *koinonia* is the essence of the Spirit's work" (184–85). Moving to his chapter on baptism into Christ's death, we must skip past an exceedingly important discussion of Barth's nonuniversalism with respect to salvation. Sensitive to Barth's preface to *CD* IV/4 in a way not exhibited by Webster, Hunsinger takes seriously the connection of this volume to the rest of the *CD.* He couches his approach in the assessment of Michael Wischogrod, who recognizes in Barth a Jewish sensibility with respect to Scripture that unashamedly listens and exposits the text without regard for the demands of relevancy. But what Hunsinger is after here is the further understanding of baptism in terms of *koinōnian* incorporation into the crucified Christ. Endeavoring to open up the close affinity von Balthasar sensed between himself and Barth, Hunsinger highlights what he calls the "overthrow" *(Aufhebung)*—in Barth most familiarly attached to his treatment of religion per se—of nature (connected with the Roman Catholic maxim that sees grace as completing nature) in a special sense formulated brilliantly by Hunsinger: "Grace perfects human nature as created only as grace destroys human nature as fallen" (270). Baptism into Christ's death is accomplished by the work of the Holy Spirit, who contemporanizes Christ in his death to us and us to Christ in his death because of the deepest possible *in nobis* action of this Spirit.

since the excellence of his work and representation of these theologians has created, apparently willingly on his part, a kind of custodianship with respect to their writings and teachings. Unfortunately, it appears that between the mainstream Anglicanism that Webster also wishes to defend, although he appears not to have a cobelligerent in Timothy Gorringe, who actually wishes to defend the appropriateness of *CD* IV/4, and perhaps the influence of Thomas Torrance,[95] who also found Barth in this volume profoundly counterintuitive, Webster fails to properly represent Barth or Jüngel in this matter, and to dire effect. This is odd because he is so acutely aware of Jüngel's courage and intent to find the substance of the gospel:

> Reading Jüngel's Christology may serve as a reminder that theology ought to be frightening, perilous—and not only because, properly undertaken, it ought to issue in intellectual, cultural and spiritual non-conformity, but because the one to whom theology gives its attention is unimaginably demanding. It is the jaggedness of Jüngel theology which most commands respect, for his real intellectual virtue is that of relentless critical interrogation of our representations of what he takes to be the heart of Christian faith.[96]

How ironic that at one of Jüngel's most passionate and courageous points, namely, in embracing and extending Barth's doctrine of baptism and the fundamental direction of the *CD* from II/2 to IV/4, Webster barely comments throughout his writings.

Webster has become particularly influential in Barthian interpretation at the point of showing the unity of ethics with dogmatics throughout the *CD*. Webster's expertise has been to show how such a massive work in theology, so wholly devoted to the knowledge of the being and action of the Triune God

95. "If we reject the idea of an intermediate reality of supernatural grace between God and man, as surely we must do, then we are left with two alternative positions for our understanding of baptism: . . . a return to a sacramental dualism between water-baptism and Spirit-baptism, in which the meaning of baptism if found not in a direct act of God but in an ethical act on the part of man made by way of response to what God has already done on his behalf . . . taken by Karl Barth, but this seems to me to be deeply inconsistent with his dynamic doctrine of the Trinity and the *opera ad extra* in creation and redemption as well as with his doctrine of the Incarnation according to which God himself has come to us within the space-time structure of our worldly existence and communicated himself personally to us there in his own living being and reality as God" (Thomas F. Torrance, *Theology in Reconciliation: Essays toward Evangelical and Catholic Unity in East and West* [London: Geoffrey Chapman, 1975], 99–100). Torrance is not actually interacting with Barth's arguments, nor is it at all clear that what he regards as counterarguments have in any way affected the persuasiveness of Barth's position. Cf. George Hunsinger, *Disruptive Grace: Studies in the Theology of Karl Barth* (Grand Rapids: Eerdmans, 2000), esp., "The Mediator of Communion: Karl Barth's Doctrine of the Holy Spirit," 148–85; and "Baptized into Christ's Death: Karl Barth and the Future of Roman Catholic Theology," 253–78.

96. John Webster, "Jesus in Modernity: Reflections on Jüngel Christology," in John Webster, *Word and Church: Essays in Christian Dogmatics* (Edinburgh: T & T Clark, 2001), 151–90, quoting 188.

in Jesus Christ, at one and the same time everywhere has for a subtext the corresponding action of the human through faith in Jesus Christ. Webster produced two major texts, the one following hard on the other: *Barth's Ethics of Reconciliation* (1995) and *Barth's Moral Theology* (1998). In the second volume, Webster repeats his contention that he lays out in more detail in the first: Barth's view of baptism was "from the beginning derailed by a focus on Barth's polemic about sacramental theology and practice, polemic that in fact was largely tangential to his main argument."[97] This is something of a bizarre comment since Barth had done so much to identify Jesus Christ as the one and only sacrament. How could Webster put a label of derailment on Barth's consistent outworking of the implications of this as he is reforming traditional notions about the obediential action of the church in baptism? Granted, Webster's purpose in the 1998 book is to continue to reorient Barth's readership according to a proper reception of the centrality of ethics in the *CD*. Yet it is at the point of the central acts of the Christian faith, like baptism, that what Barth is doing theologically is still just as important as what he is doing ethically. Webster also wants to bring out important historical information relative to the pre-*CD* Barth and to show that his work in the 1920s and 1930s, following *Römerbrief* (1919), bore a strong ethical impulse from his now-published lectures on Calvin and later those on ethics at Münster and Bonn. From this Webster wishes to show "the degree to which Barth's thinking is coherent from beginning to end" and to show that the profound development of his "theanthropological" views of *CD* IV are not "freshly-minted" convictions.[98]

There is, then, a difficulty: Webster fails to grasp fully the progressively reforming intent on Barth's part as he writes the *CD* and instead intends to show a basic coherency in Barth's theological ethics from the beginning of his work—not unlike Bruce McCormack's interest in showing the coherency of Barth's method in order to overturn misreadings of Barth's theological development. Webster is willing to admit Barth's "retractions, detours," revisiting of "old themes and self-corrections," but always to show how "very consistent" Barth's ethical vision is and at one with his theological vision since his break with liberal theology in 1915.[99] Indeed, there is no quarrel with this agenda overall; as with McCormack's interpretation of Barth, it became necessary to hold the work of the later Barth together with that of the early Barth. But this commitment to coherency and consistency can obscure Barth's keen reforming interest as a never-ending task placed on the theologian by the Word of God and the Spirit of God.

Nevertheless, what about Webster's reception of Jüngel as a Barthian interpreter, particularly in the area of Barth's ethics, more particularly as an interpreter of Barth's view of election, Jesus Christ as sacrament, the ethical possibility

97. Webster, *Barth's Moral Theology,* 2.
98. Ibid., 3.
99. Ibid.

arising from the indwelling of the Holy Spirit, and finally the significance of baptism as the inaugural act of obedience in the Christian life? Late in his essay on Barth and Luther's influence on Jüngel, Webster discusses Jüngel's exposition of Barth's ethics of reconciliation. Webster acknowledges that Jüngel's essays on Barth's view of baptism and the Christian life in *CD* IV/4 seek "to clarify Barth's intentions by lifting the texts out of the messy polemic evoked by its rejection of infant baptism, . . . important above all because they set what Barth had to say about baptism and Christian action in the context of the larger dogmatic and ethical themes of the *Church Dogmatics* as a whole."[100] He goes on to recognize the fundamental role of analogy or correspondence between divine and human action in Jüngel. Webster approvingly cites the axiomatic statement by Jüngel, *"Gott spricht—der Mensch entspricht"* (God speaks—the human corresponds). Nevertheless, greater emphasis could be put on Jüngel's locating this correspondence in action that obeys the Word of God, which also and first of all justifies the human being, so that the bond of unity between God and the human through Christ is not so much one of being as of Spirit and grace enabling action.

Webster is quite sensitive to the underlying implications of Barth's and Jüngel's reception of Barth on the matter of ethics in baptism and its impact on sacramental theology. Commenting on the ethical unity that God establishes with the human being through Word and faith, where Jüngel wishes to show Barth's giving each, God and the human, their due, Webster abruptly comments that this is Jüngel's major point,

> rather than protest against ecclesial sacramental *practice*—which is the real force of Barth's distinction between baptism with the Holy spirit and baptism with water in the last part of the *Church Dogmatics*. By distinguishing between an exclusively divine act and a corresponding fully human act, Barth's late doctrine of baptism refuses to construe divine omnicausality with divine sole causality.[101]

That God is omnicausal of human salvation does not make him the sole actor in the life of the church. Real human action in relation to God takes place in obedience to him. Analogy, quoting Jüngel, "guards the difference between God and humanity, in that it emphasizes as strongly as possible their partnership." This rings entirely true to Barth's statements in *CD* IV/4, and Jüngel is intent on following the reasoning in this volume. Curiously, Webster is drawing on Jüngel's radical chapter defending Barth's view of baptism and the entirety of *CD* IV/4; it is the elephant in the theological room, but Webster does not admit to it or explore the details of the chapter.[102] He does not acknowledge the radical nature of Jüngel's reforming program in this and

100. Ibid., 199.
101. Ibid., 201.
102. I.e., Jüngel, "Taufe," 273. Webster, *Barth's Moral Theology,* 201, focuses on only the distinction between divine and human action and the analogical relation of the one to the other.

the other attending two chapters, which embrace and extend Barth's doctrine of baptism in *Barth-Studien.* Indeed, he does not even connect with Barth's doctrine of baptism in one of his favorite essays by Jüngel, "Invocation of God as the Ethical Ground of Christian Action."[103] Webster leaves almost unacknowledged how this essay belongs to a cluster of articles by Jüngel that link correspondence, election, the sole sacramentality of Christ, the distinctions between God's work and human work and baptism as liturgical work, and his full embrace and extension of Barth's reform of baptism within an integrated complex of theological argumentation and understanding. Even in the published version of his dissertation and its second edition in 1991, Webster does not recognize what actually in Germany is well known about Jüngel inside the evangelical church. Webster seems to acknowledge together with Jüngel that Barth's doctrine of baptism is "the basis of an entire theological ethics."[104] The most Webster can say about Jüngel's approach is that his "close engagement" with Barth means that "he adopted many characteristic problems and solutions, discovering in Barth's texts an account of the relation of God and man fully alert to the realities of each"; that "Jüngel draws . . . positive affirmation of human agency out of Barth's denial of sacramental status to the human act of water baptism."[105] Yet this is the point, since according to Barth's view water baptism is how God maintains the full integrity of the human being before God and for the human self. Crucial to Webster's attention to what he does wish to report about Jüngel, however, is the latter's emphasis on an ethical relation to Christ, not through a generally grounded moral activity but through obedience to the gracious command of Christ. This perspective holds true for Barth in *CD* IV/4 as well as for Jüngel in his *Christian Life.*

The very existence of *CD* IV/4 is where a difficulty arises with Webster. It is not so much that Barth's argument in IV/4 is messy but that its effects are messy—first, for any reader who has too fully absorbed the Reformed sacramental outlook and formulations of I/1 but has not recognized the profound shift away from this outlook in II/2; and second, for anyone who is looking to Barth from within a sacramental tradition that is presumed to be beyond reform. Webster tends to privilege the posthumously published fragments of material that Barth might have included in a longer *KD* IV/4 (1967), a meditation on the first two petitions of the Lord's Prayer as the moral vision of the Christian life. But Barth had much more to write on the ethics of the Lord's Prayer; the material had simply not reached the stage of the sections on baptism and was not ready for publication. Indeed, Barth's very preface to IV/4

---

103. Eberhard Jüngel, "Invocation of God as the Ethical Ground of Christian Action: Introductory Remarks on the Posthumous Fragments of Karl Barth's Ethics of the Doctrine of Reconciliation," in *Theological Essays,* trans. J. B. Webster (Edinburgh: T & T Clark, 1989), 154–72.

104. John Webster, *Eberhard Jüngel: An Introduction to His Theology* (Cambridge: Cambridge University Press, 1991), 107.

105. Ibid., 106–7.

must be taken with greater seriousness, along with its actual inclusion in any complete copy of the multivolume *KD/CD*. If Barth had continued to write for publication and completed the *CD*, he would simply have drawn out the full implications of his presenting what belongs distinctively to the human in Jesus Christ through obedient response to the Word and command of God.[106] This would ultimately have included a perspective where the nature of the Lord's Supper matches that of baptism as liturgical framework of the ethical life in Christ of believer and church, the human believing and active yes and amen that correspond to God's own yes and amen in Jesus Christ, indeed, as in indispensable imitation of the baptism of Jesus himself for living the Christian life,[107] as *necessitate praecepti*.[108] Water baptism is the fundamental act of *imitatio Christi*. Jüngel and others are intent on taking IV/4 in its entirety as the proper trajectory of the *CD*. Webster, however, is irritated by what he regards as the "messiness"—which Barth himself might rather have called a "mess caused" by IV/4 in a "demythologised" doctrine of baptism consistent with New Testament teaching[109] and his rejection of the practice of infant baptism.[110] Webster is alert to the priority of Luther in Jüngel's thought. Although Webster curiously wishes that Jüngel would have embraced Barth's political activism more fully over against Luther's degree of passivity, he does not mention how fully Jüngel has embraced Barth's reforming activism with respect to baptism.[111] Webster

106. "Baptism is the first step of the way of a human life which is shaped and stamped by looking to Jesus Christ. It is the first step which the baptized person who has come to see Jesus Christ takes along with the community. It is also the first step which the community . . . takes along with the one baptized. In baptism a human life comes into the life of the community. . . . In all its individuality . . . it becomes the life of a member of the community" (*CD* IV/4:149).

107. Ibid., 47–50. Indeed, Barth goes on to emphasize that the act of baptism to which believers are invited by the church in the New Testament is invariably practiced *"semper ubique et ab omnibus"* (always, everywhere, and by all).

108. Ibid., 101.

109. In ibid., 11, Barth places alongside many non-Christian practices and beliefs "the liturgico-sacramental . . . mysticism which so quickly made its way as an alien body in Christianity." As he confronted sacramental theology that identifies human action with divine action, Barth regarded this as treating Christian baptism "docetically" (ibid., 102). This is true, one way or another, of Roman Catholic, Lutheran, and Reformed views in which "the meaning of baptism is to be sought and found in a divine action which is concealed in the administration by men and which makes use of this. What concerns us is the consensus that baptism is to be defined, described and explained as a mystery. This consensus needs to be demythologised. We oppose it" (ibid., 105).

110. Barth could not be more categorical on this point in the last part of *CD* IV/4: "Indeed, we have though it could be regarded as self-evident that in the work of baptism one has to presuppose, both on the side of the community and also on that of the candidates, human beings who are capable of thought and action and who may be summoned as such to conversion, obedience, hope, and the decision of faith. We could not even consider the possibility that infants might be baptised, and hence we have not even had occasion to dispute this" (ibid., 166).

111. Webster, *Jüngel*, 213 At this point, Webster could have brought out the difficult matter of Jüngel's having to be something of a one-time *Grenzgänger* (boundard walker) between the artificially and tragically separated East and West Germany as a result of the Cold War. As a

neither interacts closely with Jüngel's reception of Barth's view nor does much with Jüngel's provision of a full outlining of IV/4 as it was meant to be read, fully integrated into the *CD*. The most he will do is acknowledge Jüngel as a Protestant who restricts the term *sacrament* to Jesus, but he does not clearly attribute this to his following Barth through the lengthy arguments of the *CD*. Attributing this doctrine to "Protestant reserve"—although Lutherans are far more unreserved about their sacramental views than the Reformed—Webster acknowledges that Jüngel is "highly receptive to Barth's critique of sacramental status of baptism and also unfashionably wary about the description of the church as sacrament in recent ecumenical theology." Webster also quotes Jüngel on a point profoundly rooted in Barth's argumentation in IV/4, that worship is fundamentally moral action, the church's "first and fundamental answer to the question What should we do?"[112] Although Webster is so reticent that he does not connect the lines between Jüngel and Barth, those connections nevertheless are indispensable to understanding Jüngel and gaining a crucial interpretation of Barth.

In his most thoroughgoing discussion of *CD* IV/4 in his first book on ethics, Webster's two chapters on baptism manifest rigid refusal to engage Jüngel's essays on Barth's view of baptism and Jüngel's own massive adoption of this view.[113] Webster knows that Barth has prepared the way for his assertions about

---

son of Magdeburg in the East, the general subjugation of Germany to the dictates of the Allied Powers after World War II is a matter that can barely now be accounted for in an assessment of Jüngel's or any other German theologian's political theology in the second half of the twentieth century. As to highlighting Jüngel's sympathy with Barth on *CD* IV/4, this is never more than hinted at. That Jüngel fully embraces and extends Barth's argument on baptism and sacrament is barely accounted for. Cf. John B. Webster, "Eberhard Jüngel," in *The Modern Theologians: An Introduction to Christian Theology in the Twentieth Century,* 2d ed., ed. David Ford (Cambridge, Mass.: Blackwell, 1997), 52–66.

112. Webster, "Jüngel," 52–66.

113. John Webster, *Barth's Ethics of Reconciliation* (Cambridge: Cambridge University Press, 1995), 117. He acknowledges another article, Dieter Schellong, "Der Ort der Tauflehre in der Theologie Karl Barth's," in *Warum Christen ihre Kinder nicht mehr taufen lassen,* ed. D. Schellong (Frankfurt a.M: Stimme-Verlag, 1969), 108–42, in which Schellong notes the coherency of Barth's view with the rest of the *CD*. On this article Webster ambiguously states that it is "instructive for an understanding of the *Dogmatics* as a whole," but he does not engage either Jüngel or Schellong. Indeed, in Webster's chapter on the baptism of the Spirit—whose title at first seems to suggest a close engagement with the structure of *CD* IV/4—Webster rehearses points of view in Barth that Barth had left behind, points on sacrament and baptism, which Jüngel treated in great depth but Webster nowhere engages. One should not say that Webster leaves out Jüngel's treatment of baptism entirely. Using his own translation, Webster does quote a comment by Jüngel but does so in a way that most readers would interpret as lending support to Webster's rejection of Barth's doctrine of baptism in IV/4. Thus, Webster quotes Jüngel, "The understanding of the being of Jesus Christ as a history which has accomplished and revealed the reconciliation of all people and the world to God, which grounds Barth's doctrine of reconciliation, destroys the traditional theological concept of baptism as a sacrament" (Webster, *Barth's Ethics,* 129, quoting from Jüngel, "Thesen zu Karl Barths Lehre von der Taufe," in Jüngel, *Barth-Studien,* 291, thesis 2.1; with linkage to "Zur Kritik des sakramentalen Verständnisses der

baptism, its nonsacramental character, and the necessity of Spirit baptism and faith in the believer prior to the necessary principle of water baptism in IV/1, where Barth establishes the sole sacramentality that is in and of Christ. Indeed, Webster also cites Jüngel's statement in a work coauthored with Karl Rahner, "The being of Jesus Christ, which *ex opere operato* effects salvation, is as such the one *sacramentum fidei*."[114] Barth himself regards the saving work of God and the saving Word of God to be united fully in Jesus Christ, who is present to every believer as the Mediator such that his "history takes place in every age."[115] Hence, Webster is demonstrating how integral in fact IV/4 is for the entirety of volume IV and therefore for most of the *CD*, as Jüngel and the present work contend. What has been at stake for Barth throughout *CD* IV is absolute clarity regarding the exclusivity of divine agency in the whole of salvation apart from the mediation of any other creaturely reality than that of Jesus Christ: "God sets among men a fact which speaks for itself."[116] Indeed, in these chapters from his first book on Barth's ethics, Webster advances aspects of Barth's basic and most profoundly argued points that show his rejection of sacraments and of infant baptism in favor of the genuineness of human action in the Christian life in covenant relation with God and that therefore indicate baptism's ethical nature. For example:

> The crux of a correct answer to the meaning of baptism lies in a strict correlation and a no less strict distinction between the human action as such and the divine action from which it springs, on whose basis it is possible, and towards which it moves.[117]

Webster acknowledges and can positively defend the argument for the ethical interpretation of baptism as a genuine human response that must not disappear in the mystification of traditional sacramentalism.[118] This teaching is based on Barth's lifelong view that God is the only basis for Christian obedience and the way of life shaped by faithfulness to God. Webster also acknowledges that Barth is actually arguing from the reality of the new birth, the work of the Holy Spirit *in nobis,* over against any kind of natural religiousness, a vestige of

---

Taufe," also in *Barth-Studien,* esp. 313–14). But Jüngel is only being painfully objective about what he himself has embraced in Barth; that objectivity is essential for the plunge he takes in this second essay, "Zur Kritik," where Jüngel is unwilling to give himself or his readers any way of escaping from the reforming obligations inherent in interpreting and applying biblical norms to the church's practice of baptism.

114. Webster, *Barth's Ethics,* 128, from Eberhard Jüngel, "Das Sakrament—was ist das?" in E. Jüngel and K. Rahner, *Was ist ein Sakrament?* 37.

115. Webster, *Barth's Ethics,* 129, quoting *CD* IV/2:107.

116. Ibid., quoting *CD* IV/3:767.

117. Ibid., 131, quoting *CD* IV/4:134.

118. This interpretation underlies much of Rosato's analysis and critique of Barth, a critique Webster deftly overturns; ibid., 134–35; cf. P. J. Rosato, *The Spirit as Lord: The Pneumatology of Karl Barth* (Edinburgh: T & T Clark, 1981).

which has been retained in the traditional view of sacraments. Indeed, Webster has fastened on one of the texts that substantiates the view taken in the present work that everything is united christocentrically:

> He who may hear and follow the call of God sounded forth in this faithful work of God cannot take offence or start back; he can only worship and praise. Everything is well. The history of Jesus Christ is different from all other histories. In its particularity, singularity and uniqueness it cannot be compared or interchanged with any other. . . . Indeed, it comes with revolutionary force into the life of each and every man. As this individual history it is thus cosmic in origin and goal. As such it is not sterile. It is a fruitful history which newly shapes every human life. Having taken place *extra nos,* it also works *in nobis,* introducing a new being of every man. It certainly took place *extra nos.* Yet it took place, not for its own sake, but *pro nobis.*[119]

What God has done apart from us and yet for us he accomplishes by his Spirit in us so that we may become unalterably determined by a faithfulness that is first in God for us and then subjectively in us for God—God with us and we with God—and through the presence of Jesus Christ and the action of the Holy Spirit within us, we with God and God with us. Not that anything about human action causes the relationship but that, on the other hand, within the covenant relation, we are set free to freely move toward God and to be with God in worship and praise. Webster appears, finally, to be appreciative of Barth's argument in *CD* IV/3 that Spirit baptism, solely on terms relative to divine initiative, is sacramental action because God is the performer of this action, apart from us and yet for us and in us.[120]

At the point of sacramentality, however, Webster distances himself from Barth. In citing Calvin, who envisions the work of the Spirit within the ordinances of the church, Webster writes: "Where Calvin envisages the Spirit as operative 'within,' Barth envisages the Spirit as active *prior to* the church's agency."[121] But Webster should have included a "within" as well ("the Spirit as *active prior* to" and *within*). Yet in Barth's case this action happens not within an indirect medium of grace but directly from the side of God to the heart of the human being, by the Spirit working directly, self-mediating grace, and therefore working immediately in the life of the human being. With respect to Barth's reasoning about the nature of the truly Christian ethic grounded in God, Webster has much that is affirmative about *CD* IV/4. Webster moves to define Barth's view of the Spirit's work through its ethical dimension once the being of the human has been reset to its original being in relation to God, in freedom and eschatologically related to a future toward which the life of every human being in Christ is progressing. Webster embraces what Barth affirms

---

119. *CD* IV/4:20–21.
120. Webster, *Barth's Ethics,* 141.
121. Ibid., 142.

in the work of the Holy Spirit within human beings, but he has ever so deftly withheld approval of Barth's limitation of that work with respect to gracious media. Webster's fuller critique emerges in his chapter on water baptism.

At the level of appreciating Barth's Christian ethics and defending him against several generations of detractors for supposedly lacking an ethic, Webster is masterfully defending Barth by letting Barth speak for himself in a text that is rarely lacking in clarity and theological richness. Here, recognizing Barth's partial affinity with much sacramental theology that identifies the fundamental ethical component in baptism, Webster faults Barth for dismissing the sacramental definition of baptism and maintains that the ethical and the sacramental in baptism are not mutually exclusive. But, of course, Barth does think this is the case. Here Webster is in danger of setting Barth up for a fall. Since Barth has rejected the entire basis on which sacramental logic functions, Webster's sacramental logic cannot be a source of critiquing Barth in any adequate way. But this is precisely the way in which Webster faults Barth. Because Webster appears not willing to adopt Barth's fundamental logic, all he can do is witness to what Barth is not saying, to his rejection of water baptism as an instrument of divine work, as not bearing "any sacramental *concursus* of divine causality and mediating human agency."[122] Webster even knows why Barth is emphatic about these rejections: They alone protect water baptism from confusing a human action with a divine action, whereby the human activity becomes "docetic" (i.e., it appears to be human action but, as sacramental theologians claim in Barth's understanding, is actually divine action). While Webster is expositing Barth's arguments for the distinctive human work that is water baptism based on exegetical engagement with numerous New Testament passages, Webster is ever implying something like eisegesis on Barth's part. Barth is seeking to "make a case on exegetical grounds that . . . water-baptism is not a sacrament."[123] It will be this "seeking" that Webster will later describe as Barth's "special pleading." Again, when Barth is describing the nature of ethical action, Webster's tone becomes appreciative: "The care with which Barth describes the idea of more decision" is "instructive"[124] and its "ontological force . . . critically important: real human deciding or choosing is not arbitrary, but deciding for and choosing "the one true reality."[125] Webster honestly reports Barth's insistence that infant baptism is a "profoundly irregular" practice that blocks the succession of faith leading to the obedience that properly belongs to water baptism in the life of Christian obedience.

In this honesty, however, there is a critique that avoids the penetrating analyses and arguments of Webster's other mentor, Eberhard Jüngel, and that anticipates the dismissive comments about Barth in *CD* IV/4, which

122. Ibid., 154–55.
123. Ibid., 158.
124. Ibid., 161.
125. Ibid., 162.

characterize Webster's most recent publications, including his second volume
on Barth's ethics. After asking what the abiding value of IV/4 is—which
certainly he has a right to do—Webster does not even address its very inclusion in the *CD*, let alone Barth's own important comments in his preface
on his hopes for reform coming first from the Roman Catholic Church,
in view of what Barth must have regarded as momentous developments in
Vatican II. In a terse statement connecting Barth's view of water baptism
with "response to Jesus'" presence in the power of the Spirit, Barth extracts
baptism from its historical identification with the ecclesial representation of
grace. In effect, Barth "secularizes" baptism by giving it a radically vocational
or ethical interpretation, thereby leaving behind the last traces of the idea
of the church as *mediatrix*.[126] In the first instance, this seems to be a rather
aggressive turnabout on Webster's part, revealing an intense irritation with
Barth's relegation of infant baptism to an act of civil religion, a ritual where a
union between church and state only possibly exists. Webster acknowledges
that Barth regarded such unions as conditions in which the church "ceases
to be 'an essentially missionary and mature' church."[127] However, Webster
does not move further against Barth precisely on this matter of the nature
of baptism as or as not a sacrament. Instead, Webster directs his attention to
Barth's concern to fashion a doctrine of the human as moral agent and not
merely a recipient of grace. Here we find one last reference to Jüngel's work on
Barth's view at the point of human action corresponding to the primary divine
action, in an extensive quote translated by Webster and leaving completely
undetectable how deeply sympathetic and theologically partnered Jüngel is
with Barth on the matter of what is sacramental and what is not. Relying on
a single critique of Barth's exegesis of New Testament texts and his theological
claims,[128] Webster simply dismisses Barth's plea that Jesus' baptism implicitly
stands behind these texts. No account is given to the fact that in the preface
Barth acknowledges profound indebtedness to the persuasiveness of Markus
Barth's extensive and careful exegesis, much lengthier than the single work
referred to by Webster. Indeed, it can be argued already during the time of
Barth's writing *CD* IV/4 and certainly in the decades since that something
closely akin to Barth's exegesis and theological conclusions have emerged in
the preponderance of New Testament interpretation. In his account, Webster
far too thinly addresses the criticism that Barth betrays an individualistic
ethic. Finally, Webster sides with T. F. Torrance's unbearably short criticism
of Barth, in which Torrance expresses his uncomprehending attitude toward
Barth in this whole matter and lodges a rather reckless accusation of "dualism"

126. Ibid., 166.
127. Ibid., 167, from *CD* IV/4:22.
128. Webster, *Barth's Ethics*, 168. E. Dinkler, "Die Taufaussagen des Neuen Testaments:
Neu Untersucht im Hinblick auf Karl Barths Tauflehre," in *Zu Karl Barths Lehre von der Taufe*,
60–153.

against Barth. While Webster effectively rejects Torrance's criticism, pointing to Torrance's own exaggerations in Christology, he goes on to claim that a "carefully phrased notion of sacramental mediation," which he finds in Barth's earlier sacramental theology, is what he wants of Barth Webster reasons that Barth abandoned his earlier view because of the specter of civil religion—but of course this earlier view is not fundamental with Barth. Instead, on Barth's earlier view Jüngel is right in his concentration on *solo verbo* and *sola fide*. Barth in his later work clearly recognizes the differentiation that God himself makes between what belongs to the living and active divine Word addressed to us and what belongs to the responsive action of the human through the converting work of the Holy Spirit, active in and through us. Unfortunately, as we have seen, Webster in the end evidences an intent to avoid Jüngel on virtually all of his points of contact with Barth on baptism in IV/4. Thus, he misses an opportunity that is likely momentous in terms of both reform and ecumenical necessity.

Webster's avoidance—if not subtle suppression of valid and potentially highly influential interpretation and extension of Barth's doctrine of baptism—appears to be typical of much of the English-language treatment of the last volume of the *CD*. In addition, the utter neglect of Markus Barth's treatise on baptism, the title of which is echoed in the title of Jüngel's important essay "Die Kirche als Sakrament?"[129] must be rectified by new research into this connection between Karl and Markus (father and son). Indeed, we are simply going to have to undertake a rereading of the *CD* from the perspective of its end point in IV/4 and in relation to the elaborate features that prepare the way for Barth's reforming standpoint.

What Webster leaves obscure is the primary trajectory of Jüngel's view of correspondence in theology. The tendency of the entire collection of German essays in *Barth-Studien* is toward Barth's ethics exemplified through his doctrine of baptism in *CD* IV/4, where on account of correspondence, election, and the distinction between divine and human action, the trajectory of the entire *CD* achieves a striking degree of clarity. Not only does Garrett Paul's translator's preface leave Jüngel's extensive treatment and embrace of IV/4 unacknowledged, but that preface also says virtually nothing of this material, let alone presents it in later volumes of Jüngel's translated materials, either by Webster or with reference to his counsel.[130] Since Jüngel so extensively outlines how vitally connected IV/4 is with the *CD* after I/2 and expresses such appreciation for the persuasiveness of Barth's understanding of biblical materials, close interaction with these essays would likely not have allowed Webster to make such denigrating statements as the following:

---

129. Eberhard Jüngel, "Die Kirche als Sakrament?" *Zeitschrift für Theologie und Kirche* 80 (1983): 432–57; cf. Markus Barth, *Die Taufe—ein Sakrament? Ein exegetischer Beitrag zum Gespräch über die kirchliche Taufe* (Zollikon-Zürich: Evangelischer Verlag, 1951).

130. In Jüngel, *Barth: Legacy*, 7–10.

The fragment is rather obviously unsatisfactory. The exegesis is sometimes surprisingly shoddy, dominated by special pleading, as well as by what seems at times an almost Platonic distinction between water baptism . . . and baptism with the Spirit. . . . The basic claim . . . involves Barth in a sharp turn from the sophisticated accounts of sacramental mediation in earlier work. . . . What replaced it lacked the nuance and weightiness of earlier discussion. In one sense . . . IV/4 does not cohere with the rest of the work—neither with Barth's earlier theology of sacraments, nor with his account of the mediation of revelation, nor, most of all, with the christologically-grounded refusal to divide divinity and humanity too sharply. In another sense, however, the baptism fragment shows strong consistency with the overarching theme of the *Church Dogmatics*, God and humanity in covenant relation. For part of what stimulates Barth to make such a clear separation of water and Spirit baptism is an ethical concern: a desire to indicate that at the beginning of the Christian life there is a distinctive form of human endeavour, subservient to the work of the Spirit but nevertheless genuine and real.[131]

It is quite clear that Jüngel takes a very different view, and yet I can find no serious engagement with it on Webster's part. Webster himself is nearly incoherent in his argument when he declares on the one hand that *CD* IV/4 "does not cohere" and then on the other that it actually does show "strong consistency with *the* overarching theme" of the *CD*. Of course, what Webster says does not cohere reflects again a too-heavy reliance on *CD* I, taking it as a lens through which to read the whole, and his claim that Barth's Christology must not be extended too far into a reading of his ecclesiology such that incarnational metaphor becomes attached to the church. Christ the Mediator is not embodied in the church in any way that could be called hypostatic and therefore christological in any ontological sense.[132] Webster is keenly aware of how Jüngel grounds his anthropology in Christ, which results in a clear distinction between divine and human action, so that they are united analogically but not substantially or incarnationally. In the end, however, Webster succeeds in his strategy of bypassing Jüngel's discussion of IV/4 and its linkage with

131. John Webster, *Barth* (New York: Continuum, 2000), 157.

132. As Barth wrote in *CD* II/1, "There is indeed correspondence but no parity, let alone identity. Even in its invisible essence it is not Christ, nor a second Christ, nor a kind of extension of the one Christ. . . . It is His body, His earthly-historical form of existence. . . . Thus to speak of a continuation or extension of the incarnation in the Church is not only out of place but even blasphemous" (608ff.). Similarly, Barth writes, "But this life of the children of God is always a life for Christ's sake. The foundation of the Church is also its law and its limit. We might say that it corresponds to the *anhypostasis* of Christ's human nature" (I/2:216). From even the first volume of the *CD*, while Barth exalts the created relation between humanity and God in Christ, the existence of humanity in this relation, the church, is ontologically one of correspondence, not one of participation in the incarnation itself. This is hugely important when one then considers the nature of the church's obedience in baptism and Lord's Supper not as acts of participation in the one sacrament that is the life of Jesus Christ but as acts of correspondence that are freely enacted by faithful obedience.

the rest of the *CD* by relegating Jüngel to being perhaps overly influenced by Luther's model of humanity's passivity in relation to the divine act of justification.[133] This limitation simply cannot be borne out in the preponderance of what Jüngel does in his theology.

There is also a deficit in the English-language reading of Barth and the assistance of Jüngel's presentation of Barth, as well as necessary critical interaction with Jüngel. We find little engagement with Jüngel's critical essays on sacrament and baptism from the *Barth-Studien* at points where Jüngel's courage to extend Barth's reforming efforts on this matter would shed light on how IV/4 coheres with the rest of the *CD*. This is certainly the case with the recent work of Paul Molnar[134] and Joseph Mangina.[135] All this is of immense ecumenical significance since while Barth is rather congenially received and allowed to contribute (at least out of I/1 and I/2) to more sacramental traditions, his potential contribution to the inclusion of Baptist, Pentecostal, and charismatic traditions is quite blocked. This situation is now tragic since so much of world Christianity expresses these forms of Christian doctrinal sensibility and practice.

---

133. Webster, *Barth's Ethics*, 200–201.

134. Paul D. Molnar, *Karl Barth and the Theology of the Lord's Supper: A Systematic Investigation* (New York: Peter Lang, 1996).

135. Joseph L. Mangina, *Karl Barth on the Christian Life: The Practical Knowledge of God* (New York: Peter Lang, 2001).

7

To Be a Pilgrim Theologian

Therefore Jesus also suffered outside the city gate in order to sanctify the people by his own blood. Let us then go to him outside the camp and bear the abuse he endured. For here we have no lasting city, but we are looking for the city that is to come. Through him, then, let us continually offer a sacrifice of praise to God, that is, the fruit of lips that confess his name.

Hebrews 13:12–15

Sojourning from Pilgerstrasse

Barth became a pilgrim in his own country (Switzerland) at the moment that the country of his promotion as a Protestant theologian became the place of his dismissal from the professorial office. The "Case of Karl Barth" in Nazi Germany brought his pilgrimage there to an end in 1935. During the years from 1946 to 1955, he lived a few blocks from the University of Basel on a street named Pilgerstrasse (Pilgrim Street). The nomadic movement that had typified Barth's student years and his career in Germany (from positions in Göttingen to Münster to Bonn) meant that the *Church Dogmatics* would be primarily a Swiss project at home, yet not at home. In theology, Barth had known since his student days what liberal theological innovation was all about. The odd fate that had made him professor of Reformed theology at Göttingen, and the faculty prejudice that prevented him from teaching systematic theology and the history of dogmatics, instead had made for his sojourn through the Reformed orthodox textbook of

Heinrich Heppe. Barth's promotion had derived from his work as a theological expositor of Scripture in *Römerbrief* (1919). New theological statement was his forte, but it was grounded in Scripture. The great project of the *Church Dogmatics* would be constructed in theological exposition and with profound investigation of the church fathers, Catholic and Reformation traditions, as well as extensive considerations of modern arguments. During the years immediately following the war, Barth would confirm all suspicions of his outsider, pilgrim status with his continuing concern for the defeated Germans and with his resistance to picking the Soviets out for special opprobrium beyond all others. His willingness to stay on the journey of his theological destiny was far greater than any impulse to stop.

What Barth could do with his time was to serve God through his teaching and writing, and this meant, then, the unity of dogmatics and ethics within the *CD*. All of Barth's references to divine reality in revelation had had a strong eschatological dimension. His early years of labor after World War I on the journal *Between the Times* had reflected his earliest stirrings in this regard. As the christocentric bent in the *CD* took on flesh, so did his ethics. Everywhere the question of Christian responsibility was detectable and forthright. In a way reminiscent of his reasoning on the *analogia fidei,* Barth taught that our knowledge corresponds to God's knowledge when our thought is conformed to God's Word, and that our guidance is found in the decision-making of faithful obedience in correspondence with the sovereign decree of God to redeem the humans he has created. God endowed the human being with decision-making by grace in Christ to become a decision-making agent. Indeed, correspondence is already bound up within the *analogia relationis* of the first pair of human beings, who were created with the divine likeness in order to receive the divine command. Beginning in the dialogue that is the divine address of God through the Word to the human being, each person is to hear, then to pray, then to inaugurate a life of service through the church. Indeed, exclusively in the church does the human being act on the commands of that Word and has as its model the form of prayer. This is so because the first answer to God's Word is a prayer of confession, of agreement with God. From the moment of awakening faith and prayer, every future act of obedience in the ethics of the Christian life is a prayerful act. Instead of self-absorbed action stemming from some kind of self-conscious moralism, the Christian moves on the basis of the awakened understanding of justification and sanctification. And here we find the connection between theology and ethics, that in receiving the revelation of justification and sanctification, the understanding of these truths in Jesus Christ can be nothing other than gratitude itself, a gratitude that hastens to serve the One who has served at such great cost.

The paradigm of prayer for the ethical life of the Christian church, then, is a simple two-stage movement of reception and response. But in this paradigm is the potential for widest representation of fellow human beings.[1] The expansive-

---

    1. Cf. Paul D. Matheny, *Dogmatics and Ethics: The Theological Realism and Ethics of Karl Barth's Church Dogmatics* (Frankfurt a. M.: Peter Lang, 1990), 209–15.

ness of Barth's model of responsible ethical agency through Christ is another feature here. Although original righteousness is not restored through Christ and comes only with the eschaton, the original vocation of righteous action is reinvigorated. The vitality of the relationship with God is then one not only of obeying the commands of Christ as found in Scripture but also of applying those commands creatively across the spectrum of human life, particularly among the other sciences whose actions must be regarded as also full of moral weight. Because obedience is integral to what humble, prayer-like reception and response to the Word of God entails, one can begin to speak of the obedience that is faith. Although Barth laid great emphasis on the independent work of Jesus Christ on our behalf, this work nevertheless humanizes and liberates the believer to new obedience. In this way, theology becomes proper theology as the worship carried out in the form of obedience reflects the unity of faith and action reflected in the gospel, and the obedient Christian becomes something of a parable of the kingdom of God yet to come.

The question of human freedom liberated for freedom by the grace of God as developed in the *CD* was not an easy one for Barth originally. Anything that would reestablish human self-confidence in humanity and therefore reinvigorate the false freedom of autonomous decision-making against God was to be rejected without question. No possibility of drawing natural comparisons between the human and God could be allowed; although God acted out of the complete freedom of his being, humanity could not know even the smallest dimension of divine freedom until some force of God had righted what was so inherently wrong in the soul. Since Barth is always attending to arguments for the proper understanding of faith, what this free decision is—quite apart from an ontology of human freedom, particularly bent upon its oppositional orientation to God—meant that little ought to be said about the power of human freedom. Indeed, Barth's tendency is to speak about the freedom of a liberated human being in Christ, in the sense of being freed from the bondage of false faith and sin rather than in the freedom of constructive, positive action: "Is there any human more free or autonomous or proud than that of the men after God's own heart who according to their own confession experienced the divine activity towards them without any will or response at all on their own part?"[2] Barth continues with exclusive references to the rule of God over all things.

The references to God's freedom predominate in the *CD,* not only to witness to the glory of the almighty God but also to lay out the first leg of a dialectic that will result in a created, grace-constituted correspondence to free divine action within the human being. To the extent that the human being is living and therefore active, the Holy Spirit can establish within

---

2. *CD* III/3:148. I am paying close attention here to the outstanding work, John Webster, *Barth's Moral Theology: Human Action in Barth's Thought* (Grand Rapids: Eerdmans, 1998), 99–124.

the individual the first freedom of receiving the Word of God.[3] Since faith must be a genuine act on our part, the gift of the genuine freedom—against the false freedom of the sinner to whom Jesus Christ now comes—is graciously given. In the awakening and new life that is faith by the Holy Spirit, the human being begins not only to represent God but also to enter into partnership with him. God is acting by his divine power, willing that the human being

> should stand and walk on his own feet. He thus wills that he should believe and love and hope. He wills his hope as his own spontaneous act. He awakens him to this hope . . . "logically" from within. Hence His work can only be man's freedom for life by Him and therefore for life in hope. Far from the Christian being mastered and taken out of himself when he is awakened to hope by the power of the Holy Spirit, it is in this life in hope awakened by the power of the Holy Spirit that he really comes to himself and may be himself. The man born of God or the Spirit, called to service and living in hope, is the man who is no longer self-alienated, and therefore he is real man.[4]

Barth traces out this principle of the gift of human freedom with utmost care, not wanting to suggest in the least any limitations on the freedom of God in view of the true freedom of the human. He also enjoins vital piety of constant devotion and attention to the dominance of the Holy Spirit in the believer's life.

Taking it that *CD* IV/4 is indeed the lens through which we should read the whole of the *CD*, Barth has finally found the specific instrument by which he can identify God's pronouncement of freedom in the life of the human being: the baptism of the Holy Spirit:

> But when we look at the divine change, at the baptism of the Spirit, we can and should say no less than that it is the active and actualising grace of God. What is manifest to man in this change, what is not just confessed (we are thinking of the ἐν ἐμοί of Gal 1:16) revealed both inwardly and from within, establishing a new beginning of existence. . . . Whatever one may have to say about the other aspect of the event, namely, about the human decision which acknowledges, confirms, attests and indicates, . . . there can be no diminution of the fulness of that which is addressed to man in it. . . . The baptism of the Spirit is more than a reference and indication through image and symbol. It is more than an offer and opportunity. . . . This means that his own freedom can be freedom for a specific human decision in conformity with the liberation which has come about for him in this alteration. . . . It can be freedom for that which is commanded by God as God empowers him for it.[5]

3. *CD* II/1:257ff.
4. *CD* IV/3.2:941–42.
5. *CD* IV/4:34.

Barth is anxious to liberate this liberating truth about transformation. Having often been reticent about transformation, wanting to allow the objective benefits of the saving works of God to have their benefit quite apart from the vicissitudes of personal experience, here those experiences have a most pointed urgency: the divine change created by the Holy Spirit. Earlier in the *CD,* Barth's focus was strictly on God's creative and redemptive action within the life of the person, but always in terms such as *formation* and *direction* as objects of divine rule and free action. It is only in the last parts of the *CD* that he can speak of freedom as a human possession on account of being possessed by God's Spirit, the same Spirit who formed and directed Jesus, but in a different sense.

At work is a strong christological basis of liberation through the work of the Son of God. The pilgrimage of Jesus, the Son who in his freedom was led into the far country, like the prodigal, is offered for the sake of human liberation. The Holy Spirit works against the old self and works for the new:

> The Holy Spirit affirms the one man and negates the other. He fights for the new man against the old. He champions freedom against unfreedom, obedience against disobedience, our life against our death, the one possible thing against the many possible.[6]

And all of this is to render the human being by faith a fit creature for the service of God. But this does not come without the great cost to the Mediator, Jesus Christ, who is the agent of God's opposition to the world and the human exemplar of the same. The victory of Jesus Christ has this effect, but now without great opposition. This great sacrifice for the believers' liberty is all about the joyful service of the Christian life, until the end of this life.

Barth was always thinking of his theology as service to God. Right in the midst of his exposition, he declares:

> We have to know Him integrally and therefore in both these aspects. At every point, therefore, we have to be silent, but we have also to speak. The honour which we give Him is in both cases alike problematical. But we are summoned to both alike. We can evade neither. We have thus to recognise Him both in His hiddenness and in His self-disclosure. It will certainly be true that in both cases He remains completely unknowable to us even as we may and must know Him. In all our thinking and speaking about Him we never become His masters. We are always and must always be His servants, and indeed quite unprofitable servants. But it is also true—and this must be stated just as vigorously—that in both cases He becomes completely recognisable to us, not because of our capacity, thinking and speaking, but because of the grace of His revelation, which we cannot refuse to receive, however little we may be able to control it.[7]

6. *CD* IV/2:368.
7. *CD* II/1:342.

Throughout his life, Barth held dear a verse of Scripture, among many, but one alluded to here that appears over and over in his life and writings, Luke 17:10:[8] "So you also, when you have done all that you were ordered to do, say, 'We are worthless slaves; we have done only what we ought to have done!'" Barth constantly reminded his audience that whatever degree of correspondence the Spirit graciously creates between believers and God is at best relative and bears creaturely flaws until perfected by resurrection.

Indeed, what has begun in the baptism of the Spirit is only a beginning, "a commencement which points forward to the future," where the new has come and is coming (2 Cor. 5:17).[9] This anticipates yet another and final change, one actualized by the face-to-face encounter when "we will all be changed" (1 Cor. 15:51), no longer hampered by the dim mirror of present knowledge (1 Cor. 13:12).

> This is the absolute future which the Christian is impelled and directed by the Holy Spirit to wait for and to hasten towards in this time of his which is one long Advent season. During this time the Holy Spirit feeds him with the body of Jesus Christ which was given for him, and strengthens him with the blood of Jesus Christ which was shed for him, to nourish and sustain him for eternal life in which God will be all in all, and thus in him too. He has not yet apprehended this. The people of God, whose member he is, is the *pilgrim people of God*. "Hallowed be thy name. Thy kingdom come. Thy will be done in earth, as it is in heaven" (Matt. 6:9f)—this is his prayer. But he is constantly chasing this perfection which awaits him and comes to meet him. He is constantly running towards it. Apprehended by Jesus Christ, he constantly seeks to apprehend it.[10]

Here is the truth of the pilgrim, of pilgrim faith, of the pilgrim path, of the pilgrim community in Christ—faith as movement, and its theology of movement, dealing with the present in Christ, with its necessities, but straining toward the great fulfillment that swallows up all necessity.

Nevertheless, the nurture is for action, not for the purpose of merely enduring until the end. God's yes has come to this human being whom the Holy Spirit has reached, and in the baptism of this one is the first obedience, "the immediate first step in the new life-act for which man is empowered and to which he is summoned by the divine change." Out of this is the beginning of action that will correspond to the action of the original agent who is God. The one to whom the baptizand corresponds is Jesus Christ himself at his baptism: "Because He is committed unreservedly to subordination to God, therefore He is committed unreservedly to solidarity with men."[11] Finally, "water baptism

8. Cf., e.g., *CD* II/2:616; IV/1:701.
9. *CD* IV/4:38.
10. Ibid., 40.
11. Ibid., 58.

. . . is distinct from the baptism of the Spirit, as the human decision which corresponds to the divine turning to man, . . . a truly human work and word which proceeds from that basis, which hastens to that goal, and which is done in the freedom that God has given to men."[12] Now, whether or not Barth is to be the instrument of reform on this matter is in question. Some may call the collapsing of the two moments of baptism into one "docetic." On the other hand, many may regard this separation somehow as gnostic. What is crucial, however, is the freedom of grateful obedience now being made unabashedly at the heart of his theological program.

To be a pilgrim theologian, one is always realizing the mixture of emotion in the Christian life typical of Barth: humility and confidence. Humility, because all we are and have is of God, and all that we have to say is really of God and never, in the first instance, ourselves. Confidence, because of the certainty of God. It is not my hold on God that is certain but God's hold on me. And so toward the end of his life Barth found the humility and confidence to write this way about baptism as the consistent outflow of his dogmatic tendencies all along the way. "Thus the meaning of baptism is man's conversion—the conversion of all who have a part in it. . . . It is the common forsaking of an old way of life and the common following of a new way of life."[13] And continuing, "Since it is effected in human knowledge, thought, resolve and will, it is, of course, 'only' human. It is not divine. It is human action that simply responds to divine action. Nevertheless, it does so in an appropriate way."[14] But it is celebration and consecration. "Baptism is the oath which is taken by them in concert. If the original sense of the Latin *sacramentum* is observed, it might be called a sacrament from that standpoint. In baptism they take up their posts in the ranks of the *militia Christi* in which each . . . may be confident that he will receive as much insight and strength as is needed to fulfill the task which is assigned to him and suitable for him. . . . This is the pledge which the Christian has made in baptism in answer to God's pledge to him."[15]

The pilgrim theologian, now more than ever, is on the theological path of following the dictum of the Lord: "And he said to them, 'Therefore every scribe who has been trained for the kingdom of heaven is like the master of a household who brings out of his treasure what is new and what is old'" (Matt. 13:52). The discipline has much that is old; even the new has become old, requiring acknowledgments. But there is also the "ever new," which results from daily consecration to prayer and service. The theologian is charged to bring both kinds of treasure out of the storehouse, and the great exemplar of this was Karl Barth.

12. Ibid., 102.
13. Ibid., 138.
14. Ibid., 143.
15. Ibid., 161.

Sojourning at the Boundaries of Christian Faith

The witness that is theology is always an act of faith in which we say what we believe God has permitted us to say, as an extension of what he has commanded us to proclaim. As a consequence of this interpretive task, physical and temporal boundaries have constantly been crossed and continue to be crossed in the ongoing history of the church and the churches This is the nature of the Reformation along with the emergence of majority Christianity outside its historic boundaries: the churches of the Southern Hemisphere. As Philip Jenkins writes of them, they begin as wildly sectarian, prophetic movements but in time learn from Scripture the nature and doctrine of being church:

> As sects drift away from their origins, they in turn spawn a new generation of enthusiasts who seek to recapture the charisma and spiritual power that they believe to be integral to religious experience. Churches beget sects, which in turn become churches, until they in turn beget new and still fierier sects. The cycle has recurred many times, and will continue *ad infinitim.*
>
> As Southern churches grow and mature, they will assuredly lose something of their sectarian character and become more like the major churches, with all that implies for the nature of leadership, worship style, and so on. They will move toward the mainstream, just like Methodists and Quakers did in their day.[16]

The normalization or disappearance of most Christian sects takes place because of two factors: (1) Believers are persistent in reading the translated Scriptures without discarding parts of them or adding "new" scriptures. (2) They are open to the essentials of Christian orthodoxy in the form of the great creeds and theological works. Some degree of improved economic and political conditions is also necessary as well. The existence of these churches is the product of regional boundary breaking, even beyond the conscious missionary efforts of the established churches of the world.

But not all boundaries are good (e.g., the schismatic one established between Western and Eastern churches in 1054). This is also the case with the boundary between Jew and Christian, which Paul teaches has been destroyed through Jesus Christ: ὅτι δι αὐτου ἔχομεν την προσαγωγην οἱ ἀμφοτεροι ἐν ἑνι πνεύματι προ τον πατέρα. "For through him both of us have access in one Spirit to the Father" (Eph. 2:18). In time, then, either eschatologically or through active faith here and now, the boundary between Jew and Gentile is crossed through the gospel. The boundaries that exist and are deeply grounded in the gospel persist, however, and are not so easy to dismiss.

Perhaps the two most persistent boundaries are those surrounding other religions, particularly Islam, and "sexual identity," particularly homosexuality.

16. Philip Jenkins, *The Next Christendom: The Coming Global Christianity* (New York: Oxford University Press, 2002), 138.

Add to this mix a host of recent voices in theology, all claiming a hermeneutics of the Holy Spirit on just these matters, and one has an uncertain mix of issues. Of course, Barth's view on Judaism and Jewish identity is complex in itself, full of variations that resist a single summary statement. Certainly the most extensive work on the matter of Barth's relation to Jews and Judaism is by Eberhard Busch, *Unter dem Bogen des einen Bundes: Karl Barth und die Juden 1933–1945*[17] (Under the Bow of the One Covenant . . .). When in 1944 the Zurich rabbi Zvi Taubes appealed in direst terms for Swiss defense of Hungarian Jews, the Leonhard's Church pastor of Basel, Paul Vogt, preached to a congregation that likely included Barth on June 27:

> The repentance of the church is today's missionary mandate from God.
> Repentance is the 180-degree turn, not away from God but toward God, not away from the brother but toward the brother, not away from the Jews but toward the Jews.
> I want to raise both hands to God: Forgive us Christians for making such a mockery of Christ! Our guilt has become undeniably revealed.
> And I want to stretch out both hands toward the Jews: Forgive us Christians our Christless, Christ-alienated Christianity!
> Repentance of the church is the missionary mandate from God.[18]

This document includes a quantity of crucial information detailing the operations of the Holocaust. It gives further theological and spiritual commentary on the horrendous failure of the church in Europe toward the Jews. For Barth, moving to the farthest boundaries of what theological language can express, the Holocaust is an event uniquely analogous to Golgotha itself, where God delivered his Son over for us. His Son is again led to death in his bodily brothers and sisters. In all of this, and in the war also, the presence of God for Barth is known through the revelation of human injustice. Indeed, the mass murder of the Jews shows the depth of human opposition to God, since God reveals himself supremely through his act of electing his people.

When the war was over, Barth communicated in great detail what would constitute genuine repentance on the part of German Christians. This would be entirely under the provision of the grace and mercy of God to make a new spiritual beginning. He imagines Jesus addressing the German people:

> Come to me, you unsympathetic ones, you wicked Hitler-boys and -girls, you brutal SS soldiers, you slanderous Gestapo-scoundrels, you sad compromisers

17. Eberhard Busch, *Unter dem Bogen des einen Bundes: Karl Barth und die Juden 1933–1945* (Neukirchen-Vluyn: Neukirchener Verlag, 1996).

18. Schweizerisches evangelisches Hilfswerk für die Bekennende Kirche in Deutschland, ed., *Soll ich meines Bruders Hüter sein? Weitere Dokumente zur Juden- und Flüchtlingsnot unserer Tage* (Zollikon-Zürich: Evangelischer Verlag, 1944), 10. Since this was published by the foundation for the Confessing Church in Germany, Barth would have had and likely read a copy.

and collaborators, you herd-humans all, you who have for so long patiently and stupidly followed behind your so-called *Führer!* Come to me, you guilty and co-guilty, to what befell and must befall you, according to what your deeds are worth! Come to me, I know you well, but I don't ask who you are and what you have done. I see only that you are at the end, and abruptly from the front you must begin. I will revitalize you, precisely from zero will I now begin anew![19]

Barth would lead the way among his fellow Swiss in extending Christian friendship to repentant Germans. But neither Barth nor any uninvolved theologian in the crisis of German Nazism and Christian complicity could do for German Christian theologians what they alone would have to do. They needed to find repentance by the work of God's Spirit for the most radical misdeeds against God's chosen, God's beloved people Israel.

Indeed, without German repentance in the mid-twentieth century, it was difficult for European Christians, including Barth, to find their own repentance for anti-Semitism, let alone love for the Jews as devoted original covenant people. Barth's own theology of the Jews, the elect people of God, is at many points profoundly perceptive and redemptive and at other points not so. The theologian who most acutely brought the latter to light is Friedrich Wilhelm Marquardt, of the University of Berlin. In his own important early analysis and critique of Barth,[20] Marquardt exposes unfortunate analogies that Barth employed for the Jews: the negative reflection of God's electing action—election unto judgment, in contrast to election unto mercy (as displayed in the church).[21] This is Israel as a negative *Vorbild der Kirche*[22] (prefiguration of the church). No double predestination is present on this point but rather the election of the obdurate, those who resist God and resist their election to God. Meanwhile, the church is the presentation of mercy under election.

Contrary to any sense of a philosophical logic here, Barth instead is reflecting on the accepted and the rejected among Jesus' disciples, the latter being Judas. In the most difficult and to-be-rejected passage from the *CD,* this comparison analogizes the death of Judas with the destruction of Jerusalem and Israel's right to exist under the Roman Empire. At this juncture in the *CD,* the Israel of Jesus' day and the Israel of Jesus' death are virtually equated: Israel "is always a past

19. Quoted in Busch, *Unter dem Bogen,* 527; from Barth's *Die Deutschen und wir* (Zollikon-Zürich: Evangelischer Verlag, 1945).

20. Friedrich Wilhelm Marquardt, *Die Entdeckung des Judentums für die christlich Theologie: Israel im Denken Karl Barths* (München: C. Kaiser, 1967), e.g., 298–322; cf. similar points in Katherine Sonderegger, *That Jesus Christ Was Born a Jew: Karl Barth's "Doctrine of Israel"* (University Park, Pa.: Pennsylvania State University Press, 1992), 61–69. Sonderegger, with too negative an assessment, characterizes Barth's work at this point as "a voice medieval in character and tone, canonical, and anti-Judaic"—but it must be stressed, not anti-Jewish. The dimness of Barth's view of the existence of the synagogue is the former; his profound affirmation of God's eternal covenant and love toward the Jews refutes any charge of the latter.

21. E.g., *CD* II/2:205–33.

22. *KD* II/2:256.

and rejected people, as the people of God." Barth goes on to contrast Israel's "evil human 'tradition'" with the church's "divine 'tradition'" of proclaiming that "in its confession is the hope of Israel, the promise of its election, which always outlasts and excels and surpasses its rejection." "What the result will be is in the hand of God." And yet they are "rejected men elected in and from their rejection, men in whom Judas lived, but was also slain, as in the case of Paul. They are rejected who as such are summoned to faith. They are rejected who on the basis of the election of Jesus Christ, and looking to the fact that He delivered Himself up for them, believe in their election."[23]

One can only be reminded of the failures of any theologian. At the same time, we need to maintain the essentials of Paul's theology of Israel and mission to Israel in Romans, as Barth does. Barth is neither anti-Semitic nor anti-Jewish. Instead, he is both Pauline and apocalyptic in the vein of Luke.

But this must find its counterbalance in the constantly rehearsed and expansive line through the *CD,* the emphasis on Jesus the Jew and his special oneness with his people. Mark R. Lindsay brings this out with great detail and care.[24] As important as election is and as problematic as some of Barth's formulations are, the christological necessity of Jesus' Jewishness is brought home as the most powerful center of argumentation in the *CD:*

> The word did not simply become any "flesh," any man humbled and suffering. It became Jewish flesh. The Church's whole doctrine of the incarnation and the atonement becomes abstract and valueless and meaningless to the extent that this comes to be regarded as something accidental and incidental. The New Testament witness to Jesus the Christ, the Son of God, stands on the soil of the Old Testament and cannot be separated from it. The pronouncements of the New Testament Christology may have been shaped by a very non-Jewish environment. But they relate always to a man who is seen to be not a man in general, a neutral man, but the conclusion and sum of the history of God with the people of Israel, the One who fulfils the covenant made by God with this people.[25]

And then, because of the corporate unity of Jesus Christ with his people, Barth writes:

> For what the Christian Church is, Israel was and is before it—His possession (Jn 1:11), His body. He Himself in the one person is the crucified Messiah of Israel who as such is the secret Lord of the Church, the risen Lord of the Church who as such is the manifested Messiah of Israel. In its Old Testament form the community attests Him as the man elected and called by God who as such was invested with the sins of the whole world, and bore the judgment of God, and

23. *CD* II/2:505–6.
24. Mark R. Lindsay, *Covenanted Solidarity: The Theological Basis of Karl Barth's Opposition to Nazi Antisemitism and the Holocaust* (New York: Peter Lang, 2001).
25. *CD* IV/1:166.

in this form of a servant was truly the Lord. In its New Testament form the community attests Him as the God electing and calling man, who has not given Himself in vain, but to have mercy on His own, to set him [them] right, for him [them]. In its form as Israel it attests the justification which begins strangely and terribly in the midst of a world of sin and death, its *terminus a quo*. In its form as the Church it attests its *terminus ad quem*, its strange and glorious consummation in a new world of right and life. . . . We are dealing with two forms, two aspects, two "economies" of grace. But it is the one history, beginning there, having its centre in Jesus Christ, and here hastening to its culmination. It is the bow of the one covenant which stretches over the whole [*es ist der Bogen des einen Bundes, der sich über dieses Ganze spannt*].[26]

The asymmetry of some of Barth's earlier depictions has given way to unitary covenantal thinking. Instead of negative imaging, Israel and the Jews are presented as integral to the saving economy of God itself, to the fulfillment promised in Romans 11 and Ephesians 2, of Gentiles united to Jews, united to God through Jesus Christ. Barth, together with Paul, cannot be counted as supersessionist.[27] Yet unlike Paul, Barth wonders at the image of Israel and the divine action that such an image may reflect. This is a negative speculative exercise that does not belong to the gospel and represents, at least, a moment in theology that God no longer permits, let alone with whose love it could possibly correspond.

The question of correspondence is always operative in Christian theology as we move from doctrine to doctrine, from divine to creaturely reality, and from situation to situation. Perhaps the most curious attempt at suggesting a correspondence is the one by Eugene Rogers in his *Sexuality and the Christian Body*. In this collection of chapters, he is in deep conversation with ancient strands of Christian tradition and spirituality. With a hermeneutic of the Spirit alluding to Barth, Rogers is seeking an "irregular" dogmatics that creates possibilities for the affirmation of homosexual orientation and practice, specifically in terms of same-sex couplings and marriage.

Rogers seems a bit confused about whether Barth's expositions contain arguments of an aesthetic or "thick" descriptive character. Or perhaps Rogers will opt for Frei's more appropriate redescription of "the classical themes of communal Christian language molded by the Bible, tradition and constant usage in worship, practice, instruction and controversy . . . rather than evolving arguments on their behalf."[28] Rogers frames his case with the assumption that it partakes of the same reforming potential as voluntary celibacy for Catholic priests and the potential for female ordination. He also uses the history of

26. Ibid., 670; *KD* IV/1:749.

27. Lindsay, *Covenanted Solidarity*, 222, concludes with massive evidence against the claims of Sonderegger.

28. Eugene F. Rogers Jr., *Sexuality and the Christian Body: Their Way into the Triune God* (Cambridge, Mass.: Blackwell, 1999), 10–11; quoting Hans W. Frei, "Eberhard Busch's Biography of Karl Barth," in *Types of Christian Theology*, ed. George Hunsinger and William C. Placher (New Haven: Yale University Press, 1992), 158–59.

theology ridding itself of anti-Semitism and supersessionism for his facile reflection on perceived correspondences.

In his book, Rogers at least makes his intent "to create a convergence on Christian sexuality among traditionalists and revisionists in the sense of 'relocating their opposition as no longer at the center of things.'"[29] But, of course, Frei's very point about Barth's recognition of tradition was that its essential form and content were in place. The only burden for the churches that practice obligatory celibacy of priests, male exclusivity in ordination, or even baptism of infants, for that matter, is whether these regulatory practices are fully consistent with the nature of ministry and the experience of faith. The issue is not whether believers can at points abrogate the moral prohibitions of Scripture and tradition in favor of an otherwise rejected variation on moral formation at the deepest levels of the human psyche.

In reading Rogers's reading of Barth, it is apparent that Rogers knows there is no crack in the form or content of the *CD* that bears an opening for his construction of a convergence, let alone an affirmation, of a homosexual approach to moral formation. Roger claims that all of Barth treatments of Scripture—Genesis 1–3, Romans 1, and Christian doctrine of marriage—leave the matter abstract and actually untreated. In Barth's day, there was nothing like the expansion of theologizing on this topic as at the beginning of the twenty-first century. Yet he was singularly concrete about the matter. For multiple reasons it is odd theologically that Rogers did not quote in detail and respond to Barth's decisive interpretation in the *CD*'s few pages on

the malady called homosexuality [*der sogenannten Homosexualität*].[30] This is the physical, psychological and social sickness, the phenomenon of perversion,

29. Rogers, *Sexuality and the Christian Body*, 14.

30. This is obviously mistranslated and should read "so-called homosexuality," which presumably is what is behind Robert Jenson's terse remarks on homosexuality in his recent magnum opus: "Finally, the inclusion of the 'heterosexual' in a rule is a—perhaps now necessary—redundancy. For homoeroticism is of course not a mode of sexuality at all but an escape from it. Homoeroticism is a group of sensual techniques, devised to abstract sexuality's pleasure without commitment to its function; doubtless these are sometimes used also as visible words of affection. There could not be a monogamy—or polygamy—other than heterosexual; talk of 'same-sex marriage' is a mere triumph of Humpty Dumpty.

"We need not here resolve the question of whether there are such things as sensual 'orientations' and if so how they are acquired. What must anyway be clear is that 'homosexuality' cannot refer to the characteristic as 'the way God created me,' if 'create' has anything like its biblical sense. No more in this context than in any other do we discover God's creative intent by examining the empirical situation; as we have seen I may indeed have to *blame* God for that empirically present in me that contradicts his known intent, but this is an occasion for unbelief, not a believer's justification of the evil.

"Abstention from sexuality is not in itself an evil. Indeed, one of the blessings enabled by the church's anticipation of the Kingdom is that celibacy can be a specific vocation within her. Nor is deprivation of sexuality a sin. Abstention or deprivation is not, however, the same as defection" (Robert Jenson, *Systematic Theology*, vol. 2 [New York: Oxford University Press, 1999], 93).

decadence and decay, which can emerge when man refuses to admit the validity of the divine command. . . . In Rom. 1 Paul connected it with idolatry, with changing the truth of God into a lie, with the adoration of the creature instead of the Creator (v. 25). . . . From the refusal to recognise God there follows the failure to appreciate man, and thus humanity without the fellow-man, . . . since humanity as fellow-humanity is to be understood in its root as the togetherness of man and woman. . . . And because the nature of the Creator of nature will not be trifled with, . . . because the natural orientation on him is still in force, there follows the corrupt emotional and finally physical desire [*die korrupte physische Lust*] in which—in a sexual union which is not and cannot be genuine [*in einer Geschlechtsbeziehung, die keine ist, noch sein kann*]—man thinks that he must seek and can find in man, and woman in woman, a substitute for the despised partner. But there is no sense in reminding man of the command of God only when he is face to face with this ultimate consequence, or pointing to the fact of human disobedience only when this malady breaks out openly in these unnatural courses. Naturally the command of God is opposed to these courses. This is almost too obvious to need stating. . . . But the decisive word of Christian ethics must consist in a warning against entering upon the whole way of life which can only end in the tragedy of concrete homosexuality. We know that in its early stages it may have the appearance of particular beauty and spirituality, and even be redolent of sanctity [*Heiligkeit*]. Often it has not been the worst people who have discovered and to some extent practised it as a sort of wonderful esoteric of personal life. Nor does this malady always manifest itself openly, or, when it does so, in obvious or indictable forms. Fear of ultimate consequences can give as little protection in this case, and condemnation may be as feeble a deterrent, as the thought of painful consequences in the case of fornication. What is needed is that the recognition of the divine command should cut sharply across the attractive beginnings. The real perversion takes place, the original decadence and disintegration begins, where man will not see his partner of the opposite sex and . . . make a responsible answer, but [is] trying to be human in himself as sovereign man or woman, rejoicing in himself in self-satisfaction and self-sufficiency. The command of God is opposed to the wonderful esoteric of this *beata solitude*. For in this supposed discovery of the genuinely human, man and woman give themselves up to the worship of a false god. It is here, therefore, that for himself and then in relation to others each must be brought to fear, recollection and understanding. This is the place for protest, warning and conversion. The command of God shows him irrefutably—in clear contradiction to his own theories—that as a man he can only be genuinely human with woman, or as a woman with man. In proportion as he accepts this insight, homosexuality can have no place in his life, whether in its more refined or cruder forms.[31]

The compactness of Barth's exposition here is astounding and in many ways alludes to Rogers's main points—particularly the centrality of bodily desire,

31. *CD* III/4:166.

the aesthetics of moral formation, and the sanctification of the body. But by not exegeting the passage, Rogers can abstractly pass by it.

This passing by of Barth's discourse was apparently expedient for Rogers in suggesting that the modification of Barth's theological concept of Israel requires alteration of Barth's theological and ethical reflections on homosexuality. The irony, as Rogers points out, is that Barth had little to say about the matter. But the reason for this too is in the short passage above: "Naturally the command of God is opposed to these courses. This is almost too obvious to need stating." Certainly, if Barth's public and ecclesial context had included mass movements of sexual liberationism (or libertinism), he would have had much more to say. One ought to observe that Barth is describing his context, in which homosexuality is experimented with and openly embraced. His text does not employ any symbol of a homophobic nature, let alone of a type that would tend in the direction of violent acts of hatred.

Rogers does not accuse Barth of fomenting hatred or violence. Instead, he adopts Barth's own critical stance toward abstraction in theology, critiques his theology of Israel, and finally claims the interpretive work of the Holy Spirit as the potential source of his book's theological agenda.[32] Rogers claims that Barth's partial neglect of this issue has come from his centering the *CD* on the doctrine of election—which Rogers believes diminishes the work of the Holy Spirit. Ironically, so much of Rogers's process in combining these elements—the subtext of seeking correspondence between a theology of Israel and a theology of homosexuality, the close reading of and interaction with Barth—is simply not in evidence, for all the sophistication of a type shown by Rogers.

His discussion of a range of issues related to homosexuality contains repeated irony: While Rogers makes serious attempts to engage tradition (e.g., Thomistic or Eastern Orthodox), the texts that he should explicitly engage and refute are entirely lacking. In many respects, his approach for the better part of his book is confusing. Perhaps the riddle is solved, however, as he discusses Thomas's view of intuition in theology. Here Rogers cites "the rule for Thomas that *human beings cannot expect to come to correct conclusions on moral matters under conditions of injustice.*"[33] Rogers claims that moral justice is not being done to those who believe that homosexuality is one possible variation on biblical moral formation. Therefore, he seems to say, persons of such an orientation cannot reason themselves through their own moral predicaments without a social order that is fully accepting of homosexuals. But, of course, Rogers has created an interpretive and rhetorical scenario from which there would then be no escape and no resolution.

---

32. Rogers, *Sexuality and the Christian Body,* 166–79.
33. Ibid., 121.

Reading Again Soon

Beyond the indirect and direct attempts at covering the boundaries of Word, Spirit, and tradition in the twenty-first century, the issues of ongoing, pilgrim interpretation of the Word of God are helped immensely by Barth's example. This does not mean that we must necessarily adopt anything that he wrote. And yet his knowledge and his judgments are so valuable for us to know and to guide us. Barth assists us in finding healing after the great losses of modernist theology, whether liberal or conservative. He helps to connect us with so much living tradition that was discarded by theologians of previous generations.

Barth shows how he dealt so exhaustively and lively with these problems. But the precision and godliness of his answers are not our answers. Each generation, and indeed each believer, is responsible for fresh answers to questions of everyday that are ever new. Barth issued a well-known caution about the knowledge of God via the Holy Spirit while yet being expectant of a theology just so grounded, which is yet to be written. It will begin an entirely new tradition in Christian theology, which will begin to match the great dynamism of its expansive and variable nature, but be rooted in Word and Spirit. Barth's caution would not have been over a theology of the particular Spirit of God, the Spirit of Christ, the Spirit of the gospel, the Spirit of Pentecost. What Barth could do he did and more: all centered on Jesus Christ and his mediatorial and trinitarian role for the life of the church and the world.

BIBLIOGRAPHY

Allen, Edgar Leonard. *The Sovereignty of God and the Word of God: A Guide to the Thought of Karl Barth.* New York: Philosophical Library, 1951.

Anderson, Donald N. "The Political Ethics of Karl Barth and Reinhold Niebuhr." Ph.D. thesis, University of Chicago Divinity School, 1965.

Anderson, William P. *Aspects of the Theology of Karl Barth.* Washington, D.C.: University Press of America, 1981.

Andrews, Isolde. *Deconstructing Barth: A Study of the Complementary Methods in Karl Barth and Jacques Derrida.* New York: Peter Lang, 1996.

Anz, Wilhelm, Michael Wolter, Bernd Wildemann, and Walter Schmithals. *Existenz und Sein: Karl Barth und die Marburger Theologie.* Tübingen: J. C. B. Mohr (Paul Siebeck), 1989.

Balthasar, Hans Urs von. *The Theology of Karl Barth: Exposition and Interpretation.* Translated by E. T. Oakes. San Francisco: Communio Books, Ignatius Press, 1992.

Barth, Karl. *Christ and Adam: Man and Humanity in Romans 5.* Translated by T. A. Smail. New York: Octagon Books, 1983.

———. *Des Christen Wehr und Waffen, von Karl Barth.* Zollikon-Zürich: Evangelischer Verlag, 1940.

———. *The Christian Life: Church Dogmatics* IV, 4, *Lecture Fragments.* Translated by G. W. Bromiley. Grand Rapids: Eerdmans, 1981.

———. *Die christliche Dogmatik im Entwurf.* München: C. Kaiser, 1927; Zürich: Theologischer Verlag, 1982.

———. *Church and State.* Translated by G. R. Howe. Greenville, S.C.: Smyth & Helwys, 1991.

———. *The Church and the War.* Translated by A. H. Froendt. New York: Macmillan, 1944.

———. *Church Dogmatics*. Edited by G. W. Bromiley and T. F. Torrance. Translated by G. W. Bromiley. 2d ed. 4 vols. plus index as vol. 5, in 14 vols. Edinburgh: T & T Clark, 1975–81.

———. *Deliverance to the Captives*. Westport, Conn.: Greenwood Press, 1979.

———. *The Epistle to the Philippians*. Translated by J. W. Leitch. Louisville: Westminster John Knox, 2002.

———. *The Epistle to the Romans*. Translated by Edwyn C. Hoskyns. London: Oxford University Press, 1958. Translation of *Der Römerbrief*. 6th ed. Bern: Bäschlin, 1933.

———. *Ethics*. Edited by D. Braun. Translated by G. W. Bromiley. New York: Seabury, 1981.

———. *Final Testimonies*. Edited by E. Busch. Translated by G. W. Bromiley. Grand Rapids: Eerdmans, 1977.

———. *God Here and Now*. Translated by P. M. van Buren. New York: Routledge, 2003.

———. *God in Action: Theological Addresses*. Translated by E. G. Homrighausen and K. J. Ernst. New York: Round Table Press, 1936.

———. *God's Search for Man: Sermons*. Translated by G. W. Richards, E. G. Homrighausen, and K. J. Ernst. New York: Round Table Press, 1935.

———. *Gott ist jeden Morgen neu*. Basel: F. Reinhardt, 1978.

———. *The Holy Spirit and the Christian Life: The Theological Basis of Ethics*. Translated by R. B. Hoyle. Louisville: Westminster John Knox, 1993.

———. *Karl Barth-Rudolf Bultmann Letters, 1922–1966*. Edited by B. Jaspert and G. W. Bromiley. Translated by G. W. Bromiley. Grand Rapids: Eerdmans, 1981.

———. *Die kirchliche Dogmatik*. 4 vols. plus *Register* in 14 vols. Zollikon-Zürich: Evangelischer Verlag, 1932–67, 1970.

———. *Die kirchliche Lehre von der Taufe*. München: C. Kaiser, 1947.

———. *Komm Schöpfer Geist! Predigten von Karl Barth und Eduard Thurneysen*. München: C. Kaiser, 1924.

———. *Learning Jesus Christ through the Heidelberg Catechism*. Translated by S. C. Guthrie Jr. Grand Rapids: Eerdmans, 1981.

———. *Die lebendige Gemeinde und die freie Gnade*. München: C. Kaiser, 1947.

———. *Prayer*. Edited by D. E. Saliers. Translated by S. F. Terrien. Louisville: Westminster John Knox, 2002.

———. *Predigten 1918*. Edited by H. Schmidt. Zürich: Theologischer Verlag, 2002.

————. *Protestant Theology in the Nineteenth Century: Its Background and History.* Grand Rapids: Eerdmans, 2002.

————. *The Resurrection of the Dead.* Translated by H. J. Stenning. New York: Revell, 1933.

————. *Der Römerbrief.* Bern: Bäschlin, 1919.

————. *Theological Existence Today! (A Plea for Theological Freedom).* Translated by R. B. Hoyle. London: Hodder & Stoughton, 1933.

————. *The Theology of John Calvin.* Translated by G. W. Bromiley. Grand Rapids: Eerdmans, 1995.

————. *The Theology of Schleiermacher: Lectures at Göttingen, Winter Semester of 1923–24.* Edited by D. Ritschl. Translated by G. W. Bromiley. Grand Rapids: Eerdmans, 1982.

————. *The Theology of the Reformed Confessions, 1923.* Translated and annotated by D. L. Guder and J. J. Guder. Louisville: Westminster John Knox, 2002.

————. *This Christian Cause (A Letter to Great Britain from Switzerland).* New York: Macmillan, 1941.

————. *Trouble and Promise in the Struggle of the Church in Germany.* Translated by P. V. M. Benecke. Philip Maurice Deneke Lecture. Oxford: Clarendon, 1938.

————. *Witness to the Word: A Commentary on John 1: Lectures at Münster in 1925 and at Bonn in 1933.* Edited by W. Fürst. Translated by G. W. Bromiley. Grand Rapids: Eerdmans, 1986.

————. *Wolfgang Amadeus Mozart.* Translated by C. K. Pott. Grand Rapids: Eerdmans, 1986.

————. *The Word of God and the Word of Man.* Translated by D. Horton. Boston: Pilgrim, 1928.

Barth, Karl, and Christoph Blumhardt. *Action in Waiting.* Edited and translated by Hutterian Society of Brothers. Rifton, N.Y.: Plough Publishing House, 1979.

Barth, Markus. *Das Mahl des Herrn: Gemeinschaft mit Israel, mit Christus und unter den Gästen.* Neukirchen-Vluyn: Neukirchener Verlag, 1987.

————. *The People of God.* Sheffield: JSOT Press, 1983.

————. *Die Taufe—ein Sakrament? Ein exegetischer Beitrag zum Gespräch über die kirchliche Taufe.* Zollikon-Zürich: Evangelischer Verlag, 1951.

Becker, Dieter. *Karl Barth und Martin Buber—Denker in dialogischer Nachbarschaft?* Göttingen: Vandenhoeck & Ruprecht, 1986.

Berkhof, Hendrikus. *Karl Barths Lichterlehre.* Zürich: Theologischer Verlag, 1978.

Blumhardt, Christoph. *Action in Waiting.* Farmington, Pa.: Plough Publishing House, 1998.

Bolich, Gregory G. *Karl Barth and Evangelicalism*. Downers Grove, Ill.: InterVarsity, 1980.

Braaten, Carl E., and Robert W. Jenson. *A Map of Twentieth-Century Theology: Readings from Karl Barth to Radical Pluralism*. Minneapolis: Fortress, 1995.

Brinkschmidt, Egon. *Martin Buber und Karl Barth: Theologie zwischen Dialogik und Dialektik*. Neukirchen-Vluyn: Neukirchener Verlag, 2000.

————. *Sören Kierkegaard und Karl Barth*. Neukirchen-Vluyn: Neukirchener Verlag, 1971.

Brown, Colin. *Karl Barth and the Christian Message*. London: Tyndale, 1967.

Brunner, Emil. *Natur und Gnade: Zum Gespräch mit Karl Barth*. Tübingen: J. C. B. Mohr (Paul Siebeck), 1934.

Burnett, Richard E. *Karl Barth's Theological Exegesis: The Hermeneutical Principles of the Römerbrief Period*. Tübingen: Mohr Siebeck, 2001.

Busch, Eberhard. *Karl Barth: His Life from Letters and Autobiographical Texts*. Translated by J. Bowden. Grand Rapids: Eerdmans, 1994.

————. *Karl Barth und die Pietisten: Die Pietismuskritik des jungen Karl Barth und ihre Erwiderung*. München: C. Kaiser, 1978.

————. *Unter dem Bogen des einen Bundes: Karl Barth und die Juden, 1933–1945*. Neukirchen-Vluyn: Neukirchener Verlag, 1996.

Casalis, Georges. *Portrait of Karl Barth*. Translated by R. McAfee Brown. Westport, Conn.: Greenwood, 1981.

Chavannes, Henry. *The Analogy between God and the World in Saint Thomas Aquinas and Karl Barth*. Translated by W. Lumley. New York: Vantage, 1992.

Cochrane, Arthur C. *The Existentialists and God: Being and the Being of God in the Thought of Sören Kierkegaard, Karl Jaspers, Martin Heidegger, Jean-Paul Sartre, Paul Tillich, Etienne Gilson, and Karl Barth*. Philadelphia: Westminster, 1956.

Collins, Paul M. *Trinitarian Theology, West and East: Karl Barth, the Cappadocian Fathers, and John Zizioulas*. Oxford: Oxford University Press, 2001.

Colwell, John. *Actuality and Provisionality: Eternity and Election in the Theology of Karl Barth*. Rutherford Studies. Contemporary Theology, no 3. Edinburgh: Rutherford House, 1989.

Cootsona, Gregory S. *God and the World: A Study in the Thought of Alfred North Whitehead and Karl Barth*. New York: Peter Lang, 2001.

Davaney, Sheila Greeve. *Divine Power: A Study of Karl Barth and Charles Hartshorne*. Philadelphia: Fortress, 1986.

Demson, David E. *Hans Frei and Karl Barth: Different Ways of Reading Scripture*. Grand Rapids: Eerdmans, 1997.

Dickerman, David L., ed. *Karl Barth and the Future of Theology: A Memorial Colloquium Held at the Yale Divinity School, January 28, 1969.* New Haven: Yale Divinity School Association, 1969.

Dorrien, Gary J. *The Barthian Revolt in Modern Theology: Theology without Weapons.* Philadelphia: Westminster John Knox, 1999.

Eicher, Peter, and Michael Weinrich. *Der gute Widerspruch: Das unbegriffene Zeugnis von Karl Barth.* Düsseldorf: Patmos, 1986.

Etzelmüller, Gregor. *"—Zu richten die Lebendigen und die Toten": Zur Rede vom Jüngsten Gericht im Anschluss an Karl Barth.* Neukirchen-Vluyn: Neukirchener Verlag, 2001.

Fetzer, Antje. *Tradition im Pluralismus: Alasdair MacIntyre und Karl Barth als Inspiration für christliches Selbstverständnis in der pluralen Gesellschaft.* Neukirchener theologische Dissertationen und Habilitationen 32. Neukirchen-Vluyn: Neukirchener Verlag, 2002.

Feuerbach, Ludwig. *The Essence of Christianity.* Translated by G. Eliot. Library of Religion and Culture. New York: Harper, 1957.

Finke, Anne-Kathrin. *Karl Barth in Grossbritannien: Rezeption und Wirkungsgeschichte.* Neukirchen-Vluyn: Neukirchener Verlag, 1995.

Fisher, Simon. *Revelatory Positivism? Barth's Earliest Theology and the Marburg School.* Oxford: Oxford University Press, 1988.

Ford, David. *Barth and God's Story: Biblical Narrative and the Theological Method of Karl Barth in the "Church Dogmatics."* Studien zur interkulturellen Geschichte des Christentums 27. Frankfurt am Main: Lang, 1981.

Frei, Hans W. *Theology and Narrative: Selected Essays.* Edited by G. Hunsinger and W. C. Placher. New York: Oxford University Press, 1993.

Freudenberg, Matthias. *Karl Barth und die reformierte Theologie: die Auseinandersetzung mit Calvin, Zwingli, und den reformierten Bekenntnisschriften während seiner Göttinger Lehrtätigkeit.* Neukirchener theologische Dissertationen und Habilitationen 8. Neukirchen-Vluyn: Neukirchener Verlag, 1997.

Frey, Arthur. *Cross and Swastika: The Ordeal of the German Church.* Translated by J. S. McNab. London: Student Christian Movement Press, 1938.

Freyer, Thomas. *Pneumatologie als Strukturprinzip der Dogmatik: Überlegungen im Anschluss an die Lehre von der "Geisttaufe" bei Karl Barth.* Paderborner theologische Studien 12. Paderborn: Schöningh, 1982.

———. *Zeit—Kontinuität und Unterbrechung: Studien zu Karl Barth, Wolfhart Pannenberg und Karl Rahner.* Bonner dogmatische Studien 13. Würzburg: Echter, 1993.

Gärtner, Friedrich. *Karl Barth und Zinzendorf: Die bleibende Bedeutung Zinzendorfs auf Grund der Beurteilung des Pietismus durch Karl Barth.* Theologische Existenz heute, eine Schriftenreihe, n. F., 40. München: C. Kaiser, 1953.

Gemmer, Anders. *Sören Kierkegaard und Karl Barth.* Stuttgart: Strecker und Schröder, 1925.

Genest, Hartmut. *Karl Barth und die Predigt: Darstellung und Deutung von Predigtwerk und Predigtlehre Karl Barths.* Neukirchen-Vluyn: Neukirchener Verlag, 1995.

Gollwitzer, Helmut, and Hellmut Traub, eds. *Hören und handeln: Festschrift für Ernst Wolf zum 60. Geburtstag.* München: C. Kaiser, 1962.

————. *Reich Gottes und Sozialismus bei Karl Barth.* Theologische Existenz heute, n. F., 169. München: C. Kaiser, 1972.

Gorringe, Timothy. *Karl Barth: Against Hegemony.* Christian Theology in Context. Oxford: Oxford University Press, 1999.

Goud, Johannes Frederik. *Emmanuel Levinas und Karl Barth: Ein religionsphilosophischer und ethischer Vergleich.* Abhandlungen zur Philosophie, Psychologie und Pädagogik 234. Bonn: Bouvier, 1992.

Groll, Wilfried. *Ernst Troeltsch und Karl Barth: Kontinuität im Widerspruch.* Beiträge zur evangelischen Theologie: theologische Abhandlungen 72 München: C. Kaiser, 1976.

Gunton, Colin E. *Becoming and Being: The Doctrine of God in Charles Hartshorne and Karl Barth.* Oxford Theological Monographs. New York: Oxford University Press, 1978.

Hack, Christina. *Groter dan ons hart: De verhouding van God en mens bij Karl Barth en Emmanuel Levinas, met het oog op het nieuwe tijds denken.* Zoetermeer: Boekencentrum, 1993.

Haga, Tsutomu. *Theodizee und Geschichtstheologie: Ein Versuch der Überwindung der Problematik des deutschen Idealismus bei Karl Barth.* Forschungen zur systematischen und ökumenischen Theologie 59. Göttingen: Vandenhoeck & Ruprecht, 1991.

Hamer, Jérôme. *Karl Barth.* Translated by D. M. Maruca. Westminster, Md.: Newman Press, 1962.

————. *Karl Barth, l'occasionalisme théologique de Karl Barth: Étude sur sa méthode dogmatique.* Paris: Desclée, de Brouwer, 1949.

Härle, Wilfried. *Die Theologie des "frühen" Karl Barth in ihrem Verhältnis zu der Theologie Martin Luthers.* Bochum: Wilfried Härle, 1969.

Hart, John W. *Karl Barth versus Emil Brunner: The Formation and Dissolution of a Theological Alliance, 1916–1936.* Issues in Systematic Theology 6. New York: Peter Lang, 2001.

Hart, Trevor A. *Regarding Karl Barth: Toward a Reading of His Theology.* Downers Grove, Ill.: InterVarsity, 1999.

Hempel, Christa. *Rechtfertigung als Wirklichkeit: Ein katholisches Gespräch: Karl Barth, Hans Küng, Rudolf Bultmann und seine Schule.* Europäische Hochschulschriften, Reihe 23, Theologie 55. Bern: Herbert Lang, 1976.

Hendricks, William L. "The Concept of Death in the Theology of Karl Barth." Ph.D. diss., University of Chicago, 1972.

Hennecke, Susanne. *Der vergessene Schleier: Ein theologisches Gespräch zwischen Luce Irigaray und Karl Barth.* Gütersloh: Kaiser, Gütersloher Verlagshaus, 2001.

Henry, David Paul. *The Early Development of the Hermeneutic of Karl Barth as Evidenced by His Appropriation of Romans 5:12–21.* NABPR dissertation series 5. Macon, Ga.: Mercer University Press, 1985.

Herberg, Josef. *Kirchliche Heilsvermittlung: Ein Gespräch zwischen Karl Barth und Karl Rahner.* Disputationes theologicae 5. Frankfurt am Main: Peter Lang, 1978.

Herwig, Thomas. *Karl Barth und die ökumenische Bewegung: Das Gespräch zwischen Karl Barth und Willem Adolf Visser't Hooft auf der Grundlage ihres Briefwechsels, 1930–1968.* Neukirchen-Vluyn: Neukirchener Verlag, 1998.

Heubach, Joachim, ed. *Luther und Barth.* Erlangen: Martin-Luther-Verlag, 1989.

Hoyle, Richard Birch. *The Teaching of Karl Barth: An Exposition.* London: Student Christian Movement Press, 1930.

Hromádka, J. L. *Evangelium für Atheisten.* Mit einem Nachwort von Karl Barth. Arche nova. Zürich: Verlag der Arche, 1969.

Hubert, Hans. *Der Streit um die Kindertaufe. Eine Darstellung der von Karl Barth 1943 ausgelösten Diskussion um die Kindertaufe und ihrer Bedeutung für die heutige Tauffrage.* Europäische Hochschulschriften, Reihe 23, Theologie 10. Bern: Herbert Lang, 1972.

Hunsinger, George. "Baptism and the Soteriology of Forgiveness." *International Journal of Systematic Theology* 2 (2000): 247–69.

———. *Disruptive Grace: Studies in the Theology of Karl Barth.* Grand Rapids: Eerdmans, 2000.

———. *How to Read Karl Barth: The Shape of His Theology.* New York: Oxford University Press, 1991.

Jehle, Frank. *Ever against the Stream: The Politics of Karl Barth, 1906–1968.* Translated by R. and M. Burnett. Grand Rapids: Eerdmans, 2002.

———. *Lieber unangenehm laut als angenehm leise: Der Theologe Karl Barth und die Politik, 1906–1968.* Zürich: Theologischer Verlag, 1999.

Jenson, Robert W. *Alpha and Omega: A Study in the Theology of Karl Barth.* New York: Nelson, 1963.

———. *God after God: The God of the Past and the God of the Future, Seen in the Work of Karl Barth.* Indianapolis: Bobbs-Merrill, 1969.

Jeong, Sung Min. *Nothingness in the Theology of Paul Tillich and Karl Barth.* Lanham, Md.: University Press of America, 2003.

Johnson, William Stacy. *The Mystery of God: Karl Barth and the Postmodern Foundations of Theology.* Louisville: Westminster John Knox, 1997.

Jüngel, Eberhard. *Barth-Studien.* Zürich: Benziger, 1982.

———. *God's Being Is in Becoming: The Trinitarian Being of God in the Theology of Karl Barth: a Paraphrase.* 2d ed. Translated by J. Webster. Grand Rapids: Eerdmans, 2001.

———. *Karl Barth: A Theological Legacy.* Translated by Garrett E. Paul. Philadelphia: Westminster, 1986. Translation of *Barth-Studien.* Zürich: Benziger, 1982.

———. *Karl Barths Lehre von der Taufe: Ein Hinweis auf ihre Probleme.* Zürich: EVZ-Verlag, 1968.

Karelse, Leddy. *Dwalen: Over Mark C. Taylor en Karl Barth.* Zoetermeer: Boekencentrum, 1999.

Kim, Heup Young. *Wang Yang-ming and Karl Barth: A Confucian-Christian Dialogue.* Lanham, Md.: University Press of America, 1996.

Kinder, Ernst. *Natürlicher glaube und offenbarungsglaube: Eine Untersuchung im Anschluss an die Glaubensphilosophie Fr. H. Jacobis.* München: C. Kaiser, 1935.

Kirschbaum, Charlotte von. *The Question of Woman: The Collected Writings of Charlotte von Kirschbaum.* Translated by John Shepher. Grand Rapids: Eerdmans, 1996.

Klappert, Bertold. *Israel und die Kirche: Erwägungen zur Israellehre Karl Barths.* In Memoriam Hans Joachim Iwand (1899–1960). München: C. Kaiser, 1980.

———. *Versöhnung und Befreiung: Versuche, Karl Barth kontextuell zu verstehen.* Neukirchener Beiträge zur Systematischen Theologie 14. Neukirchen-Vluyn: Neukirchener Verlag, 1994.

Köbler, Renate. *In the Shadow of Karl Barth: Charlotte von Kirschbaum.* Translated by K. Crim. Louisville: Westminster John Knox, 1989.

Kress, Christine. *Gottes Allmacht angesichts von Leiden: Zur Interpretation der Gotteslehre in den systematisch-theologischen Entwürfen von Paul Althaus, Paul Tillich und Karl Barth.* Neukirchen-Vluyn: Neukirchener Verlag, 1999.

Krötke, Wolf. *Der Mensch und die Religion nach Karl Barth.* Theologische Studien 125. Zürich: Theologischer Verlag, 1981.

———. *Sünde und Nichtiges bei Karl Barth.* Theologische Arbeiten 30. Berlin: Evangelische Verlagsanst., 1970.

Küng, Hans. *Justification: The Doctrine of Karl Barth and a Catholic Reflection.* Translated by T. Collins, E. E. Tolk, and D. Granskou. Philadelphia: Westminster, 1981.

Kupisch, Karl. *Begegnung mit Karl Barth: Eine historisch-politische Betrachtung.* Theologische Existenz heute, n. F., 62. München: C. Kaiser, 1958.

Laak, Werner van. *Allversöhnung: Die Lehre von der Apokatastasis: Ihre Grundlegung durch Origenes und ihre Bewertung in der gegenwärtigen Theologie bei Karl Barth und Hans Urs von Balthasar.* Sinziger theologische Texte und Studien 11. Sinzig: Sankt Meinrad Verlag für Theologie C. Esser, 1990.

Lange, Peter. *Konkrete Theologie? Karl Barth und Friedrich Gogarten "Zwischen den Zeiten" (1922–1933): Eine theologiegeschichtlich-systematische Untersuchung im Blick auf die Praxis theologischen Verhaltens.* Basler Studien zur historischen und systematischen Theologie 19. Zürich: Theologischer Verlag, 1972.

Leitch, James W. *A Theology of Transition: H. R. Mackintosh as an Approach to Barth.* London: Nisbet, 1952.

Lindbeck, George. "Barth and Textuality." *Theology Today* 43 (1986): 361–76.

Lindenlauf, Herbert. *Karl Barth und die Lehre von der "Königsherrschaft Christi": Eine Untersuchung zum christozentrischen Ansatz der Ethik des Politischen im deutschsprachigen Protestantismus nach 1934.* Spardorf: R. F. Wilfer, 1988.

Lochman, Jan Milic, and Martin Rohrkrämer. *Freundschaft im Widerspruch: Der Briefwechsel zwischen Barth Karl Josef L. Hromádka und Josef B. Soucek, 1935–1968.* Zürich: Theologischer Verlag, 1995.

Lohmann, Johann Friedrich. *Karl Barth und der Neukantianismus: Die Rezeption des Neukantianismus im "Römerbrief" und ihre Bedeutung für die weitere Ausarbeitung der Theologie Karl Barths.* Theologische Bibliothek Töpelmann 72. Berlin: De Gruyter, 1995.

Lowrie, Walter. *Our Concern with the Theology of Crisis: The Fundamental Aspects of the Dialectical Theology Associated with the Name of Karl Barth.* Bohlen Lectures. Boston: Meador Publishing, 1932.

Macken, John. *The Autonomy Theme in the Church Dogmatics: Karl Barth and His Critics.* Cambridge: Cambridge University Press, 1990.

Mackintosh, H. R. *Types of Modern Theology: Schleiermacher to Barth.* London: Nisbet, 1937.

Mangina, Joseph L. *Karl Barth on the Christian Life: The Practical Knowledge of God.* New York: Peter Lang, 2001.

Marquard, Reiner. *Karl Barth und der Isenheimer Altar.* Arbeiten zur Theologie 80. Stuttgart: Calwer, 1995.

McCord, James I., and T. H. L. Parker, eds. *Service in Christ: Essays Presented to Karl Barth on His Eightieth Birthday.* Grand Rapids: Eerdmans, 1966.

McCormack, Bruce L. "Beyond Foundationalism and Postmodern Reading of Barth." *Zeitschrift für dialektische Theologie* 13 (1997): 67–95.

———. *Karl Barth's Critically Realistic Dialectical Theology: Its Genesis and Development, 1909–1936.* Oxford: Clarendon, 1995.

————. "Revelation and History in Transfoundationalist Perspective: Karl Barth's Theological Epistemology in Conversation with a Schleiermacherian Tradition." *Journal of Religion* 78 (1998): 18–37.

McLean, Stuart D. "Elements of Dynamics and Form in the Thought of Karl Barth and Jacques Maritain." Ph.D. diss., University of Chicago, 1968.

————. *Humanity in the Thought of Karl Barth.* Edinburgh: T & T Clark, 1981.

Mechels, Eberhard. *Analogie bei Erich Przywara und Karl Barth: Das Verhältnis von Offenbarungstheologie und Metaphysik.* Neukirchen-Vluyn: Neukirchener Verlag, 1974.

Meijering, E. P. *Von den Kirchenvätern zu Karl Barth: Das altkirchliche Dogma in der "Kirchlichen Dogmatik."* Amsterdam: J. C. Gieben, 1993.

Metzger, Paul Louis. *The Word of Christ and the World of Culture: Sacred and Secular through the Theology of Karl Barth.* Grand Rapids: Eerdmans, 2003.

Molnar, Paul D. *Karl Barth and the Theology of the Lord's Supper: A Systematic Investigation.* New York: Peter Lang, 1996.

Moltmann, Jürgen, ed. *Anfänge der dialektischen Theologie.* Theologische Bücherei-Systematische Theologische 17. München: C. Kaiser, 1977–87.

Moosbrugger, Otto. *Das Problem der speziellen Ethik bei Karl Barth: Der Ansatz zur speziellen Ethik, speziell zur Lehre vom Gebot Gottes des Schöpfers, und die Argumente gegen die theologische Naturrechtslehre in der "Kirchlichen Dogmatik" Karl Barths.* Bonn: Rheinische Friedrich-Wilhelms-Universität, 1972.

Mueller, David L. *Karl Barth.* Peabody, Mass.: Hendrickson, 1972.

Neuser, Wilhelm H. *Karl Barth in Münster, 1925–1930.* Zürich: Theologischer Verlag, 1985.

Norden, Günther van. *Die Weltverantwortung der Christen neu begreifen: Karl Barth als homo politicus.* Gütersloh: C. Kaiser, 1997.

Oblau, Gotthard. *Gotteszeit und Menschenzeit: Eschatologie in der Kirchlichen Dogmatik von Karl Barth.* Neukirchen-Vluyn: Neukirchener Verlag, 1988.

Oden, Thomas C. *The Promise of Barth: The Ethics of Freedom.* Philadelphia: Lippincott, 1969.

Ogletree, Thomas W. *Christian Faith and History: A Critical Comparison of Ernst Troeltsch and Karl Barth.* New York: Abingdon, 1965.

O'Grady, Colm. *The Church in Catholic Theology: Dialogue with Karl Barth.* London: G. Chapman, 1969.

Osborn, Robert T. *Freedom in Modern Theology.* Philadelphia: Westminster, 1967.

Oshima, Sueo. "Theology and History in Karl Barth: A Study of the Theology of Karl Barth in Reference to the Philosophy of Martin Heidegger." Ph.D. diss., University of Chicago, 1970.

Osthövener, Claus-Dieter. *Die Lehre von Gottes Eigenschaften bei Friedrich Schleiermacher und Karl Barth.* Theologische Bibliothek Töpelmann 76. New York: W. de Gruyter, 1996.

Otterness, Omar G. "The Doctrine of Sanctification in the Theology of Karl Barth." Ph.D. diss., University of Chicago, 1969.

Pangritz, Andreas. *Karl Barth in the Theology of Dietrich Bonhoeffer.* Translated by B. and M. Rumscheidt. Grand Rapids: Eerdmans, 2000.

Parker, T. H. L. *Karl Barth.* Grand Rapids: Eerdmans, 1970.

Pauck, Wilhelm. *Karl Barth, Prophet of a New Christianity?* New York: Harper & Brothers, 1931.

Plasger, Georg. *Die relative Autorität des Bekenntnisses bei Karl Barth.* Neukirchen-Vluyn: Neukirchener Verlag, 2000.

Prolingheuer, Hans. *Der Fall Karl Barth, 1934–1935: Chronographie einer Vertreibung.* Neukirchen-Vluyn: Neukirchener Verlag, 1977.

Reinisch, Leonhard, ed. *Theologians of Our Time: Karl Barth [and Others].* Notre Dame, Ind.: University of Notre Dame Press, 1964.

Roberts, Richard H. *A Theology on Its Way? Essays on Karl Barth.* Edinburgh: T & T Clark, 1991.

Rodin, R. Scott. *Evil and Theodicy in the Theology of Karl Barth.* New York: Peter Lang, 1997.

Rogers, Eugene F. *Thomas Aquinas and Karl Barth: Sacred Doctrine and the Natural Knowledge of God.* Notre Dame, Ind.: University of Notre Dame Press, 1995.

Rosato, Philip J. *The Spirit as Lord: The Pneumatology of Karl Barth.* Edinburgh: T & T Clark, 1981.

Rothen, Bernhard. *Die Klarheit der Schrift.* Göttingen: Vandenhoeck & Ruprecht, 1990.

Rumscheidt, H. Martin. *Revelation and Theology: An Analysis of the Barth-Harnack Correspondence of 1923.* Cambridge: Cambridge University Press, 1996.

———, ed. *Karl Barth in Review: Posthumous Works Reviewed and Assessed.* Pittsburgh: Pickwick Press, 1981.

Salmann, Elmar, and Aniceto Molinaro. *Filosofia e mistica: Itinerari di un progetto di ricerca.* Roma: Pontificio Ateneo S. Anselmo, 1997.

Schlemmer, Hans. *Von Karl Barth zu den deutschen Christen.* Gotha: L. Klotz, 1934.

Schmitt, Keith Randall. *Death and After-Life in the Theologies of Karl Barth and John Hick: A Comparative Study.* Amsterdam: Rodopi, 1985.

Scholl, Hans, ed. *Karl Barth und Johannes Calvin: Karl Barths Göttinger Calvin-Vorlesung von 1922.* Neukirchen-Vluyn: Neukirchener Verlag, 1995.

Schwöbel, Christoph. "Theology." In *The Cambridge Companion to Karl Barth,* edited by John Webster, 17–36. Cambridge: Cambridge University Press, 2000.

Selinger, Suzanne. *Charlotte von Kirschbaum and Karl Barth: A Study in Biography and the History of Theology.* University Park, Pa.: Pennsylvania State University Press, 1998.

Shofner, Robert D. *Anselm Revisited: A Study on the Role of the Ontological Argument in the Writings of Karl Barth and Charles Hartshorne.* Leiden: Brill, 1974.

Sigurdson, Ola. *Karl Barth som den andre: En studie i den svenska teologins Barth-reception.* Stockholm: B. Östlings bokförlag Symposion, 1996.

Smart, James D. *The Divided Mind of Modern Theology: Karl Barth and Rudolf Bultmann, 1908–1933.* Philadelphia: Westminster, 1967.

Smith, Steven G. *The Argument to the Other: Reason beyond Reason in the Thought of Karl Barth and Emmanuel Levinas.* American Academy of Religion Academy Series 42. Chico, Calif.: Scholars Press, 1983.

Spencer, Archibald James. *Clearing a Space for Human Action: Toward an Ethical Ontology in the Early Theology of Karl Barth.* New York: Peter Lang, 2001.

Starkloff, Carl F. *The Office of Proclamation in the Theology of Karl Barth: A Study of Preaching Authority as Service to the Word of God.* Les publications sériées de l'Université d'Ottawa 93. Ottawa: University of Ottawa Press, 1969.

Steck, Karl Gerhard. *Karl Barth und die Neuzeit.* Theologische Existenz heute, n. F., 173. München: C. Kaiser, 1973.

Stroble, Paul E. *The Social Ontology of Karl Barth.* San Francisco: Christian Universities Press, 1994.

Süss, René. *Een genadeloos bestaan: Karl Barth over het Joodse volk.* Kampen: J. H. Kok, 1991.

Tae, Seung-Chul. *Die göttliche Ontologie des Menschen bei Karl Barth: Zum "allein möglichen" Weg einer theologischen Lehre vom Menschen.* Europäische Hochschulschriften, Reihe 23, Theologie 609. New York: Peter Lang, 1997.

Tempelman, Andrew D. "The Conditions of Intelligible Analogical God-Language in the Theologies of Paul Tillich, Eric Mascall, and Karl Barth." Ph.D. diss., University of Chicago, 1972.

Thiemann, Ronald. "Response to George Lindbeck." *Theology Today* 43 (1986): 377–82.

Thompson, John. *Christ in Perspective: Christological Perspectives in the Theology of Karl Barth.* Grand Rapids: Eerdmans, 1978.

———. *The Holy Spirit in the Theology of Karl Barth.* Allison Park, Pa.: Pickwick Publications, 1991.

————, ed. *Theology beyond Christendom: Essays on the Centenary of the Birth of Karl Barth, May 10, 1886.* Allison Park, Pa.: Pickwick Publications, 1986.

Thorne, Phillip R. *Evangelicalism and Karl Barth: His Reception and Influence in North American Evangelical Theology.* Allison Park, Pa.: Pickwick Publications, 1995.

Tippelskirch, Dorothee C. von. *"Liebe von fremd zu fremd": Menschlichkeit des Menschen und Göttlichkeit Gottes bei Emmanuel Levinas und Karl Barth.* Alber-Reihe Thesen 22. Freiburg [Breisgau]: Alber, 2002.

Toren, Bernard van den. *Breuk en brug: In gesprek met Karl Barth en postmoderne theologie over geloofsverantwoording.* Zoetermeer: Boekencentrum, 1995.

Torrance, Alan J. *Persons in Communion: An Essay on Trinitarian Description and Human Participation, with Special Reference to Volume 1 of Karl Barth's Church Dogmatics.* Edinburgh: T & T Clark, 1996.

Torrance, Thomas Forsyth. *Karl Barth: Biblical and Evangelical Theologian.* Edinburgh: T & T Clark, 1990.

————. *Karl Barth: An Introduction to His Early Theology, 1910–1931.* London: SCM, 1962.

Van Til, Cornelius. *Barth's Christology.* Philadelphia: Presbyterian & Reformed, 1962.

————. *Christianity and Barthianism.* Philadelphia: Presbyterian & Reformed, 1962.

————. "Has Karl Barth Become Orthodox?" *Westminster Theological Journal* 16 (1954): 135–81.

————. *Karl Barth and Evangelicalism.* Philadelphia: Presbyterian & Reformed, 1964.

————. *The New Modernism: An Appraisal of the Theology of Barth and Brunner.* Philadelphia: Presbyterian & Reformed, 1946.

————. "Review of *Kirchliche Dogmatik IV/1,3,*" *Westminster Theological Journal* 22 (1959): 64–69.

Vogel, Heinrich. *Freundschaft mit Karl Barth: Ein Porträt in Anekdoten.* Zürich: Theologischer Verlag, 1973.

Wallace, Mark I. "The World of the Text: Theological Hermeneutics in the Thought of Karl Barth and Paul Ricoeur." Ph.D. diss., University of Chicago, 1986.

Ward, Daryll. "The Doctrine of Election in the Theologies of Friedrich Schleiermacher and Karl Barth." Ph.D. diss., University of Chicago, 1989.

Ward, Graham. *Barth, Derrida, and the Language of Theology.* Cambridge: Cambridge University Press, 1995.

Webb, Stephen H. *Refiguring Theology: The Rhetoric of Karl Barth.* Albany, N.Y.: State University of New York Press, 1991.

Webster, J. B. *Barth's Early Theology: Scripture, Confession, and Church.* Edinburgh: Continuum, 2004.

———. *Barth's Ethics of Reconciliation.* Cambridge: Cambridge University Press, 1995.

———. *Barth's Moral Theology: Human Action in Barth's Thought.* Grand Rapids: Eerdmans, 1998.

———, ed. *The Cambridge Companion to Karl Barth.* Cambridge: Cambridge University Press, 2000.

Werner, Martin. *Das Weltanschauungsproblem bei Karl Barth und Albert Schweitzer: Eine Auseinandersetzung.* Bern: P. Haupt, 1924.

Willis, Robert E. *The Ethics of Karl Barth.* Leiden: Brill, 1971.

Willis, W. Waite. *Theism, Atheism, and the Doctrine of the Trinity: The Trinitarian Theologies of Karl Barth and Jürgen Moltmann in Response to Protest Atheism.* American Academy of Religion Academy Series 53. Atlanta: Scholars Press, 1987.

Wittekind, Folkart. *Geschichtliche Offenbarung und die Wahrheit des Glaubens: Der Zusammenhang von Offenbarungstheologie, Geschichtsphilosophie und Ethik bei Albrecht Ritschl, Julius Kaftan und Karl Barth (1909–1916).* Beiträge zur historischen Theologie 113. Tübingen: Mohr Siebeck, 2000.

Yocum, John. *Ecclesial Mediation in Karl Barth.* Barth Studies. Burlington, Vt.: Ashgate, 2003.

Yoder, John Howard. *Karl Barth and the Problem of War.* Nashville: Abingdon, 1970.

INDEX